Developing Leaders for
Urban Ministries

American University Studies

Series VII
Theology and Religion
Vol. 147

PETER LANG
New York • San Francisco • Bern • Baltimore
Frankfurt am Main • Berlin • Wien • Paris

Edgar J. Elliston
J. Timothy Kauffman

Developing Leaders for Urban Ministries

PETER LANG
New York • San Francisco • Bern • Baltimore
Frankfurt am Main • Berlin • Wien • Paris

Library of Congress Cataloging-in-Publication Data

Elliston, Edgar J.
  Developing leaders for urban ministries / Edgar J. Elliston,
J. Timothy Kauffman.
      p. cm. — (American university studies. Series VII, Theology and
religion ; vol. 147)
    Includes bibliographical references and index.
    1. City clergy.   2. City churches.   3. Theology—Study and teaching.
I. Kauffman, J. Timothy,   II. Title.   III. Series.
BV637.5.E55   1993   253'.07—dc20   92-41297
ISBN 0-8204-2076-X   CIP
ISSN 0740-0446

Die Deutsche Bibliothek-CIP-Einheitsaufnahme

Elliston, Edgar J.:
Developing leaders for urban ministries / Edgar J. Elliston; J. Timothy
Kauffman.—New York; Berlin; Bern; Frankfurt/M.; Paris; Wien: Lang,
1993
    (American university studies : Ser. 7, Theology and religion ; Vol.
147)
    ISBN 0-8204-2076-X
NE: Kauffman, J. Timothy: American university studies/07

The paper in this book meets the guidelines for permanence and
durability of the Committee on Production Guidelines for
Book Longevity of the Council on Library Resources.

∞

© Peter Lang Publishing, Inc., New York 1993

Printed in the United States of America.

Acknowledgments

As with any project developed over time, many have contributed to the formation of this book. We want to acknowledge those contributions. We have had willing assistance from more men and women who lead in the equipping of leaders for urban ministries than we expected. The leaders of the ministries cited in this text are only a few of the people we could name. Tom Wolf and Carol Davis of the Church on Brady have allowed multiple times of observation, submitted to questioning, and shared documents. John Perkins encouraged us to visit the Harambee Center and then willingly shared about the formation of that ministry in northwest Pasadena. Michael Matta and Ron Benefiel have provided not only time and documents for us, but links into the city to provide bases for understanding. Roy LeTourneau provided key insights into the Encounter with God ministries and the equipping of leaders in Lima, Peru. Elizabeth McKerihan who served with the Alliance Bible Institute in Lima, Peru added many additional insights and corrections. Mary Thiesen and Fred Stoez furnished insight about World Impact ministries. All of these people were intimately acquainted with these ministries.

In addition many students contributed to our questioning about the issues of urban ministries. Church leaders who were studying with us from cities in Asia, Africa, Latin America, Europe and North American have alerted us to many issues just mentioned in this book.

To our faculty colleagues in the School of World Mission of Fuller Theological Seminary, we are grateful for the granting of a sabbatical for the drafting of the manuscript. To Heidi Burns we are grateful for the shepherding of this project through the complexities of publisher relations. Anne White provided not only the word processing, but also the typesetting support. Nancy Thomas provided editorial and proofreading support.

We are grateful to our Lord who has begun to raise our consciousness about the equipping of leaders for ministry in the cities.

J. Timothy Kauffman
Edgar J. Elliston

TABLE OF CONTENTS

List of Boxed Examples

List of Figures

List of Tables

List of Abbreviations

APU	Azusa Pacific University
ATM	Automated Teller Machine
C&MA	Christian and Missionary Alliance
CCC	Crenshaw Christian Center
CCCMTI	Crenshaw Christian Center Ministry Training Institute
CEFI	Charles E. Fuller Institute
CEU	Continuing Education Units
CTP	Church Training Program
ICAA	International Council for Accrediting Agencies
IE	Informal Education
LAN	Local Access Networks
LMI	LeTourneau Ministries International
NIV	New International Version
NRSV	New Revised Standard Version
NTS	Nazarene Theological Seminary
PTE	Programme on Theological Education
TEE	Theological Education by Extension
TEF	Theological Education Fund
TEV	Today's English Version

PREFACE

As we looked for written guidance about designing urban Christian leadership, we found many criticisms of traditional theological education as well as calls for renewal. We read many challenges to seminaries to be recontextualized for an urbanizing world. Many training programs effectively address a wide range of Christian urban leadership development needs. Because of their contextualized nature, however, they cannot be simply copied with an appropriate fit elsewhere. Because of their specific applications, they would be unlikely to fit expanded purposes. Materials about curriculum design abound, but little of it is applied directly to the equipping of Christian leaders for urban ministries.

This book, then, aims at providing a framework for identifying the foundational issues to initiate or improve a leadership development curriculum for an urban area. We hope to offer some basic educational principles and recommendations that may be used to design both theologically sound and contextually appropriate curricula to equip Christian leaders who live and work in cities.

We too believe that many current forms of theological education are too closely linked to contexts which no longer exist. Graduates of these programs are often well equipped to serve in settings that became extinct decades ago. However, we do not approach this task as in a hopeless morass, because many new effective equipping models are attempting to adjust to the new realities of our urbanizing world. While it is difficult to introduce change in existing institutions, some of these institutions are facilitating the formation of either new institutions or new ways of equipping urban leaders.

While no single model will fit universally, new insights into established educational principles can be gained by looking at some successful urban leadership development models. These principles can then be used to design or redesign and bring renewal into contextualized leadership development models.

We have sought to maintain a metropolitan perspective that allows application to minority population groups and to the poor, as well as to the more affluent and people in power. We have sought to keep the perspective at a theoretical level that may be used monoculturally, interculturally, cross-culturally, and in multicultural contexts. We have sought to be sensitive to worldview and cultural issues.

Our ministries have included both urban and rural ministries in Germany, Ethiopia, Kenya, and the United States. Our own training in traditional institutions has sensitized us to work toward the formation of new approaches in theological education. Consulting has taken us further afield. We write this book as an invitation to others to join in the conversation and the equipping of men and women to serve Jesus Christ as leaders in all the cities of the world.

Edgar J. Elliston
J. Timothy Kauffman
January, 1991

INTRODUCTION

Purpose

This chapter introduces the questions, definitions, assumptions and basic value perspectives of this book. Its purpose is to introduce the principal concerns for the developing Christian leaders for urban ministries so that the reader may be able to design a contextually appropriate leadership development curriculum for urban ministries. It aims at informing trainers and educators both in local churches and training institutions. Leaders in parachurch agencies engaged in urban ministries may find this text helpful for their nonformal and informal equipping as well.[1]

Key Issue

The primary question is "**How** should Christian leaders be equipped to serve in an urban ministry?" In dealing with the question of how to equip leaders in an urban ministry we have not assumed either a particular place, type of ministry, or kind of leadership. These key concerns will be addressed briefly in this text as variables. We view the single "cook book" or "formula" approach for urban leadership development as a common mistake. We share the conviction that traditional theological education is not well suited for the equipping of urban Christian leaders. Robert Ferris's arguments demonstrate why the traditional forms produce nonfunctional or dysfunctional graduates.[2] Other well known evangelical authors have called for new ways of equipping men and women for urban ministries.[3]

The "how" is addressed from a strong theological, contextualized base. The result—a leadership development process—should be similar from one context to another in that it will emerge out of and be built on the authoritative word of God. However, it will never be the same in terms of form because of a myriad of local differences.

Key Questions

To address this primary issue several related questions must be addressed:

1) **From what perspective will leadership be addressed?**
   What is a leader? What is a **Christian** leader? What distinguishes a Christian leader from other leaders? What is distinctive
   about an **urban** Christian leader?

2) **What are the characteristics of an urban context that
   should affect the ways Christian leaders are developed?**
   In what ways should the increasing diversity in ethnicity, changing class and moral dynamics, and the increase of isolation and insulation affect leadership development for the Church?

3) **What are the biblical/theological foundations on which
   urban Christian leadership should be developed?** Do
   these foundations share a common hermeneutic with theological
   education?

4) **What are the significant curricular issues facing the
   equipping of urban leaders?** How can one successfully inte-
   grate formal, nonformal and informal curricula into urban leadership development programs? Are some forms more effective
   than others? Why?

5) **What characterizes the task facing urban leaders?** What
   are the biblical mandates that have been given to the church and
   to Christian leaders in the city?

Assumptions

The following six assumptions form a set of key perspectives and present
the basis for this book. We address these assumptions in detail in the text.

1. **Some commonalities exist among Christian leaders and
   with Christian leadership in urban settings, whatever
   the cultural context.** Whether one is serving in an urban setting in India, Colombia, Nigeria, the USA, or Italy, all Christian
   leaders will have certain things in common such as the same authoritative word of God, the same leadership mandates, the same
   theological values for leading, and the same Spirit of God who
   guides and empowers.

2. **The basic principles of leadership development apply to
   the formation of urban Christian leaders whatever their**

type and culture. The specific educational forms will differ widely to allow for local cultural and worldview differences. However, the basic curricular principles identified in this text may be widely applied to local settings to assist in the design of effective contextualized leadership development programs.

3. **The specifics of equipping or training must always be contextually adapted for optimal effectiveness.** No single educational program design is universally applicable. Differences in worldview, resources, local ministry goals, the educational level of the learners, learning styles, and a score of other variables when combined prevent a single educational form from being optimally effective in multiple settings.

4. **Basic biblical/theological/revealed values are normative for all Christian leaders, although the cultural or leadership forms by which these values will be expressed will vary widely in different cultural contexts, even within the same urban area.** Christians rely on the same revelation although some issues are perceived differently because of their worldview differences. The revelation initiated by and provided by God remains as the normative standard by which Christian leadership and leadership development are to be judged.

5. **While differences exist between Christian and non-Christian leadership in most situations, there are also many commonalities.** These commonalities are based on the leaders' shared worldview assumptions in any given cultural context. These commonalities all help one to learn from the local non-Christian leaders and from local leadership patterns. Many local leadership patterns will prove highly informative for Christian leadership. Because of these commonalities Christians should be informed not only of the published materials about local leadership, but the unpublished practices and values as well.

6. **While many commonalities exist among Christian and non-Christian leaders in a given situation, there are also critical distinctives.** A different set of values guides Christian leaders. Their ultimate goal is different. Their set of critical relationships differs. And, their potential influence means (power) differ from those of their secular counterparts. These distinctives limit the potential use of secular leadership and management doctrines.

Definitions

While the following terms will become clearer through this book, the following definitions will provide an initial orientation.

Equip

Equip refers both to the instruction given to the emerging leader, to the preparation of the context, and to the fitting of the emerging leader into the leadership context. While several biblical concepts combine to help us understand the important function of Christian leadership development, one Greek word is particularly helpful. The word, *katartidzo*, is translated as "equip," "train," "prepare," and "mend" (as with nets) (cf. Eph. 4:13; Lk. 6:40 and 2 Ti. 3:16–17). This word carries the idea of making complete, contextually fitting, correcting or outfitting. The idea of contextually appropriate preparation is involved. The same word is used for the mending of nets (Mt. 4:21 and Mk. 1:19).

Urban

Urban refers to a geographical area characterized by a high population density and a multiplicity of interconnected social systems such as transportation, food, communications, education, energy production and distribution, commerce, law enforcement, and others. "Sub-urban" and "urban" are not distinguished because the "sub-urban" areas comprise an integral part of urban areas. The urban perspective of this book includes, but is not limited to, inner-cities, slums, minority ethnic groups, and the poor and the oppressed. Urban ministries should then reach the entire range of people who live in the metropolitan areas, from the white collar executive to the homeless and the immigrant. These ministries should reach into the walled compounds of the wealthy and the cardboard shelters of the street people. The perspective is "metropolitan" rather than "inner-city."

Ministry

Ministry refers to any leadership status and role in the church that aims to contribute to the life and purpose of the church. It may relate to small group leaders whose primary function is in a church sports program or to the denominational leader who is responsible for policy-making and administration. Ministry is intended to be wholistic in which three key relationships come into focus: 1) one's relationship with God through Jesus Christ, 2) one's relationship with one's neighbors, and, 3) one's relationship to the local context (cf. Figure). The primary relationship is the one a person has with God through Christ, because unless this relationship is right, none of the others can be. Also this relationship is primary in its eternal implications. However, all three are integrally related so that unless relations with others and with the context or environment are right, one's relationship with God suffers and one's ministry effectiveness is minimized. The converse is also true. Ministry effectiveness is enhanced as these three relationships become aligned.

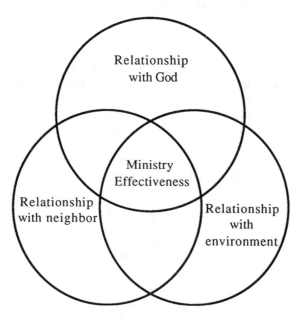

Relationship with God

Ministry Effectiveness

Relationship with neighbor

Relationship with environment

FIGURE ONE
KEY RELATIONSHIPS

Urban Ministry

Urban ministry is serving to establish or reestablish and develop these foundational relationships in an urban area. This ministry rests on two different, but complementary, biblical imperatives: 1) making disciples of all nations and 2) loving one's neighbor. The specific forms of ministry will be diverse and not confined to any given specialty (pastor, evangelist, social worker).

Leadership

Leadership can be defined as a process of influence. The process always includes several key components: leaders; followers; a situation in which they interact; means for influence that emerge from the leader and from the community of leaders and followers; values; time for the interactions to occur; and goals that the leaders and followers seek to achieve.

Leadership is a complex influence process in which leaders and followers interact in a context or a series of contexts over time. Within this context the leaders exercise influence with the followers toward a mutually desired goal. The effectiveness of the leadership process is contingent on a wide variety of contextual variables, some of which are influenced by the leaders and followers and some over which they have no influence.

Clinton offers a useful definition of leadership which in part sets the "complex contingency"[4] leadership perspective of this text:

> Leadership is: 1) a dynamic process over an extended period of time, 2) in various situations in which a leader utilizing leadership resources, 3) and by specific leadership behaviors, 4) influences the thoughts and activity of followers, 5) toward accomplishment of person/task aims, 6) mutually beneficent for leaders, followers and the macro context of which they are a part.[5]

In addition to these six important components in Clinton's definition, two critical variables must be added. The first is the worldview of the leader, the followers and the community in which they live. Within this worldview one can find perspective, philosophy, or values. Worldview heavily influences one's hermeneutic or way of interpreting all of one's perceptions, including what is read from God's word and what is expected and experienced in the city. Theological perspective also flows out of one's worldview. A second consideration is the interactional dynamics of the variables. One cannot separate the influence of the leader, the followers, and the situation from values and means of influence. All are inextricably interwoven in a dynamic influence process.

Christian Leader

A *Christian leader* is a person who is committed to Jesus Christ "with God-given capacity and with a God-given responsibility to influence a specific group of God's people toward God's purposes for the group."[6]

Christian Leadership

Christian leadership differs from secular, business, or political leadership. Ward captures this difference by writing,

> a leader is one who ministers; a leader *serves* through the gifts of the Holy Spirit, not in terms of prowess, not in terms of accomplishments or acquired knowledge, but in terms of what God is doing through his or her life. Leadership in the church is servanthood.[7]

Leadership models for the church "must be supported by Scripture and evaluated in terms of accountability to Christ."[8] While Christian leaders share the culture and most of the worldview of their secular counterparts, several distinguishing marks characterize them. Their values revolve around a different set of standards. The influence means include the use of spiritual power and the formation of spiritual authority. Other distinctives appear in the goals. The Christian's goals have an eternal dimension, whereas a non-Christian's goals are related more to the culture, the organization, or to the leader's personal desires.

Many biblical images of leaders serve to expand our understanding of Christian leadership. These word pictures allow us to see facets of the complexity of leadership that are often missed in propositional definitions. Jesus used thirty-five such images (metaphors, and other figures of speech) to describe the disciples as they were training to be leaders. Additional images appear in the Epistles. Notably, the images used in the gospels when the disciples were under training never include any terms usually associated with leadership or the assertion of power. In fact Jesus, in warning them about the abuses of the leadership patterns of the Pharisees, told them that they had "but one leader" (Mt. 23:1–12). In that context he told them that they were to be servants.

Definitions from a Western deductive and linear way of thinking are absent in the Scriptures and foreign to much of the present non-Western world. The absence of propositional definitions does not mean, however, that the complexities of leadership are not appreciated or understood. Rather, these complexities are treated with imagery which allows local contextual application and expansion.

Multiple metaphors are like the facets of a finely cut diamond. Each reflects a face with its distinctive hues, but is defined by other metaphors which reflect other hues. The brilliance and depth of color in each facet is conditioned by all of the facets of the stone, by how they are shaped and how they are positioned toward the light. The facets on a diamond are cut to a variety of shapes and sizes depending on the internal design of the stone and the stone cutter's purpose. Only when taken together is the whole understood.

Through the whole of the Scriptures scores of metaphors and other figures of speech are used to describe leaders and followers. Three key biblical metaphors reveal the larger facets of a Christian leadership perspective: servant, shepherd and steward. These three metaphors have different cultural referents today and so require close exegetical attention to see clearly their original brilliance and subtle hues, and to know how to apply them in today's situations.

The same key images serve in this book as a foundation for understanding Christian leadership: servant, shepherd, and steward. These metaphors may present some difficulty for many urban leaders because of unfamiliarity with the biblical referents.

Servant

The spiritual leader is one who voluntarily submits to the sovereign authority (lordship) of Jesus Christ, to obey Him as directed for His benefit. The leader's capacity (giftedness), role, status, placement, and tenure are all under the sovereign authority of Jesus Christ and overseen by the Holy Spirit. The service is for Christ's pleasure and results in the good of the church and the ultimate good of the servant. However, along the way the servant may experience harassment, inconvenience, and various kinds of testing. The agenda is the Lord's, not the servant's, nor that of the other believers who also may benefit from the service. Richards notes the key and *critical* concept underlying Christian leadership and ministry as "one of service and support of others."[9]

To be a leader one must first learn to be a follower. To continue to be a leader one also must continue to be a follower. Followership also appears in the Scriptures as servanthood.

The picture of a servant emerges out of several terms to describe different kinds of servants in the first century. A servant or slave, *doulos* is utterly accountable for obedience toward his master. A servant, *diakonos*, follows instructions particularly regarding the task at hand, such as the waiting on tables. The servanthood of *huperetes* particularly recognizes the authority of one's superior. The servant, *leitourgos*, recognizes the organizational structure over him.

Shepherd

While largely unfamiliar to the urban setting, the picture of a shepherd provides an understanding of additional critical facets of Christian leadership. Spiritual leaders are called and commissioned to function as shepherds. They are to tend the flock of God. This tending includes a variety of functions that follow the analogy of shepherding, such as feeding (teaching), nurturing (exhorting, reproving, correcting, comforting), protecting, congregating (maintaining group cohesion), leading or guiding, calling to follow, knowing by name, modeling and leading in hope. Shepherds are not only called and commissioned to function in these positive ways, they are warned against taking advantage of the flock for personal gain, lording it over the flock, leading for money, and being careless (cf. 1 Pe. 5:1–5; Eze. 34).

Steward

A third undergirding idea for Christian leadership is stewardship. Spiritual leaders are entrusted with the message of the gospel, gifts for ministry, and a ministry or missiological task to do. They are entrusted with other resources of the kingdom including the people whose energies they guide, the facilities and physical resources in their care, and the as yet unmeasured spiritual power God has made available through His Spirit. The commission is seen in terms of a "trust" or a "stewardship." The leader is seen then as a trustee. Trustees are expected to guard what has been entrusted to them (1 Ti. 6:20). They are expected to employ the trust to the owner's advantage and according to His will. The functioning of Christian leaders ought to be seen in terms of obediently serving, shepherding, and stewarding as directed by what God has revealed.

When referring to these metaphors one must be careful not to assign either negative or positive meanings that would be out of character for the original context. For example, servants might be seen today in terms of having less competence, trustworthiness, accountability, or scope of authority than allowed in the contexts of the first century church. One also may confuse to whom the servant is responsible. Unfortunately, many Christians see the accountability of Church leaders only in terms of the church administrative structures and not to God.

Similarly, the whole idea of shepherding is frequently foreign to the urban dweller. Many people in a city have never seen a sheep, goat, or cow except in photographs. Their view of what a shepherd is and does is severely limited and often grossly mistaken. In both cases the idea of strong leadership is often felt to be largely absent.

Current church growth literature advocates "strong" leadership.[10] However, the advocacy of strong leadership does not negate the biblical imagery. Indeed, strong leadership must be exercised in the light of the biblical imagery. Strong leadership does not require the leader to be autocratically authoritarian or dictatorial.

Because of limited views of leadership and only a passing acquaintance with secular leadership or management literature, many church leaders assume that strong leadership only means "authoritarian" as opposed to "democratic" leadership. Others would see strong leaders as explained by "Theory X" rather than "Theory Y" perspectives.[11] Following the same line of thinking, some would see strong leaders as highly "task" oriented rather than "relational" in their leadership style.

These simplistic understandings of leadership do not justly treat either the biblical foundations or current secular leadership thinking. "Strong" or, preferably, "effective" spiritual leaders influence in ways that are both contextually and theologically appropriate. Current secular leadership thinking focuses on the transformation of the whole leadership context with integrity.[12] In transformational leadership, 1) the leader, 2) the interactive and mutually influential relationships with the followers, 3) the attention that must be given to the leadership situation and the broader context, 4) the appropriate (value-driven) use of spiritual, personal, and positional power, come into focus.

The ideas of complexity in leadership and contextualization are not new. Both Jesus and the leaders in the early church led with an awareness of these complexities. They explained the complexities of leadership with a wide range of metaphors.[13]

They displayed the importance of contextually preparing or developing the people who would lead. Their training-related language contains both a strong contextual and semantic base for fitting the leaders to the situation. Many anecdotal and instructional examples could be given.

Types of Leaders

Christian leaders may be classified into five general types, described in this section as Types I through V.[14] Critical distinguishing variables include the nature of their ministries (whether direct or indirect), sphere of influence, use of influence or power, roles, status, type and amount of related training, degree of professionalization, and distribution. They also differ significantly in terms of kinds of experience they have. They are not, however, distributed on a value scale. All are highly valued and considered essential before the Lord and in the church (1 Co. 12). Figure Two and Table One show the essential distinctions of these five kinds of leaders.[15]

Different cultural contexts will require significantly different descriptions of these kinds of leaders. Some variables that will affect the ways these leader types will be defined include: the age, size, and polity of the church, and the culture(s) in which the church functions (broader culture and specific corporate culture).

Hofstede suggests four sets of variables that affect the way leadership is perceived and the way it functions: 1) Power Distance, 2) Uncertainty Avoidance, 3) Individualism-Collectivism, and 4) Masculinity-Femininity.[16] Each of these four variables will lead to a reshaping of the five kinds of leaders that are described below.

Some specific factors within each type of leadership are generic and will apply differently in different church contexts. For example, expectations about the issues of training, levels of professionalization, being salaried or not will vary from church to church in different subcultural contexts.

Another variable that ought to be seen through each type of leader is spiritual/ministry maturity. While one may be spiritually mature as a Type I leader and have a mature ministry, other types of leaders emerge from this base. One may be called to be another kind of leader and progress through the various types of leadership en route to maturity in ministry. However, one should not assume that a Type I or II leader is immature spiritually or in terms of ministry development. However, one would expect that as one emerges as a Type IV or Type V leader that there would be a greater degree of maturity. One would expect a convergence of giftedness, status, and role in one's ministry as ministry maturation continues.

The leaders who serve in each type of leadership are not limited by gender. While both cultural and theological debates continue about specific statuses and roles (e.g., elder, pastor), we find no biblical justification to distinguish between men and women based on giftedness, or the basis of leadership in the church. In a given community, because of the local worldview, theological position, or church polity, it may not be deemed wise to install either men or women in certain statuses or roles. However, neither in terms of a descriptive perspective nor from our theological perspective, do we find any reason to assign or to restrict categorically either men or women from a given type of leadership simply because of gender. Traditionally, women often have been limited to Types I and II, whereas all five types have been open to men.

While age is not a primary variable in understanding leadership, it does play a role. The spiritual and social maturity required for each type of leadership emerges out of life experience. Generally, more spiritual and social experience is required as an entry-level for each successive type of leader. However, one should not assume that as one becomes older one automatically transitions from one type of leader to another. One can point to exceptions, but men and women who would be Types IV and V are generally more than thirty-five years old. Conversely, entry into Types I and II may come as early as the teens or twenties. Cultural constraints play an important part regarding age as well.

Type I—Small Group Leaders

Type I leaders voluntarily serve without pay in a local, limited sphere of influence. They have direct or face-to-face ministry. They are nonprofessionals as they relate to their ministry. These roles generally do not require specialized or formal training. While not needing a high level of training, these roles remain the most numerous leadership roles in the church. Typical nonprofessional roles include small group leaders, Sunday school teachers, choir directors, organists, and youth sponsors. The number of people influenced by a Type I leader is limited from one to ten. The comprehensiveness of their influence or range of lifestyle issues is limited. However, the intensity or degree of their influence is potentially high. Type I leaders typically have more contact with nonbelievers than other leaders. They provide a critical component of any evangelistic endeavor. The larger the number of well-trained, dedicated Type I leaders, the greater the potential for growth.

Type II—Leaders of Multiple Small Groups

Type II leaders voluntarily serve without pay in a local, churchwide sphere of influence. Their ministry is direct or face-to-face. They serve as paraprofessionals; that is, they work alongside professionals with either mature experience or some specialized training. Elders, deacons, department heads, or ministry managers of larger ministries in a local congregation generally fit into this category. The extent of their influence reaches beyond their immediate associates to multiple related small groups. The comprehensiveness of their influence is potentially greater than the Type I leader. The intensity or profundity of their influence is potentially high.

Paraprofessional leaders serve in the place of professionals. Paraprofessionals serve in several professions, such as paramedics and paralegals. They have had specific, but limited training. In growing churches in the Two-Thirds World this kind of leader often carries the heaviest burden of leadership. Frequently, the church cannot afford higher level training or the salaries sometimes expected by the higher trained leaders. In a church situation paraprofessionals may or may not be employed.

Generally, Type II leaders are not employed. An example of a paraprofessional is a trained "lay counselor" who serves alongside the professional on a part-time basis and who would refer cases too difficult to the professional. Itinerant evangelists, colporteurs and catechists would fit into this category in many Two-Thirds World countries.

The equipping of both Type I and II leaders is absolutely essential if any ministry in the city is to be successful and durable. Otherwise, the clergy burns out attempting to do more and more while becoming less and less adept. Ministry in the city will either break down the artificial walls of separation between clergy and laity, or capitulate to secular and other religious forces.

Type III—Pastors of Small Churches

Type III leaders of churches in a Western context are generally paid and working full time in western churches. Many Type III leaders in cities and in the Two-Thirds World are often bivocational. Pastors of small congregations fit in this category, and most urban pastors find themselves in small churches. They have a local community sphere of influence. Their primary sphere of influence is direct, but they have some indirect ministry. They would be considered as semiprofessional because they would typically have met the minimal requirements, such as a basic theological education, spiritual maturity, and ministry experience, to enter a paid pastoral status and role. The extensiveness of their influence would reach beyond the local church into the community. The comprehensiveness of their influence is generally wide among the people in their sphere of influence. The intensity of their influence is potentially high.

Type IV—Pastors of Large Churches

Type IV leaders are typically pastors of a multistaff or multiple cell congregations[17] or administrators of small agencies. They have a regional sphere of influence in other congregations or agencies. Their influence is mostly indirect. They are considered as professionals, having completed their formal training and shown both their competence and commitment. The extensiveness of their influence reaches beyond the people with whom they have direct contact. The comprehensiveness of their influence is probably at its peak. The intensity of their influence, while great in a specific area, may be much less in other areas.

Type V—National/International Leaders

Type V leaders serve in national or international roles. Their ministry is indirect beyond a second level. They may influence through organizational policy making, publishing, or through mass media. They may know the kinds of people being influenced but not personally know many of them.

They are also considered as professionals. The extensiveness or scope of their influence is greater than any other type of leader in terms of the number of people influenced. The comprehensiveness of their influence is generally less with their increasing specialty. The intensity of their influence is high with only a few individuals and in limited areas and tends to decrease toward the outer reaches of their sphere of influence.

One may chart the distribution of the five kinds of leaders based on the number of people to whom a person can effectively relate and effectively influence. For the sake of simplicity, and to suggest some guidelines, the following table presents one such approach. (See Table One.) One basic assumption is that a given person has a limited potential for direct regular face-to-face influence. The number of people one may regularly directly influence at a worldview level may range between ten and twenty. Another assumption is that a set of five levels of leaders is adequate to describe types of leadership in both the church and parachurch structures.[18]

TABLE ONE
RELATIVE DISTRIBUTION OF LEADER TYPES
FOR A CHRISTIAN COMMUNITY OF 100,000[19]

Leaders who relate face to face with	5 people	10 people	15 people	20 people
Number of leaders required:				
Type I	20,000	10,000	6,667	5,000
Type II	4,000	1,000	444	250
Type III	160	100	30	13
Type IV	32	10	2	1
Type V	6	1	0	0

This distribution, while imperfect, does suggest the relative numbers of each kind of worker. The sheer numbers of people involved in Types I and II should capture our attention. Rambo,[20] while only treating Types IV and V, supports need for the limited number of these kinds of leaders. For the following table the assumed size of the community to be served is 100,000 people.

Ministry Factor

	Type I	Type II	Type III	Type IV	Type V
	←————————————————————————————→				

Direct/Indirect

Direct ←————————————→ Direct/indirect ←——→ Indirect ——→

Payment

Unpaid ←————————————→ Generally paid ←→ Full-time paid ——→

Professional

	Non-pro-fessional	Para-pro-fessional	Semi-pro-fessional	Professional ——→	

Sphere of Influence

	Small Group	Congregation	Community	Region Nation	International

Training

Little ←——→ Minimal ←→ Increasingly trained————————→
Pastor's

Typical Functions

	S.S. Teacher	Elder Dept. head	Pastor of small congre-gation	Pastor in large church	Admin-istrator of a large agency

Use of characteristics of power
Intensiveness

High   Lower
←————————————————————————————→

Comprehensiveness

Lower   Higher   Decreasing
←————————————————————————————→

Extensiveness

Low   High
←————————————————————————————→

FIGURE TWO
CONTRASTIVE CONTINUUM OF TYPES OF LEADERS

The vast majority of church workers needed are Types I and II. These people generally have the lowest entry-level skills and knowledge, may be less motivated, are culturally or socially within the context that is the focus of the development, and have the least accessibility to/from formal educational institutions (geographically, politically, economically, academically, and/or socially). They often lack the resources for training and are the least visible. These leaders, however, have the greatest potential for effective ministries among those who are not yet Christians. They have more relationships with those in secular society. Types III, IV and V must take special initiatives to develop relationships with people outside the church because typically most of their friends and associates are Christians.

In taking Types I and II leaders and attempting to change or develop them into Types III, IV or V, several dysfunctional results may emerge: 1) Too many may be trained for existing status/role positions. 2) The potential for local influence decreases. 3) A greater passivity often emerges locally along with a greater level of dependency. 4) The most able leaders are drained from the local leadership increasing the difficulty for the Types III, IV, and V leaders to influence locally. 5) The cost/benefit ratio investment of our training programs may continue to be skewed in favor of the more highly trained people.

Churches have often reversed the priority of assigning training resources with the distribution of these five kinds of leaders. The greater resources are assigned to the few (Types IV and V) because they are in positions of power and much more visible, whereas little is allocated to the development of Types I and II who outnumber Types IV and V.

Leadership Training

The intent of training leaders to serve in an urban context carries a series of major risks both for the church and for the people who would submit to training. Training is the more technological side of education in which the content, skill, and attitude development is focused on an application to a specific context. Johnson distinguishes education and training by writing,

> Training implies learning for use in a predictable situation; education implies learning for use in an unpredictable situation. The development of a training curriculum begins with a job analysis in which the tasks to be done and the knowledge skills and attitudes needed to do them are identified. The uses of training [are] ... replicative and applicative. The uses of education are associative and interpretative.[21]

While training is a critical part of the development of urban leaders, training by itself does not produce leaders. Training carries a certain mythical character in modern-information laden societies. People sometimes mistakenly believe that they can train a person to do anything or to be anything by simply having a person master the basic information and skills related to a given task.

This **Leadership Training Myth** serves to deceive us by suggesting, "We can train people to be effective leaders." If you read and believe the promotional literature about the management training seminars and workshops or the various M.B.A. programs offered in virtually any urban center in the world, you may come to believe that anyone can be trained to be an effective leader in any context. All a person needs is the right information, the right skills, and the proper motivation.

While developers of Christian leadership may not be so crass about their advertising, in practice that is what Christian leaders and theological educators often imply. Recruiters both in the churches and from Christian institutions suggest that they can make effective Christian leaders out of whoever may enter their training programs.

Fred Fiedler, who has probably supervised more contemporary leadership related research than anyone else not long ago published an article entitled, "Leadership Training Does Not Produce Leaders."[22] Kouzes and Posner[23] further debunk this myth.

Preview

The formation of Christian leadership in an urban setting requires a theological base. Once the theological foundation has been settled, one can begin to look at local curricular issues and the design of equipping structures. The following chapters seek to provide this kind of introductory perspective. Chapter two briefly describes several contemporary effective leadership equipping models. These case studies serve to illustrate how the issues raised in this text are treated in real contexts. Chapter three describes the theological perspective used in this text to form the primary perspective for equipping Christian leaders for the city. Chapter four describes characteristics of the urban context which impact on the equipping of leaders. Chapter five examines the educational foundations for developing urban leaders. Chapter six describes some ways to view needs. Chapter seven outlines some methods for equipping urban leaders. Chapter eight offers some suggestions related to developing content, skills and being in leadership development.

Notes

[1] Nonformal education refers to planned learning which is structured in short cycles and generally not aimed at a degree. Conferences, workshops, and seminars are typical nonformal types of education.

Informal education refers to unplanned, enculturative, and relationship based learning experiences which occur in daily life. They do occur in and around planned learning, but are not limited to planned learning experiences. Informal educative experiences can be facilitated, but not planned or they become nonformal or formal.

Formal education is associated with schooling. It has a longer cycle and often is designed to provide academic credit toward a diploma or degree.

[2] Robert W. Ferris, *Renewal in Theological Education: Strategies for Change* (Wheaton: The Billy Graham Center, Wheaton College, 1990), pp. 45–126.

[3] Roger S. Greenway, "Content and Context: the Whole Christ for the Whole City," pp. 85–106; Harvie M. Conn, "The Kingdom of God and the City of Man: A History of the City/Church Dialogue," pp. 9–59, and "Christ and the City: Biblical Themes for Building Urban Theology Models," pp. 222–286; Sidney H. Rooy, "Theological Education for Urban Mission," pp. 175–207; in *Discipling the City: Theological Reflections on Urban Missions*, ed. Roger S. Greenway (Grand Rapids: Baker Book House, 1979). Also see: Roger S. Greenway, "Don't Be an Urban Missionary Unless," *Evangelical Missions Quarterly* 19: 2 (April, 1983): 86–94; "Cities, Seminaries, and Christian Colleges," *Urban Mission* 3: 1 (September, 1985): 3.

[4] Current contingency leadership theories describe the complex and dynamic interactive relationships among the leader, followers, and situation. Each contributes to the other two. The leader through patterned behavior or style influences followers in a structured context toward a goal which benefits both as well as the wider context. The followers allocate the right to be influenced to the leader and provide the benefits of social recognition and goal achievement. The situation provides the organizational and social structures, worldview and values which constrain, guide, and facilitate the influence process.

5 J. Robert Clinton, *Leadership Emergence Patterns* (Altadena, CA: Barnabas Resources, 1986), p. 14.

6 J. Robert Clinton, *The Making of a Leader* (Colorado Springs: NavPress, 1988), p. 127.

7 Ted Ward, "Facing Educational Issues," *Church Leadership Development* (Glen Ellyn, IL: Scripture Press Ministries, 1977), p. 13.

8 Ted Ward, "Servants, Leaders and Tyrants," *Missions and Theological Education in World Perspective*, eds. Harvie M. Conn and Samuel F. Rowen (Farmington, MI: Associates of Urbanus, 1984), pp. 19–40.

9 Lawrence O. Richards, *A Theology of Christian Education* (Grand Rapids: Zondervan Publishing House, 1975), p. 231.

10 C. Peter Wagner, *Leading Your Church to Growth* (Ventura, CA: Regal Books, 1984).

11 McGregor developed two complementary theories which serve to explain the motivation behind leader behavior. His Theory X and Theory Y focused on the assumptions that leaders make about their followers and their followers' motivations. Given the assumptions that one makes about one's followers, the leader's behavior can be predicted.

While not using the word, McGregor suggested that one's worldview ("cosmology") deeply affects how a leader will relate to followers and how a leader will behave. His two theories, Theory X and Theory Y, illustrate two contrastive views of people. Both are intended to be descriptive of the ways leaders view their followers. McGregor uses Maslow's hierarchy of needs to show that Theory X is often an inappropriate approach because a person's basic needs are met and yet the leader is not allowing the follower to develop in the meeting of higher level needs. He suggests that moving from a Theory X perspective motivation is questionable for people whose physiological and safety needs are met and whose social-esteem and/or self-actualization needs are more prominent (Paul Hersey and Kenneth H. Blanchard, *Management of Organizational Behavior Utilizing Human Resources*, 4th ed. (Englewood Cliffs, NJ: Prentice Hall, 1981), p. 48).

A Theory X oriented leader would, according to McGregor, be more task oriented, directive, authoritarian, and focus on motivation by financial rewards or threats of punishment.

A Theory Y oriented leader, however, would be expected to be more democratic, participative, and considerate. She/he would work to facilitate the growth of the followers.

Douglas McGregor, *The Human Side of Enterprise* (New York: McGraw Hill, 1960).

Assumptions about Human Nature
from McGregor's Theory X and Theory Y

Theory X	Theory Y
1. Work is inherently distasteful to most people.	1. Work is as natural as play, if the conditions are favorable.
2. Most people are not ambitious, have little desire for responsibility and prefer to be directed.	2. Self-control is often indispensable in achieving organizational goals.
3. Most people have little capacity for creativity in solving organizational problems.	3. The capacity for creativity in solving organizational problems is widely distributed in the population.
4. Motivation occurs only at the physiological and safety levels.	4. Motivation occurs at the social, esteem and self-actualization levels, as well as the physiological and security levels.
5. Most people must be closely controlled and often coerced to achieve organizational objectives.	5. People can be self-directed and creative at work if properly motivated.

(Based on Paul Hersey and Kenneth H. Blanchard, *Management of Organizational Behavior Utilizing Human Resources*, 5th ed. (Englewood Cliffs, NJ: Prentice Hall, 1988), p. 55.)

[12] One only has to read any of the more influential books about leadership, such as Hollander's *Leadership Dynamics*, Burns' *Leadership*, Kouzes and Posner's *The Leadership Challenge*, Gary Yukl's *Leader-*

ship in Organizations, Badaracco and Elsworth's *The Quest for Integrity in Leadership*, Paul Hersey and Kenneth Blanchard's *Management of Organizational Behavior*, or Bernard Bass' revised edition of Stogdill's classic *Handbook of Leadership* to see these ideas illustrated.

13 One must also be careful not to assume that these metaphors exhaust the richness or diversity of Christian leadership in its authority, tasks, relationships, or other complexities. These metaphors only provide three of the larger facets of the diamond of leadership God intends. They reflect a limited amount of truth. Other metaphors complement and enlarge the brilliance of God's revelation. They range across relationships (e.g., son, child, joint heir) to things showing interconnectedness (e.g., temple, building, living stone) to vocations (e.g., watchman, athlete, soldier) to animals (e.g., sheep, doves, goats). The list is long. When considered together the metaphors delimit each other so the shape, wholeness, and richness of Christian leadership emerges.

14 Donald A. McGavran in 1969 described five kinds of leaders needed for growing churches in a lectureship at Columbia Bible College at Columbia, SC. Edgar J. Elliston and W. Michael Smith, *An Outline for Program Planning and Evaluation* (n.p., 1976) described a leadership training program around five kinds of leaders; Lois McKinney, "Training Leaders," *Discipling through Theological Education by Extension*, ed. Virgil Gerber (Chicago: Moody Press, 1980), pp. 179–191; and J. Robert Clinton, *Leadership Training Models Manual* (Altadena, CA: Barnabas Resources, 1984) have variously described five kinds of leaders who are needed for the Church community.

15 It should be noted that while the number five serves as a useful way to classify the types of leaders, a local situation may in fact require a different number. Furthermore, the ways that leaders are classified may require a very different kind of classification system because of the cultural situation. For example, leaders could be classified into prophet, priestly, and kingly categories in terms of their functioning. The lexical categories in a given language will also condition how leadership should be classified.

16 Geert Hofstede, "Motivation, Leadership, and Organization: Do American Theories Apply Abroad?" *Organizational Dynamics* (Summer, 1980), pp. 42–62.

Power Distance is "the extent to which a society accepts the fact that power in institutions and organizations is distributed unequally."

Uncertainty avoidance is "the extent to which a society feels threatened by uncertain and ambiguous situations and tries to avoid these situations by providing greater career stability, establishing more formal rules, not tolerating deviant ideas and behaviors, and believing in absolute truths and the attainment of expertise." Individualism "implies a loosely knit social framework in which people are supposed to take care of themselves and their immediate families." Collectivism is "characterized by a tight social framework in which people distinguish between ingroups and out-groups; they expect their in-group (relatives, clan, organizations) to look after them, and in exchange for that they feel they owe absolute loyalty to it." Hofstede describes "masculinity" as a cultural characteristic as "assertiveness, the acquisition of money and things, and not caring for others, the quality of life, or people." On the other hand, he describes "feminine" cultures as the direct opposite of these "masculine" characteristics. The combination of these configurations deeply affect how leaders are distributed (i.e., both the numbers of leaders in each type and the number of types), the perceived distance between the types of leaders, as well as the status and role sets of each type of leader.

[17] Single cell congregations generally peak at about 200 members.

[18] See Donald A. McGavran and Win Arn, *How to Grow A Church* (Glendale, CA: Regal, 1974), pp. 89–97; Edgar J. Elliston and W. Michael Smith, *An Outline for Program Planning and Evaluation*, (n.p., 1976); and McKinney.

[19] Adapted from Edgar J. Elliston, ed., *Christian Relief and Development: Training Leaders for Effective Ministry* (Dallas: Word Books, 1989), p. 190.

[20] David Rambo, Church Growth Lectures: "Patterns of Bible Institute Training Overseas"; "Theological Education by Extension: What is it Accomplishing?"; "Crisis at the Top: Training High Level Leaders"; "Leadership for the Cities: Facing the Urban Mandate," Fuller Theological Seminary, 1981.

[21] Mauritz Johnson, Jr., "A Schema for Curriculum," *Curriculum and Evaluation*, Arno A. Bellack and Herbert M. Kliebard, eds. (Berkeley: McCutchen Publishing Corporation, 1977), p. 9.

[22] Fred E. Fiedler, "The Trouble with Leadership Training is that it Doesn't Train Leaders," *Leadership and Social Change*, William R.

Lassey and Richard R. Fernandez, eds. (La Jolla, CA: University Associates, 1980), pp. 238–246.

23 James M. Kouzes and Barry Z. Posner, *The Leadership Challenge: How to Get Extraordinary Things Done in Organizations* (San Francisco: Jossey-Bass Publishers, 1987).

CHAPTER TWO

MODELS FOR EQUIPPING LEADERS FOR URBAN MINISTRIES

This chapter identifies some actual urban leadership training models. These models then serve to exemplify the training issues and illustrate the theory presented in this book. We selected them on the bases of the following criteria:

1) *Diversity of Purpose.* Each model has a different purpose, yet each falls within the broad theological mandates described in this text for urban ministries.

2) *Diversity regarding other critical curricular issues.* We selected these models to illustrate differences regarding the following curricular issues: content, control, venue, costs, resources, timing, delivery system, learner selection, teacher selection, and spiritual formation.

3) *Effectiveness.* Each urban training model presented here illustrates an effective approach in accomplishing the stated purpose of that particular model.

These cases display the potential for variety and the importance of configuring the program design to fit the local situation. We assumed that no given leadership development program, however well designed, will optimally fit in multiple contexts. Every context requires specific curricular adjustments to be both effective and efficient.

The case descriptions in this chapter provide only a brief overview of each situation. Additional descriptive information appears in the boxed text in the later chapters. As of the writing of this text, all these training models were functioning. Readers are invited to contact the responsible persons at any of these programs for further information or to participate in them. Addresses are provided in the notes related to each case description.[1]

Besides the diversity of training approaches, these cases differ in their theologies. It is not the purpose of this book to evaluate, commend or criticize the theological perspective of any group. The leaders in all these models agree with the basic theological foundations undergirding the development of leaders as employed in this text.

These case studies are divided for this book into primary and secondary categories. The primary case studies appear more extensively through the text for illustrations. The secondary examples provide breadth and illustrate significant distinctive features. The categorization of these equipping models does not reflect a value judgment on their effectiveness or importance to the Kingdom. Many other case studies could be cited. The selection process was difficult because many effective equipping programs are producing outstanding results. Some of these programs, however, were not immediately accessible to the authors for observation.

Crenshaw Christian Center Ministry Training Institute

The Crenshaw Christian Center is an independent, African-American, charismatic mega-church in South Central Los Angeles. The church has a campus of thirty-two acres on which its worship center, parking, schools, and other facilities are located.

Frederick K. C. Price serves as the senior pastor of this congregation. Besides his preaching ministry with the church, he has a nationally televised preaching ministry and serves as the president of the Crenshaw Christian Center Ministry Training Institute (CCCMTI). He also provides significant leadership for about one thousand independent charismatic churches across the United States.

The purpose of the CCCMTI is to equip men and women for Types I, II, and III leadership in a local church. The program is designed in three major sequential divisions. The first division, the Helps Ministry School, aims at equipping Type I leaders. These adults are at an entry-level in terms of ministry in the local church. This program is a three-month, seven-course curriculum of day or evening classes open to anyone who wants to understand and be more effective in the ministry of helps. "Helps" are specific tasks done by individuals that assist the appointed ministers in performing their God-given assignments. Helps include the tasks performed by ushers, counselors, nursery workers, Sunday school teachers, and the like.

Participants in this helps training program must make two commitments: First, they must commit themselves to participate in the full course. And, second, they must complete the course work before they receive any ministry assignment in the Crenshaw Christian Center.

The second year and second division of the school focuses on Bible content and interpretation. This Bible training program aims to equip lay adults who will be serving in Bible teaching roles in the local church. It is a one or two-year curriculum of day or evening classes for emerging leaders who want a greater knowledge of the faith and Bible deliverance message. To be admitted, extensive prior biblical knowledge is not required, just a sincere desire to learn. This program fulfills the prerequisite for admission to the next level.

The third division, the School of Ministry, begins the third year and aims at equipping men and women for full-time paid ministries in the church. It is a one year, twenty-four course curriculum of day or evening classes designed to train men and women who have a genuine call to full time ministry in one or more of the fivefold ministry offices. Students are eligible for admission to this program only after completion of the School of the Bible or transfer from an equivalent program.

Beyond these three schools, CCCMTI provides a Correspondence Study Program comprised of twenty-five courses, designed for people who cannot attend the residential program. This independent course study program consists of taped lectures from the classroom along with textbooks.

> Two hundred eighty-two students from ten denominations and eleven states enrolled in the CCC Schools during the year 1990. Of this number, 162 enrolled in the School of the Bible and twenty-seven enrolled in the School of Ministry. We also had twenty-seven students who enrolled in our Helps Ministry School.[2]

One strength of this program centers on the issue of student selection. The selection process becomes increasingly demanding in terms of commitment with each succeeding step. While a commitment to complete each step or each division is expected, the third year students are expected to be able to recognize clearly and articulate their calling into ministry. They are expected to be involved in ministry during the training. Rigorous standards of performance, dress, and moral conduct are expected of all the students.

Another notable strength of the program is the recognition of the need for specific equipping for men and women with entry-level knowledge, skills, and perspective for any ministry in the church, whether it is ushering or working with audio-video ministries. Specific training, then, is designed for each of these kinds of ministries and given in this early stage of training.

The equipping of leaders moves through a clear sequence in which the learner learns about a particular service, faithfully does it, and then is equipped for an expanded ministry.

The faculty of the CCCMTI numbers twelve. With only two exceptions all of the faculty members have other pastoral responsibilities in the

Crenshaw Christian Center, such as in the youth or visitation programs. Faculty members come with both ministry experience in the local church, a high-level commitment to ministry, and leadership experience in other professions. They come from backgrounds of law, law enforcement, social work, and education. The dean, Ranjit DeSilva, comes from Sri Lanka where he was the founding president of the Lanka Bible College. He had a distinguished career there in evangelism and church planting. One or two of the faculty members are alumni of the Crenshaw Christian Schools. The selection of faculty has displayed a high-level commitment to equipping people for effective ministry. It has not focused on academic credentials, but rather on effectiveness in ministry. The faculty has an awareness that, quoting from Luke 6:40, "when a student has been fully trained, he will be like his teacher." The Crenshaw Christian Center Schools clearly intends to equip men and women who will have a high-level commitment to ministry, confidence in their calling, and gifted abilities to serve.

Charles E. Fuller Institute

The evangelistic ministry of Charles E. Fuller began in 1925. In 1943 he organized the Fuller Evangelistic Association to help other missionary organizations and to multiply his evangelistic ministry. Fuller Theological Seminary was founded soon afterward to support and encourage the training of ministers. The Charles E. Fuller Institute of Evangelism and Church Growth (CEFI) emerged in 1980 out of the Fuller Evangelistic Institute. Located in Pasadena, California, a team of professional consultants and researchers coordinate the efforts of over forty staff associates strategically located across North America. With a clear purpose of helping the Church plant new churches and grow, CEFI unites academic excellence and evangelistic zeal. And, while not depicted as an "urban" church growth institute, most of CEFI's focus is in urban areas.

CEFI helps churches from many different denominations apply result-oriented ideas to specific problems. Each of CEFI's services has been tested in local churches. These services aim to meet practical needs in both local congregations and denominations. The staff uses current diagnostic and training resources. CEFI is especially concerned that churches receive the kind of advice that will help them to grow. Some CEFI materials are designed to be self-administered so churches can solve problems accurately and economically. Others are best applied with the assistance of a trained consultant.

The methods CEFI uses focus around what will be accessible to busy church leaders. CEFI packages its delivery system for the instruction in four major components: 1) workshops and seminars, 2) church diagnostic analysis, 3) church growth training modules, 4) specialized consulting, and, 5) materials production and distribution.

The workshops/seminars are one to three days long and are conducted in major urban centers around the US. These workshops/seminars focus on very specific topics. They seek to bring both a theoretical understanding so the participants can explain the problem being addressed and a set of practical actions to be taken that emerge out of the theoretical framework. For example, the seminar "Breaking the 200 Barrier," provides an explanation of why that barrier exists and then positive steps that may be taken to break it. CEFI designs these nonformal seminars so a person can receive Continuing Education Units (CEU's) or, with an arrangement with the D.Min office of Fuller Theological Seminary, academic credit.

More than 25,500 people have participated in CEFI seminars since 1983. To date CEFI has offered these seminars in about thirty-five cities. The average attendance of the twenty-one different seminars offered before February, 1991 ranged from fifteen to ninety-two with an overall average of 188. Some popular seminars have been given more than thirty times whereas some specialized seminars have only been given once.

Church growth training modules use custom designed materials dealing with over twenty different topics. They can be used by one church or by several churches working together. Each set of materials guides a pastor and a lay task force through practical instruction and specific application. The result is that good ideas are discovered and implemented. The modular training strategy is an economical way for a church to receive the help of an experienced church growth professional.

CEFI's focus on consulting provides a means of educating and equipping church leaders to address their local situation effectively. CEFI not only sends people as consultants from CEFI to congregations and denominations, but equips church leaders to become church growth consultants. Church growth consultants are available to help churches develop personalized strategies. Specialized consultations meet the unique needs of a specific client. The consultant's goal is to develop solutions to the problems that are limiting the church's effectiveness. This kind of specialized consultation is also available for districts and denominations.

The collection, production, and distribution of church growth related materials serve both the participants in the seminars and workshops as well as church leaders who cannot join in these learning experiences. These materials appear as notebooks, books, cassette tapes, and video tapes. CEFI provides the most current church growth literature and self-help materials. Training materials and seminar leader's guides are also available so churches can conduct their own training events on several topics.

A church analysis helps a local church understand its growth trends, measure volunteer involvement, evaluate programs, staff and facilities, and discover its potential for ministry in its community. It is a personalized comprehensive service that includes data gathering, a consultant's visit, extensive interviewing, and a written report.

The intended learners for CEFI's programs are Types III and IV leaders. The focus is on strategic planning and leadership. Most of the participants would be expected to have completed their theological education and be settled in a congregational ministry. While others are not specifically barred, the program aims at church leaders. Age and gender are not issues. Over the past eighteen years, many participants have been women.

The Charles E. Fuller Institute is a nonprofit ministry. An endowment and gifts of individuals and groups support its research and development. The cost of services varies according to the specific needs of each church. Participants bear the delivery and administrative costs of the CEFI programs. Other funds come from an endowment that provides funding for research and development of new curricula. The design of the financial structure then means that only the people who have made a significant financial commitment to the seminar attend the individual workshops/seminars. A typical three day seminar will cost about $250, that includes a notebook, the fees, and some light refreshments. Participants also must pay for room and board that CEFI will arrange if travel is required.

Control within CEFI may be seen in two different dimensions. As with other Christian organizations, it has a board of trustees and administrative structure. However, because fees and the sale of materials provide its operational expense, it is highly market driven. The community being served heavily influences what is taught. A market is seen as a combination of felt needs and a willingness to pay for meeting these needs.[3]

CEFI, as an urban training institution, has not focused on the poor or the multicultural dimensions of American cities. Its focus has primarily been with Anglo middle class evangelical churches. However, within this church community leaders who have worked with CEFI have reported significant positive changes in their growth patterns.

The 1990–1991 schedule of seminars included the following topics:

> How to Break the 200 Barrier
> Beyond 400
> Beyond 800
> Strategies for Starting New Churches
> How to Have a Prayer Ministry
> Basic Consulting Skills
> Drawing People in through "Felt Need" Events
> Conflict and Change in the Established Church

> Small Groups—Training Lay Pastors to Lead Home Groups
> Who Pastors the Pastor?
> Assimilation: Closing the Back Door
> Small Groups: A New Strategy
> Reaching Baby Boomers
> Reaching the Unchurched in the 1990s
> Preaching to the Unchurched

Some cities scheduled for these events include Los Angeles, Philadelphia, Seattle, Atlanta, Indianapolis, Cincinnati, Chicago, Toronto, Dallas, Vancouver, and San Francisco.

The Church on Brady

The Church on Brady is a Southern Baptist church in Los Angeles. It began meeting on January 3, 1943. The church has grown slowly, adding buildings in 1947, 1952, 1958, and 1987.

The church has a history of starting new congregations. When the present fellowship hall was opened in 1947, a Spanish mission church emerged out of that congregation. This outward-looking perspective continued until the 1960s, when

> Pressures in a changing community shattered the dream. It faded. The 60s were hard times for our church. It was the death of a vision. Many left. Few people hung on through that decade. It seemed like the end.
>
> Then God brought a man, Bro. Tom [Wolfe]. He was the right man at the right time. Revival came. Within fourteen years the dreams of the founders were fulfilled in even greater proportions than they ever dared to think.[4]

While many churches are larger, the Church on Brady has come to national recognition through its innovative and committed response to the community where it exists. The funeral for the congregation had been planned in the mid 1960s, and yet in the 1990s the church stands as an example of how a local congregation may not only serve within the community, but move through a local community to establish many other churches.

> The leadership of the church seeks to be obedient rather than just "creative." The church of our Lord is not called to be innovative. The church is called to be faithful. Thus it has never been the goal of the Church on Brady to be known as an innovative church, as such. Our goal has been to reach those around us for Jesus Christ and to extend the Kingdom of our Lord. During our stumbling attempts to do that well, others have credited us with being "nontraditional" or "innovative."[5]

Brady Response to a Changing Community

As the culture changed dramatically around the church, the leadership made a commitment to move out **into** the community rather than to move out **of** the community. They believed God is unchanging and His expectations for faithfulness in the community are unchanging. Recognizing the profound changes in the community led them to believe that they had to change to meet those changes. The Church on Brady, recognizing that it is no longer in a churched culture, felt compelled to reposition itself as in a mission culture.

The American culture and particularly the culture in East Los Angeles is no longer a "churched culture." The Church on Brady no longer sees itself in a churched culture, but in a "mission culture."[6]

Callahan cites three characteristics of an unchurched or mission culture: "1) the value of church is not among the major values of the culture, 2) a substantial number of persons are not seeking out churches on their own initiative, 3) a majority of persons live as though the church does not substantially matter."[7]

> Most professional ministers are trained to deal with matters inside the church. However, in a mission culture they are called to move out and deal with matters outside the church, in the mission culture.

> On a mission field, leadership is best understood as facing outside, addressing the world, not inside, focusing only on the church. The pastor on mission will participate actively, personally interacting with the society and training the church membership to be on mission in the unchurched culture.

> Thus leaders will be more proactive, less reactive; more intentional, less passive; more relational, less organizational; more missional, less institutional. For in a mission culture, the church must go to the world, whereas in a church culture, the church can organize for the world to come to the church.[8]

The profound cultural changes that came into the American culture in the 1960s and the dramatic population shifts in East Los Angeles led the leadership of the Church on Brady to be obedient in the new context. "The conviction is sincerely held by our leadership that the church that does not clearly, concretely, and courageously face those changes will wither into irrelevance."[9]

The Church on Brady states as its purpose the intent "to become a spiritual reference point east of downtown Los Angeles and a sending base to the ends of the earth."[10] The ministry philosophy of the Church on Brady undergirds its principles, policies, and strategic approach not only to the community, but to the equipping and sending of men and women to plant churches in other parts of the world as well. The Church on Brady seeks to be a full service church that is fully obedient to the Great Commission and to the Great Commandment.

As God's people on assignment, the Church on Brady:

*Lives by apprenticeship
Some learn in order to know.
We learn in order to do.

*Thinks in congregations
Some think in individual congregations.
We think in multiplying congregations.

*Exists by being laity dependent.
Some involve people in their programs.
We depend on people fulfilling their callings.[11]

Developing Leaders in Context

The Church on Brady is responding in its context to develop leadership. At least three kinds of leaders are deliberately equipped in the Church on Brady training programs: 1) Type I leaders for small groups, 2) Type II leaders who link small groups and become paraprofessional congregational leaders, and, 3) Type III leaders who initiate new congregations through the formation of small groups or pastors.

Beyond the Anglicized European stock from northwest Europe, Los Angeles County has more than 150 other ethnic groups identified in communities within the county. Some populations of these ethnic groups are substantial. Outside their home countries Los Angeles provides the largest city in the world of Mexicans, Armenians, Koreans, Filipinos, Salvadorians, and Guatemalans. Los Angeles is the third largest Canadian city. It has the largest Gypsy, Iranian, Cambodian, and Japanese communities in the United States. More Samoans live in Los Angeles than in American Samoa. It has the largest Russian Jewish population outside the Soviet Union and Israel.

The religious mosaic is no less complex. Within the metropolitan area of Los Angeles are some of the largest churches in the United States. Buddhist temples, Hindu temples, Muslim mosques, Satanic centers, cultic temples, humanistic centers, Native American worship centers, and others comprise major parts of the mosaic.

Los Angeles is a major training center for Christian organizations. Bible institutes, Bible colleges, Christian colleges, Christian universities, seminaries that serve the Orthodox, Catholic, evangelical, and charismatic communities are present. These institutions serve not only the Anglo community, but the Hispanic, Armenian, Egyptian Orthodox, Chinese, and Korean communities; they also teach in their languages.

Los Angeles is expected to have more ethnic groups represented than any other city in the world by the year 2000. Demographers predict it will continue to grow at 2.1 percent per year, double the national growth rate. By A.D. 2000 the aging Anglo population, then a minority, will be dependent upon the Hispanic and Asian populations who will be in the majority.

The Church on Brady training program seeks to equip a person to plant churches in an urban setting in which outside financial assistance is not given. The purpose sets the program apart from most formal educational programs and from church-based nonformal programs. While adaptable in other urban areas, it has been designed carefully to fit into the East Los Angeles context. This context is mixed ethnically with an Hispanic majority.

Learner Selection

The selection of people to be trained in the leadership training program occurs in at least two ways: 1) existing leaders take note of the people from within the congregation and encourage them to participate in the equipping, and 2) people from outside the congregation come to the church to be trained for these ministries. People coming from outside may be seminary graduates, Christian college graduates, or lay people.

The basic training that is available to everyone at the church focuses on the beginning stages of leadership training. The selection process continues as the individuals' commitment is observed in faithfulness in the formation of small groups and participation in training sessions. The training sessions have taken on an increased formal character because the Church on Brady has recently entered an arrangement with Grand Canyon University in Phoenix to offer a Master's Degree in Urban Studies. This academic credential provides a formal means by which some graduates may apply for work in other countries.

People who are learning to organize small groups in the congregations with the Church on Brady, are not put on salary, so that they will learn how to organize self supporting churches from the very beginning without creating dependencies.

The selection process continues in a competency-based approach by which the learner must demonstrate the ability to establish small groups and congregations before graduating. If the person cannot establish small groups that will multiply, it is believed that the person should not be sent to establish new congregations as a church planter.

Curriculum Design at the Church on Brady

The educational program at the Church on Brady consists of several elements. The foundational base of the church's discipleship is its Church Training Program (CTP). Leaders formulated the CTP in 1976 as a comprehensive plan for training. The CTP courses focus on four areas: Maturity (character), Message (convictions concerning God's Word), Ministry (skills), and Missions (bases for cross-cultural ministry and skills). Other educational components include sermons, articles, specialized training for leaders, individualized ministry counseling and projects, seminars, mission trips, internships, and apprenticeship training.[12]

A key component both in the ministry of the church and the training of church planters is the small group program. Small group leaders are required to take a ten-week leader's course designed to equip them for leading a small group before a ministry assignment is given in a small group.

> This training includes such things as grounding in the purpose of share groups, basic leadership qualifications, dynamics of leadership reproduction, evangelism philosophy and skills, basic counseling skills and responsibilities, input on issues such as divorce, reconciliation, and remarriage, tongues, the second coming and other doctrinal issues.[13]

> Leaders are also required to attend monthly training sessions. These sessions focus on key issues in small groups. For example, one recent training session focused on reproducing leadership. It focused on helping leaders answer the tough questions of whom they would select as potential leaders, when and how they would train and model for them.[14]

Emerging leaders are provided both experiential input, affective related input, and reflection. Development of character, convictions, and competence form primary concerns. The ministry director evaluates these three concerns before any ministry assignments are made. In this way, deficient areas are identified, goals for growth are set and projected training and service are mapped out.[15]

> The general policy of the church is to give a higher level of responsibility before or at approximately the same time as a higher level of training. Thus, before being given training in leading a leader has already begun serving (at least informally) in that capacity. In this way, the staff seeks to insure that individuals are eager for more input. Share group leaders, for example, are given the responsibility of nurturing the members of their group and leading them toward an evangelistic lifestyle that reaches unbelievers for Christ. The catch word that every share group leader is taught is that as the leader goes, so goes the group. The effect of this kind of responsibility is that the share group leaders feel a good deal of pressure to "produce," and because of this they are usually eager for input that will help them do so.[16]

The ministry philosophy of the Church on Brady prevents the leadership from simply filling empty slots. Davis notes that

> we believe that God has gifted the Body to accomplish what He has called it to
> . . . . Therefore, we try to discern what gifts a person has with a specific area
> of ministry within the church's overall program. This means that the ministry is
> actually shaped to a degree by the gifting of its leaders.[17]

Church members who demonstrate commitment and spiritual growth are encouraged to accept an entry-level type of responsibility such as "ushering or preschool care, building maintenance or assisting leaders in various areas."[18] "We believe in Luke 16:10 . . .," Davis notes, "so we watch a person to see if they are faithful in the little things before we give them greater responsibility."[19]

Initially, a verification of committed faithfulness is sought. As faithfulness is demonstrated, greater responsibilities are assigned. In this next assignment of person's apparent giftedness is taken into consideration.

Spiritual Formation

The spiritual formation focus of the Church on Brady requires long term attention because many of the leaders are converted out of very difficult situations including personal abuse, substance abuse, and immoral lifestyles. Much of the foundational spiritual formation occurs in the small share groups. These groups continue to contribute to the spiritual and ministry formation of the merging leaders as well as other participants. Mutual accountability is expected.

The element of spiritual formation may be seen in the purpose statement:

> The purpose of share groups is to win unbelievers to Christ by providing accountability among believers for a transformed life personally and an evangelistic lifestyle.[20]

Spiritual formation is also a focus "in the 'maturity' concentration of the church training program. The courses in this concentration focus on spiritual and character development."[21] The course description for "Essentials of Knowing Christ," illustrates this focus:

> The goal of this course is to firmly establish each class member in the joyous
> habit of daily Bible study and prayer. Attention will be given to mutual accountability, effective methods, personal application and common hindrances to
> success.[22]

The primary equipping model which has characterized the training over the past years is an apprenticeship model. This model has served well in the multicultural context of East Los Angeles. It has also demonstrated its durability across the different levels of instruction in the equipping of leaders.

> The commitment of the church to the apprenticeship style training model is per-haps the backbone of the whole program and is, indeed, a refreshing change form the cognitively dominated programs propagated by seminaries and Bible schools. It is a return to the Biblical model, and something that needs to be mul-tiplied to other training institutions.[23] . . . While the apprenticeship model is effectively used by upper-level leaders, it is more unconsciously (as opposed to consciously) employed by many mid-level leaders in the church as a means of training younger leaders.[24]

LeTourneau Ministries International

LeTourneau Ministries International (LMI) is an interdenominational mis-sion support organization whose purpose is to "help urban churches in Latin America with programs of evangelism discipleship and church growth."[25] LMI does not send missionaries, but rather works through ex-isting evangelical missions and local churches as a consulting and funding agency.

The mission statement for LMI is very clear and to the point: "To help urban churches evangelize their nation."[26] The objective is:

> To help existing missions and national churches in each of twenty countries of Latin America establish a network of strong, aggressive, evangelistic churches that when left alone will have the vision and potential to continue to evangelize and establish churches throughout their nation. This means that they will have the leadership and resources necessary to carry out this task without any further help from outside. We are estimating at this time that each country will need as-sistance in building at least thirty to forty facilities each of 1,000 to 1,500 seat-ing capacity in order enable them to produce the resources necessary to continue accomplishing the task without us.

A primary focus of LMI is the provision and planning for funding for new church planting. However, a critical component of their overall con-sulting and planning is the leadership development for urban churches.

LMI Foundations

Beginning in 1973 with the Linze church in Lima, Peru, basic ministry and strategic positions were formed in cooperation with the Christian and

Missionary Alliance in that city. One of conscious decisions was the multiplication of churches rather than the addition of members to a single congregation. A second strategic perspective was the recognition of the need for facilities for urban church planting. As LMI continued to assist with funding the new church buildings, demand soon outstripped the available resources. In response to this demand a new principle was incorporated into the strategy. The principle was simply that new churches would commit twenty percent of their income to contribute to the building of new churches in other places. Three strategic perspectives contribute to the overall approach of LMI in urban centers in Latin America: 1) biblical perspectives, 2) continent/national strategies, and 3) local church strategies.

Biblical Perspectives of LMI

LMI works with churches and missions from what they call "three biblical anchors": 1) New Testament and Model, 2) Commission Oriented, and 3) Local Congregation Centered.

New Testament and Model

The strategic urban approach of the Apostle Paul in the first century is seen as a primary model for the church today. Initially, he visited urban centers to establish churches. On his second missionary tour he continued to focus on the encouragement of these urban churches.

Commission Oriented

The priority of LMI in its consulting and support is the Great Commission. "The intent of this program is to, as the commission states, "*make disciples*." This demands a balance of evangelism and discipleship follow-up. There must be the reproduction of new life on a regular basis, but there must also be a systematic approach to maturing each one of these converts."[27] LMI then has a heavy focus on evangelism and what is termed "discipleship" or "leadership development."

Local Congregation Centered

The New Testament model for evangelism was in the context of local bodies of believers. The local church is the "one institution which God states in

His word He will bless. Social and educational works are not wrong but we believe if we build the local church properly, it will be able to provide these other things to its own community, thus, enhancing its testimony and drawing more people to make decisions for Christ."[28]

Continental/National Strategy

Four specific principles serve to guide the methodology and leadership development of ministries supported by LMI: 1) small cultural steps, 2) concentration, 3) middle class foundations, and 4) capital city focus.

Cultural Small Steps

The small step principle seeks to "use all our manpower . . . in its most productive role."[29] The greater the distance between a person's own culture and the receptor culture, the more difficulty the person has in making the adjustment. The greater the cultural distance, the more time is spent in simply trying to exist in the host culture. One result is a great loss of efficiency which affects the effectiveness of the ministry in question, whether that person be a missionary, a national pastor or church worker. However, when one crosses a cultural boundary which is not distant, the potential for effective ministry to occur more quickly is enhanced. Latin American urban centers are similar in many ways to North American urban centers. Culturally, urban centers in Latin America are closer to urban centers in North America than rural regions in Latin America would be to those in North America. However, the difference between people who live in rural areas in Latin America and people who live in urban regions in Latin America is not great.

> When the nationals in the capital are won to Christ and challenged properly, they go to secondary or provincial cities—a very small step for them since this is where most of them originally lived. Those in the providence cities are won, and they in turn go to the smaller cities and even to the jungle settings. The nation is won through everyone taking only a small step. If we are to reach the world we must wisely use the resources we are given.[30]

Concentration

The concentration principle seeks to "throw all our resources into one place."[31] In the past, mission strategies have often followed a rural perspective in which missionaries are strategically located geographically covering wide areas among people who are widely dispersed. However, the LMI, using an urban strategy perspective, seeks to concentrate all of its "resources and personnel into one place to develop a successful thriving ministry that will be capable of reproducing itself. By concentrating all our efforts and resources on one church, more people are reached with the message of the gospel and we are able to find, challenge and train qualified national leadership to continue to work using the 'small step' methodology."[32] The perspective is to build a strong foundation which has "the potential to grow far beyond our previous strategies and also to become indigenous much quicker."[33]

Middle Class Foundations

The middle class receives the initial focus of church planting attention. "Winning the middle class provides insurance in two key issues facing the continuation of any program, leadership, and resources."[34] Neither missionaries, who are outsiders, nor people in the lower class, who lack education, a financial base, and national leadership potential, are seen to have the potential for changing the nation. Leadership that will affect the whole nation will likely emerge out of the middle class. People out of the middle class are able to support the work and lead it in a way that others will follow. "When a strong base is built, then they can reach more widely in both directions—both down to the poor and up to the very rich. They are more effective in their own hometowns than a missionary could ever be and can infiltrate the centers of power to make a national impact for Christ."[35] To date more success has been seen in the evangelization of the urban poor than the urban rich through this strategy.[36]

Capital City Focus

The great concentrations of people live in the capital cities in Latin America. Typically, across Latin America between one-third and one-half of a nation's people live in the capital city. For any strategy to influence a nation in Latin America, it is critically important to recognize that "almost anything of any importance has its origin in the capital city."[37] The networks of relationships from the capital city reaches into virtually every remote area and certainly into every town and city in the nation.

In Latin America capital cities have a high concentration of centralized government. Educational resources are located in capital cities. The capital cities provide the primary linkages for both national and international trade. And the national cities provide the heaviest concentration of people who are in the middle class.

Local Church Strategy

The primary and most effective agency for evangelism is the local church. With a concentration of resources in the capital city to establish between twenty and forty local congregations which number between a 1,000 and 1,500, LMI seeks to implement its national strategies.

The equipping of leaders in the local congregation who will implement the basic strategic perspectives is critically important to LMI's overall approach. LMI has identified eight points which are brought into focus for all of the leaders in the new churches that are being established. These eight points include 1) prayer, 2) team ministry, 3) location, 4) attractive buildings, 5) momentum evangelism, 6) discipleship, 7) missionary vision, and 8) financial responsibility. Every point has an urban missiological foundation. Together these eight points are described in LMI literature as the "Encounter With God" strategy.

Prayer

"Divine guidance is an absolute essential in the preparation as well as the working out of programs of evangelism and church growth."[38] Prayer is enlisted from two sources: from the members of the new emerging congregation and from other supporting congregations, including those in North America.

Team Ministry

Team ministries for local congregations are built from the very beginning. The pulpit is shared among the pastoral team. "This provides continuity, a breadth of experience, less missionary paternalism, greater efficiency, and a smoother and less dramatic pastoral transition."[39] LMI in Lima built its strategy on the already strong foundation of the Christian and Missionary Alliance (C&MA) presence.

Location

The location of local congregations is a critical issue in the overall strategy within the capital city. In Latin America "where most people travel on public transportation, if a church is located even one block off the main avenue where the bus routes flow, its future growth and ministry is surely endangered."[40]

LMI insists that "any congregation expecting to be a part of the Encounter With God program finally establish herself on a main avenue. The strategic location makes two important contributions to the spreading of the Word of God; accessibility (easy to find) and credibility (everyone is aware of their presence)."[41]

To establish local congregations that will grow rapidly and have the potential for establishing other congregations, "it is a far better investment to build where the greatest number of people can be reached and influenced with the message of the gospel than to limp along off the beaten path just to save money."[42]

Attractive Buildings

Just as the location of local congregations is a critical issue, so also the facilities are seen to be very important in the overall plan. The buildings should be "attractive enough to draw the middle and upper class but not so elaborate as to turn off the lower class."[43] Strategically located churches with attractive buildings then become a part of the overall strategy.

Momentum Evangelism

Location and aesthetically pleasing buildings do not guarantee church growth. However, evangelism which builds on the ever widening networks of relationships in the city does provide a key. Momentum in evangelism combines

> the best features of mass evangelism and local church evangelism. Those who are saved the previous month now bring their friends, relatives and acquaintances the next month. Those that are saved that month are added to the ranks in bringing others the following month. As the months unfold momentum is gained and church attendance literally explodes. The chain reaction of evangelism can sweep through homes and communities much more effectively than if a campaign were held only once or twice a year.[44]

This part of the strategy has come under criticism in some urban centers, such as Mexico City because the middle class people there find the evangelistic crusades every month too taxing on their already busy schedule. There other evangelistic methods have proven to be more effective to maintain the momentum.

Discipleship

"The discipling of believers is vital and of equal importance with evangelism."[45] The discipleship equipping approach of these churches does not aim at the maintenance of new believers, but rather the equipping of new believers for leadership, first in small groups, then in larger groupings in the local congregations. "New converts are immediately and continuously encouraged to attend the Bible academy which has special classes two evenings a week. Initially new believers are taught basic truths to ground them in their new found faith. Then they are led into deeper study of individual books within the Bible and finally into studies which will develop them as church workers."[46] The Bible academies in local churches provide a key ingredient for infrastructural growth and spiritual growth which are both basic to continued numerical growth.

Leadership development is "one of the two ingredients of vital importance to the continuance of the strategy." Theological Education by Extension ("TEE") greatly aids the equipping of lay people for leadership through an extensive home study curriculum. The TEE materials and programs are administered out of these local Bible academies.

The equipping of Type III and IV leaders is done in the Alliance Bible Institute whose objective is the development of future urban pastors and Christian education workers. The curriculum in the Alliance Bible Institute is designed to be taken over a six year period, three evenings a week so that the learners can work, pay for their own studies, and remain in ministry while they are studying. Students are expected to take on increasing leadership responsibilities and ministry through the course of the six year equipping program. Initial ministry assignments may be brief voluntary assignments. However, by the third year more significant long term commitments are expected. Many upper division students are employed as part-time associates in the churches.

The redesign of this Bible institute's delivery system and approach to learner selection away from a more traditional approach led to a multiplication of more mature students who enter with both ministry experience and a clear sense of call to the ministry. Since the redesign, the institute has not had a problem with declining enrollments.

Missionary Vision

As new congregations are established a strong emphasis is placed on commitment to a missionary vision. "The formation of new daughter congregations in the capital city by each local church is not an option but an essential aspect of growth. They are committed not to build bigger and bigger but to multiply themselves by the 'hiving off' of members to form the nuclei for these new churches."[47] The vision does not only include the formation of new churches in the local city but in other cities and towns as well. The clear intent is to move across a whole nation, beginning from the capital city.

Financial Responsibility

"The development of churches which are financially accountable and eventually free of all forms of subsidy" is an integral part of LMI's strategy. LMI does not support any ongoing expenses of the churches or pastoral salaries. It only supports the construction of church evangelistic centers and some overall program coordination costs.

LMI's fiscal policies have aided the formation of new congregations in Peru.

> We feel a young church that is receiving resources for land and buildings must also commit herself to help other new churches. Rapid inflation in most Latin American countries makes it impractical for churches receiving financial assistance to consider they are receiving a dollar and cents loan to be paid back within a stipulated period at a given interest rate. Instead as buildings are completed she commits herself to a program of mutual assistance paying into a revolving fund of at least twenty percent of her monthly income. This commitment is perpetual—until Christ returns.[48]

This fiscal commitment appears on the surface to be a very good and valid idea. However, in some situations this policy has become a stumbling block to expansion. In Mexico City, for example, the policy of committing twenty percent of the church's income in perpetuity to other church buildings has not been popular with the Mexican leadership and is viewed as a limiting factor.

Old First Church
Los Angeles First Church of the Nazarene

Probably the most crucial and, at the same time, heartrending decision an "Old First Church" can ever make is to decide whether it will stay in its urban setting or follow its parishioners to the safer, and for them, more predictable and controllable suburbs. History has shown that most go. However, some stay. The story of Los Angeles First Church of the Nazarene chronicles a typical church which had to make that decision.

Historical Background

Founded in 1895 by Phineas F. Bresee, this congregation soon became involved in a nationwide revival movement which ultimately resulted in the unification of several regional clusters of churches to become the Church of the Nazarene.[49]

Mission to the poor was a major issue for Bresee. He connected social work and evangelism in the first days of the church:

> We were convinced that houses of worship should be plain and cheap, to save from financial burdens, and that everything should say welcome to the poor. We went feeling that food and clothing and shelter were the open doors to the hearts of the unsaved poor, and that through these doors we could bear to them the life of God. We went in poverty, to give ourselves—and what God might give us—determined to forego provision for the future and old age, in order to see the salvation of God while we were yet here. God has not disappointed us.[50]

The congregation's first building was in the middle of downtown Los Angeles. However, through a combination of growing pains and changing neighborhoods, the church moved twice out of downtown, each time believing it had moved far enough from the urban problems, only to find itself again overtaken. Their present location at Third and Vermont is halfway between downtown and Hollywood.

During the first half of this century the church grew and prospered. By 1954, church membership peaked at 702. The congregation's clientele was no longer even marginally poor. They were doctors, professors, and millionaires. The entire denomination enjoyed prestige and status.

In the mid-sixties, urban growth again began to overtake the congregation. Decline set in. Pastors became frustrated and discouraged at not being able to "turn it around." By 1976 membership was less than half that of 1954. Even though the church still had influence, the grey pall of inevitable death was becoming visible.

The church board, sensing this threat, began considering alternatives. Ron Benefiel, the present pastor, commented about when the philosophy of ministry began to change:

> When the church was in decline, they decided to call Paul Benefiel as their pastor. He had been a good pastor, but he did not bring prestige to the pulpit. I believe it was because he has a Master's Degree in Sociology. They knew they were dying and were not going to recapture the old glory, and they wanted someone who could help the church minister to the community. I'm convinced they didn't know all that meant, but that is when the transition took place.[51]

The calling of Paul Benefiel in 1974 was the first step in this church's rediscovering its mission to the poor of Los Angeles. This time, however, the decision to minister to the community was only the first step. Many more related decisions were to follow.

The Components of Leadership Training

Once First Church made the decision to become a community based church,[52] the question arose, "How can the church make the transition?" People used to being served now realized that they were the servants.

Retraining Lay Leadership

With time a new vision of ministry emerged which, in addition to worship, included service to the immediate community. Slowly, a palette of holistic ministries was added. Some were designated to serve the community as a whole, and others were aimed at particular needs within the church.

Ethnic Leadership Development

The church established four ethnic congregations over ten years. A vital ministry, similar in proportion to that experienced in the "glory" days replaced despair. The difference is that leadership includes major ethnic groups of the community. In addition to an English-speaking congregation there are presently a Korean , a Spanish-speaking and a Filipino congregation. All are considered part of First Church.

The church is divided into different ethnic congregations, but all members belong to the larger church. There are several reasons for this. First, people generally prefer to find Christ within their own language and cultural context. Second, according to Ronald Benefiel, "We see the need of cultivating a sense of unity, purpose and commitment to Jesus Christ in the midst of our cultural heterogeneity."[53] Third, rapid demographic changes would have a renewed negative impact on the morale of the larger church body.

To start a new ethnic congregation within this model, in addition to the commitment of the parent church, three criteria had to be filled: First, the demographics had to be right. Secondly, the congregation had to be prepared to start this new work. Thirdly, it was very important to find the right leader for each new congregation. For church planting, the pastor had to be someone who had a heart for evangelism.[54]

This model presents both problems and solutions:

1. It avoids what often becomes a problem in a "one church building—many congregations" model; the renter—tenant concern. This avoids that for which ministry to the community was created to bypass—the "us against them" syndrome.

2. Paternalism can become a concern in a multiethnic congregational structure. The senior pastor has to be able to release the other congregations to do what is necessary for ministry in their culture. This freedom requires firm relationships between the members of the pastoral staff and a secure senior pastor.

3. The "one service, simultaneous translation" model is flawed, because one ministers mainly to marginal people who feel more comfortable in the host culture than in their own. The majority of those in the target culture are most comfortable hearing the gospel within their own cultural context.

Within the multicongregational organizational structure, Los Angeles First Church of the Nazarene has created a Charter which calls for a "Super Board" to be made up of representatives from each self-supporting congregation. This council has authority over building use, maintenance costs, utility costs, and joint programming. In other details, such as transportation, joint decisions are also made. The key for membership distribution on the council is based on the congregations' membership, Sunday morning attendance, and financial giving from the previous year.[55]

Church Planting

First Church has a close working relationship with the Union Rescue Mission. That places them ministering to the poor and destitute of the city. They have returned to the Skid Row area where an Institute graduate began contextualized church services in an inner-city park which ministered to street people. The pastor lives in the immediate vicinity.

Another congregation was planted in Exposition Park. Its ministry began with Caribbean Blacks, but with changing demographics, the church now ministers to a predominantly Central American population. To help meet expenses, to establish a more permanent presence, and to minister to the material needs of their community, they have opened a Thrift Store.

Bresee Institute

The Bresee Institute officially began in the summer of 1983. The initial purpose was to prepare "men and women to minister more effectively within the urban context."[56]

> The Bresee Institute is an extension of the ministry of L.A. First Church of the Nazarene. It functions as an urban ministry training center, drawing upon the ministries of the inner-city church, urban ministry people, formal training institutions, and other Christian organizations . . . . The training staff are all involved in urban ministries and work with the Bresee Institute on a part-time basis.[57]

Graduate credit is offered both through Nazarene Theological Seminary (NTS) and Azusa Theological Seminary (APU) School of Theology. Bresee Institute provides the faculty, which has adjunct faculty status with APU.

> The purpose of the Bresee Institute is to train Christian men and women, lay and clergy, to minister to the people in the city by equipping them to recognize and solve urban problems in the context of Christian community.[58]

In another purpose statement a new definition of what it means to minister to a multicultural and poorer community in a holistic and meaningful way was developed:

1. To prepare individuals who are committed to ministering to urban areas for Christian leadership.

2. To equip individuals for urban and cross-cultural ministry with the appropriate skills necessary to effectively impact the urban environment.

3. To assist mid-career ministers already involved in the urban setting in developing new ministry skills while continuing their ministry.

4. To create formal interdenominational evangelistic thrusts that would indeed improve the spiritual and material tone of the urban context, i.e., Los Angeles.[59]

The Bresee Institute represents a trend in contemporary metropolitan settings. With its complex inter-organizational relationships, the Bresee Institute is not a separate legal entity, but rather a division of Los Angeles First Church and the P. F. Bresee Foundation. It is also related to Azusa Pacific University, Nazarene Theological Seminary, and informally linked to Fuller Theological Seminary. It also has formal links with a growing number of undergraduate institutions.

Finances are handled through the P. F. Bresee Foundation or through affiliation with accredited educational institutions. Since the Bresee Institute is located on the campus of the Los Angeles First Church of the Nazarene, costs for facilities are minimized and availability of facilities is maximized.

Within this framework, six levels of programming have emerged: 1) graduate course work; 2) graduate internship; 3) undergraduate urban studies; 4) summer internship; 5) an orientation-to-the-city program; and 6) seminars, workshops, conferences, and consultations. Although the Bresee Institute was initiated through the vision of the local church, the training and the ministry are an interdenominational effort.

Los Angeles Urban Ministries/Study Center—Urban Concentration

The Bresee Institute Graduate Program is designed to be a part of the Master of Arts or Master of Divinity degree program offered through APU. The Bresee Institute offers six to eight courses with APU Graduate School of Theology providing academic credit. Each requires three hours of class time a week, in addition to field trips into the community, and twelve hours of supervised ministry per week.

All courses are based on the action-reflection model, and experiential learning is treated in different ways. Often the instructors arrange individual appointments with people who are active in ministry or the community. All of the course require reflection papers.

The ministry experience component of the curriculum reflects both the philosophy of education at the Bresee Institute and the philosophy of education at APU. The APU Graduate School of Theology catalog states,

> The Graduate School of Theology is committed to an experiential learning model. The Master of Divinity and Master of Ministry Programs are designed with the intentional integration of biblical, theological and ministerial studies. Students are required to devote at least twelve hours per week for the duration of their degree program to some form of supervised ministry.[60]

The ministry experience requirement relates not only to ministry courses, but also urban anthropology, sociology, and urban planning courses as well.

The Graduate Internship

It is possible for the student to take courses without being an intern; however, all interns must take the course work. The interns are expected to

participate in ministry at least twenty hours per week over the two semes-
ter period.

Dynamic reflection is a critical component of the intern program, and
it occurs between the supervisor and intern in biweekly debriefing sessions.
"The purpose is to evaluate the context of the ministry with its particular
needs and the interns actual performance in ministry."[61]

The internship program aims at the stimulation of spiritual growth.[62]
The interns are expected to attend and participate in worship services,
Bible studies and other growth related activities of the church where they
are working during the time of the internship program. The intern's supervisor is expected to keep track of the intern's spiritual growth and
progress.

The Bresee Institute for Urban Training Summer Internship

The summer internship at the Bresee Institute is an eight week program for
undergraduates or recent graduates. It parallels the graduate internship.

This program is also based on the action-reflection model. The morning program normally includes lectures, videos and other kinds of input
for reflection and spiritual formation. The afternoon periods are given to
ministry and participation in community activities.

Undergraduate Program

The summer internship program is designed for college juniors and seniors
who indicate interest in urban training. The program provides the intern
with an introduction to the city and the opportunity to learn about and participate in the life and outreach of Los Angeles First Church and the Bresee
Institute.[63]

Christian Leadership Formation

Spiritual formation is addressed in the intern-supervisor relationships. The
times of reflection involving personal spiritual growth, the class-time input, the seminars, and the ministry experience all contribute to the ongoing
spiritual development of the participants.[64] A significant number of the
graduates have become leaders in L.A. First Church. Some have come into
the programs headed for secular jobs, yet many of those have opted for active ministry of various sorts.

Learner Selection

The Bresee Institute works with Types I, II, and III leaders. These leaders come from a variety of experiences. Some are pre-service. Some are in-service or mid-career and some have interrupted their ministries to participate in the training programs. However, the training programs are primarily aimed at pre-service students.

Faculty Selection

Each of the faculty members at the Bresee Institute has a graduate degree in some area of urban studies plus urban ministry experience. These degrees range from Ph.D.s in Sociology and Urban Planning, to a M.S.W., and an M.A. Instructors combine in their training both theology and social sciences. The range of their ministries includes pastoring, teaching, working in evangelism, and a various social ministries among the poor. The social ministries include food distribution, community organization and development, and relief and rehabilitation through such organizations as the LA Mission, Union Rescue Mission, and World Vision.

Summary—First Church of the Nazarene/Bresee Institute

The result of the change in focus has not only revolutionized the ministry of the church, it has also transformed the lives of individuals and the way they cherish their church. The decision of many interns to stay after completing their studies shows they are convinced that meaningful ministry is taking place. Certainly the urban setting brings with it a high degree of mobility and change. However, people are no longer leaving the church out of frustration, fear, or even lack of identification with the ministry of the church because they live in the community.

Harambee Christian Family Center

John and Vera Mae Perkins moved to Pasadena in 1982, after twenty-three years of Christian community development in Mississippi. Their goal was to retire, but John was challenged anew by the need he found in a high crime and drug community, and they established the Harambee Christian Family Center. Harambee is a Swahili word which means, "Let's get together and push!" It is an East African rallying cry that calls people together to solve a problem.[65] Perkins, a popular public speaker, described his first impressions of the community:

> This "microcosm of decay," is typical of the new emerging "underclass" in any urban area in the world. I looked into the eyes of . . . neighbors and saw their basic worth, and their unrealized potential drowning in hopelessness.[66]

They chose a place to live, staked out a ten block neighborhood, and went to work. John held community meetings to find out what the perceived needs were, and Vera Mae, a gifted children's worker, opened Bible clubs in their garage. There they gathered a group of dedicated volunteers who share time, skills, and knowledge to challenge spiritually impoverished youth to develop the disciplines necessary for realizing their leadership potential.

Within two years, they had put together a facility with four contiguous houses which became a campus on which a learning complex was developed. Crafts, a print shop, typing, piano, sewing, cooking, a computer learning center, the performing arts, and many more courses are offered to youth. The staff lives on campus. Many classrooms have been added, and an outdoor amphitheater was created as an alternative activity for the summer street scene. The Harambee Christian Center is not a church. The Center supports and is supported by many local churches.

Harambee Center Creed

The creed of the Center expresses the members' commitment to encouraging and helping each other, and to working together to elevate all people caught in the cycle of poverty:

> We are what we make of ourselves,
> We will no longer fit the mold that has been prepared for us,
> We will strive for a completeness in Christ that will compel us to stand against the social and economic injustices of our time,
> We will identify and understand our heritage, thus affirming our family,
> We will broaden our educational and technical skills,
> We will learn to use the economic system to free our people from the poverty cycle,
> We will never discourage, but always encourage our sisters and brothers,
> Then, we will join hands and move together to change our society.
> HARAMBEE! HARAMBEE! "Let's get together and push!"[67]

Governing Body and Funding for the Center

The Center is governed by a twenty-four member Board of Directors that provides oversight of the Center's operations. The funding comes entirely from money, goods, and services donated by individuals and churches. The Center receives no government funding.

Harambee Programming

The programming includes attention to youth, families (particularly single parent families), and community leaders. All of the programs aim at the building of a Christian community.

Youth Program

The staff and the approximately eighty volunteers see "parenting" as an important part of their ministry. They work hard to create a family atmosphere. Some of the staff and volunteer groups are graduates of the program. One of the guiding principles is that as one receives, there is a responsibility to reinvest one's self. The Center is open seven days a week for the youth.

Adult Literacy Tutoring

Adults in the neighborhood have shown great interest in the adult literacy program. The Center provides trained tutors who meet weekly with each participant in a one-on-one setting to assist with reading and writing skills. The tutor and the student meet at a mutually convenient time and place.

Monthly Business Luncheon

The Center holds a monthly business luncheon for local community leaders. During their time together, information is shared with business and community leaders about the concerns and the needs of Northwest Pasadena. It also affords an opportunity to build coalitions to meet those needs and concerns.

Summer Day Camp

In the summer, the Center provides an eight-week, six-hour a day program for about sixty-five children who spend their time enhancing reading skills in an atmosphere of play. The children also participate in organized crafts, sports, field trips, tutoring, and overnight camp outs. This program provides many opportunities for volunteer involvement and the development of small groups or Type I leaders. The time commitment is flexible.

Home for Female Ex-Offenders

In July of 1991, Harambee bought an adjacent house, renovated it and is using it as a home for female ex-offenders who are beginning a new life with Christ. The house is now debt-free.

Summary—Harambee Christian Family Center

The Harambee Christian Family Center is a community-oriented development model which addresses all age levels and all levels of society. It seeks to introduce Christian values into economically disadvantaged communities and to develop leaders who will become both role models for the younger generation and catalysts for transformational change in those very communities.

One foundational principle the Center teaches and practices is the delegation of community leadership responsibilities to people as they emerge as leaders. Emerging leaders are expected to return to their community the kind of leadership benefits they themselves have received. A large number of the professionals who are volunteering their time at the Center were young people who now have college and advanced degrees. The Center has made a significant difference in their lives and they now in turn are seeking to continue the transformation process in the communities from which they came.

Perkins also attempts to encourage other churches in the area to begin similar programs. Grace Methodist Church, for example, adopted a ten square block area adjacent to the Harambee area. The concept is to have a whole chain of such programs "pushing together." Crime has been reduced, and drug traffic has been drastically curtailed in the area.

John Perkins recently spoke to the Harambee family:

> After being here for more than eight years now, we can see the problem clearly. The breakdown of the family is at its root. Ninety percent of Northwest

Pasadena's African American children are growing up without a father in the home. Although numerous mothers are surviving well as single parents, the majority, we feel, are not. This is evident in the attitudes of both children and teenagers . . . We at Harambee are incredibly thankful for the many wonderful people who have joined us in our struggle.[68]

World Impact

Keith Phillips initiated World Impact as a ministry to the children and the youth of South Central Los Angeles. The aim is spiritual reproduction and the development of leadership in the ghettos of America's cities. It has since been reproduced in several other cities.

World Impact seeks to provide long-term commitment and ministry to the poor of the city. This is done by having missionaries move into the community and become permanent residents. Missionaries have been living and ministering in Watts for over twenty years. Modeling the Christian lifestyle, being available by having an open door policy, holding Bible studies, and spending lots of time learning and understanding the needs and longings of the people of the community are the grassroots approach of this ministry.

Several levels of training have been developed by World Impact to meet the needs of staff instruction and spiritual formation for ministry. Areas of training include cultural sensitivity, Bible study techniques, lifestyle evangelism, and discipleship training.

Staff Training

Each person who joins the organization as a staff member is placed in a highly structured two-year staff training program. Those who do the training are called "one-on-one leaders," who themselves will likely still be in training themselves in the organization.

During their first three months, every new staff member is on probation. The organization deliberately gives new people low status servant functions, such as washing dishes, and cleaning and maintenance. This serves as a means both of testing commitment and providing opportunities for learning World Impact values and perspectives.

The highly structured program not only calls for definitive activities, it also determines how long each of these tasks should take to complete. For example, viewing video tapes and debriefing with one's mentor are part of the first stages of a new staffer's training. These activities are highly structured, as illustrated in the following instructions:

1. View introduction to the New Staff Tape (1 1/2 hours).
2. View World Impact Strategy Tape. (1 hour)
3. View Safety Tape (1 1/2 hours).
4. Read the Employee's Training Manual. (5 hours)

Upon reaching a predetermined level of discipleship, each new staff member is assigned a new recruit to mentor in the same way he/she was mentored. This model reflects 2 Timothy 2:2: *"And the things you have heard me say in the presence of many witnesses entrust to reliable men who will also be qualified to teach others."* World Impact's leadership formation program has proven, over time, to be extremely effective. The aim is that every staff member and new disciple, become capable of reproducing herself or himself in the person they disciple.

The Ministry Phase

At an appropriate point in their training, staff members are paired up and moved into the neighborhood where they will be ministering. There they will host Bible clubs and Bible studies, and spend time with the people of the community. By doing this they are consciously identifying with the people to whom they wish to minister. In their relationships at home they have an opportunity to model what a Christian family looks like. They are available when crises arise in the ghetto society where fear is an integral part of life.[69]

Types of Ministry

There are many types of structured ministry at World Impact. Some of the fundamental and formational ministries are: 1) Bible groups for the children and young people in the community, 2) Bible study for adults, which is meant for the parents of the children reached through the Bible groups, 3) camp and farm experience for both children and youth, 4) Christian schools, 5) vocational training centers, and 6) new projects such as a home for unwed mothers, well child clinics, dental services and a home for abandoned children.

Training

Leadership training takes place on several levels. First, the formal spiritual dimension begins with the staff and is extended through them to the youth and then to the parents. Secondly, there is the informal modeling of an incarnational Christian lifestyle in the community. The first two levels have resulted in many of the children and youth becoming staff members themselves. Thirdly, there are schools and vocational training centers which back up, in a practical way, the offer of a way to new life in Christ.

Schools—World Impact has elementary schools in Newark, New Jersey, and Los Angeles, and a Junior High School in Los Angeles. The schools began with the commitment to nurture inner-city young people in wisdom, stature, and favor with God and man. Each teacher is on staff and considers him or herself to be a missionary.[70]

Vocational Training—In communities where the light of hope has been dimmed, it takes more than words to rekindle that hope. The goals for vocational training are to help young people to 1) become employable, 2) have a constructive outlet after school and on weekends, and 3) earn extra money. The private sector is contracted for entry-level jobs so that their graduates have employment possibilities.[71]

World Impact Strategy

The strategy of World Impact is three-fold: 1) evangelism, 2) follow-up, and 3) discipleship. This process may take as long as five to ten years.[72]

Lifestyle Evangelism

Involvement in evangelism includes everything a person is and does: sharing God's love in Bible clubs with the children and teens, in the adult Bible studies, while distributing emergency food and clothing, tutoring, or while playing basketball. World Impact's lifestyle is evangelism. Whenever an opportunity presents itself, as people become convicted of sin, they are lead to repentance and commitment to Christ.

Follow-up

Every person who accepts Christ enters into a follow-up relationship with a staff member. This is the beginning of the payoff of the initial training. Each new convert is taught how to live the Christian life through Bible study, prayer, Scripture memorization, meditation on God's word and worship.

Discipleship

After the urban Christian is taught how to feed him or herself spiritually, they enter a discipleship relationship. In this training they learn how to teach others to grow in Christ. Each staff member is committed to long term ministry in the ghetto. This process may take as long as five to ten years. However, the staff missionaries are allowed this way to observe the spiritual growth in their young people and the multiplication that results when each young person goes out and does the same. Many become themselves missionaries to the ghettos of North American cities.

Financing

The staff members raise their own support in a faith mission fashion. Gifts and donations from individuals and corporations supply operating expenses. The Christian elementary schools, junior high school, vocational center, and other endeavors, however, are financed through tuition, scholarships, and work-related income.

Summary—World Impact

World Impact is an outward-oriented development model which, through endeavoring to minister to children and young people in economically disadvantaged communities, has, in addition, developed its own staff members into leaders. In order to meet the spiritual needs of the many new converts, both children and adults, World Impact has begun holding larger scale worship services in the communities.

Notes

1 Crenshaw Christian Center, 7901 South Vermont, Los Angeles, CA 90005; Charles E. Fuller Institute for Evangelism and Church Growth, P.O. Box 91990, Pasadena, CA 91109-1990; The Church on Brady, 715 South Brady Avenue, Los Angeles, CA 90022; LeTourneau Ministries International, Box 26200, Colorado Springs, CO 80936; Bresee Institute, 3401 West Third Street, Los Angeles, CA 90004; Harambee Christian Family Center, 1581 Navarro Avenue, Pasadena, CA 91103; World Impact, 2001 South Vermont, Los Angeles, CA 90007.

2 Ranjit DeSilva, "CCC Schools," *Crenshaw Christian Center: Annual Report 1990* (Los Angeles: Crenshaw Christian Center, 1990), p. 10.

3 Carl George, interviewed by Edgar J. Elliston, February 22, 1991.

4 Church on Brady, *Day of the Congregation* (Los Angeles: The Church on Brady, 1990), p. 4.

5 Ibid., p. 5.

6 Kenneth L. Callahan, *Effective Church Leadership: Building on the Twelve Keys* (New York: Harper and Row, 1990).

7 Ibid., pp. 19–20.

8 Church on Brady, p. 6.

9 Ibid.

10 Ibid., p. 1.

11 Ibid., p. 8.

12 Peter B. Morehead, "An Analysis of the Leadership Training Program at the Church on Brady" (n.p., 1986).

13 Ibid.

14 Ibid.

15 Ibid.

16 Ibid.

17 Ibid.

18 Ibid.

19 Ibid.

20 Ibid.

21 Ibid.

22 Ibid.

23 Ibid.

24 Ibid.

25 *Review of LeTourneau Ministries International* (Colorado Springs, CO: LeTourneau Ministries International, 1991), p. 27.

26 Ibid., p. 5.

27 Ibid., p. 11.

28 Ibid.

29 Ibid., p. 12.

30 Ibid.

31 Ibid.

32 Ibid.

33 Ibid.

34 Ibid., p. 13.

35 Ibid.

36 Elizabeth McKerihan, interviewed by Edgar J. Elliston, February 19, 1991.

37 *Review of LeTourneau Ministries International*, p. 13.

38 Ibid., p. 14.

39 Ibid.

40 Ibid., p. 15.

41 Ibid.

42 Ibid.

43 Ibid., p. 16.

44 Ibid.

45 Ibid., p. 17.

46 Ibid.

47 Ibid., p. 18.

48 Ibid.

49 C. Douglas McConnell, *The Bresee Institute for Urban Training: A Study in the Analysis of Urban Training* (M.A. thesis, Fuller Theological Seminary, 1985), pp. 60–61.

50 Timothy L. Smith, *Called unto Holiness* (Kansas City: Nazarene Publishing House, 1962), p. 114.

51 Ronald Benefiel, transcript of interview by Timothy J. Kauffman, July 28, 1986, p. 12.

52 Ibid.

53 Ibid., p. 8.

54 Ibid., p. 7.

55 Ronald Benefiel, "Multi-Congregational Structure for First Church of the Nazarene, Los Angeles, California" (n.p., 1989).

56 Fletcher Tink, *The Bresee Institute for Urban Training Brochure* (Los Angeles: Bresee Institute for Urban Training, 1983), p. 1.

57 McConnell, pp. 6–62.

58 Tink, p. 2.

59 Bresee Institute, "Promotional Literature" (Los Angeles: Bresee Institute, n.d.).

60 Azusa Pacific University Graduate School of Theology *Catalog* (1984), p. 2.

61 McConnell, p. 98.

62 Fletcher Tink, "Internship Arrangements at the Bresee Institute" (n.p., 1984), p. 6.

63 Tink, *The Bresee Institute for Urban Training Brochure*, p. 3.

64 McConnell, pp. 171–172.

65 John Perkins, "The Harambee Christian Family Center" (n.p., n.d.).

66 Ibid.

67 Ibid.

68 John Perkins, *Harambee News*, 6: 2 (Summer 1991), p. 1.

69 World Impact, "Ministry Information" (Los Angeles: World Impact, Inc., n.d.).

70 World Impact, *World Impact Bulletin* (Los Angeles: World Impact, Inc., August, 1988).

71 Ibid.

72 As of this writing the World Impact staffs in some cities are linking converts to local evangelical churches, whereas in other cities the focus has shifted to the planting of new churches. The evolution into an urban church planting mission is a recent development within the World Impact organization.

CHAPTER THREE

FOUNDATIONAL PERSPECTIVES FOR DEVELOPING URBAN CHRISTIAN LEADERS

The beginning point of reference for developing urban Christian leadership comes from a biblical/ theological mandate. A theological base undergirds the purpose, the clarification of roles and status, the task-related values and perspectives, and the leadership development processes. One can

This chapter seeks to establish a set of foundational perspectives for developing leaders for urban ministries. These perspectives form the value bases and touch the theological foundations of this book. These perspectives then serve as a vantage point for considering training and broader curricular issues.

turn to secular literature to find ways to answer many leadership questions. However, whenever secular literature or the local urban situation provides the primary answers, the resulting leadership is likely to be less than fully Christian. Both the local urban context and insights from other disciplines are important for the contextualization of the leadership development process. However, in order for leadership to be Christian and to aim at accomplishing God's purpose in a local urban setting, the primary values must come from a biblical base.

The trend in the West over the past 150 years has moved from the study of leaders and their lives to the study of leadership. The study of leaders remains important because the character qualities, motivation, behavior, and competencies of the leader greatly impact the effectiveness of their leadership. However, more recent studies have shown that leadership effectiveness does not depend solely on the character and actions of the leader. Rather, the interactions of the followers and the influences of the leadership situation also greatly influence a leader's impact. Many complexities are involved.

The Scriptures employ a wide range of metaphors to bring specific leadership qualities into focus, while recognizing the complexities. The

Scriptures provide value bases for both the leader as a person and for the subject of leadership in general. The Scriptures also provide the critical perspectives about the context in which Christian leaders develop and serve. This section, therefore, seeks to introduce some foundational perspectives on which urban Christian leadership may be developed and by which Christian leaders should be expected to serve.

Other authors address more extensively issues such as a Christian's view of the city, the relationship between the "cultural" and "evangelistic" mandates[1] and spiritual warfare in the city.[2] This book primarily focuses on the development of leaders in an urban setting.

Contextualizing Christian Leadership Development

The identification and application of these biblical values is an ongoing concern for the Church in every age and place. Gilliland writes,

> True theology is the attempt of the church to explain and interpret the meaning of the gospel for its own life. By its theology the church seeks to answer questions raised by the Christian faith using the thought, values, and categories of truth that are authentic to that place and time.[3]

Church leadership development is a part of the broader contextualizing of the gospel. Until the leadership patterns and structures of a church fit the contemporary situation and measure up to the biblical standard, the process of contextualization is not finished. The International Council of Accrediting Agencies that provides international guidance for accrediting theological education developed a Manifesto which calls for the contextualization of theological education. It suggests that the content, structures and operation of theological education "show that they exist in and for their own specific context."[4]

Educational institutions and training programs can be controlled from within the context. They can be supported from within the context. And they can be planned within the context. Yet they may never fit that situation because often they were originally designed from a foreign worldview.[5] Designing educational programs from a foreign worldview often excludes consideration of internal issues. Contextualization of leadership development programs then help guard against imperialistic or irrelevant approaches that produce dysfunctional leaders.

> Contextualization must be understood as a principle that will characterize mission along the whole theological continuum. The first messages, the early and later discipling, the formation of the church for witness including ethical concerns and social action—all this comes under the discipline of contextualization.[6]

The design and implementation of contextualized leadership development for the church in urban areas may employ the same models that are
used in other dimensions. However, the same strengths and weaknesses that
apply to the contextualization of theology for the Church apply to the design and implementation of curriculum and instruction in the Church.
Gilliland suggests that an understanding of

> culture is absolutely essential if we are to know the way a people see their world
> and what they consider to be real. Culture shows where values are and what
> kinds of needs a people have. Culture also helps us understand where changes
> are taking place. All of this corresponds to the human dimension involved in the
> incarnation . . . . It is easy to view culture as a completely trustworthy vehicle
> of truth. To suppose that culture is an adequate guide to all truth is erroneous.
> Often those who study cultures, especially outsiders to the culture, are unpre-
> pared to see the contradictory elements which the Gospel must judge and trans-
> form. No culture is above the highest revelation of God which we have in
> Christ and the Scriptures.[7]

While anthropology can help us understand the urban culture, an understanding of the culture alone will not provide an adequate base for designing appropriate leadership development for the church in that culture.

Another contextualization model, the adaptation model, has been
widely used in the design of leadership development programs. The design
of training programs for urban ministries has suffered from this model because it takes an existing structure and makes only the minimal adjustments
necessary to fit that structure in a new situation.

A Christian college in Harare, the capital city of Zimbabwe, seeks to
develop leaders who will minister in that city as well as in the other cities
of Zimbabwe. The curriculum, the administrative structure, the facilities,
the library all look very similar to the US college on which it was patterned. The language of instruction, the form and content of the lectures,
the lengths of the class periods, the grading procedures are the same, with
only minor changes. This urban training program has not been exception-
ally effective. Gilliland identifies the faulty assumption as one "philosophi-
cal framework within which all cultures can talk to each other."[8] Unfortunately, this model does not seriously consider the differences in worldview.

When one goes to a different place, a difference in worldview may be
expected. However, geography does not cause nor guarantee differences in
worldview. The African-American woman who works as an attorney on
the twenty-eighth floor of a downtown office building certainly has a different worldview from the Colombian immigrant woman who cleans her
office, although they may be the same age and work in the same building.
When working in a city, one cannot assume that because the city has complex systems that the worldviews that undergird those systems correspond

to the worldviews of any other city in the world. One *can* assume that the educational system designed for one time and place by and for Christian leaders will not automatically fit in another time or place.

Two models of contextualization serve in this text to provide additional insight for the design and implementation of leadership development programs. The first of these is what Gilliland calls, the "Synthetic Model:"

> The synthesis is in the bringing together of four basic elements—the gospel, Christian tradition, culture and social change. The product comes from the dialogue between these, using the insights of the people themselves. There is a recognition that no culture exits in a vacuum but is influenced by other cultures and contexts; so it is important to recognize the elements that are shared with others. No cultural setting is complete, it needs the complementary features of other contexts. The advantage of the Synthetic Model is that it is through the dialogical process that a real appreciation for truth arises.[9]

The second contextualization model that we are using in this text comes from Paul G. Hiebert's article, "Critical Contextualization."[10] This model has

> the advantage of taking both the culture and the scriptures seriously and asks the church as a body to participate in the hermeneutical task. Critical contextualization confronts the double-edged risk of too much permissiveness in the role of culture on the one hand and the outright rejection or denial of traditional belief and practice on the other. Uncritical contextualization risks syncretism or a suppression of old forms that go underground. Critical contextualization first exegetes the culture and then turns to a fresh study of corresponding biblical themes.[11]

A Christian's View of the City

People who live in urban areas are as much a part of God's concern as any other people. Neither the place of residence; the density of the population; the existence or absence of complex social, economic or political networks; the abundance of physical, social, or spiritual needs—in short *nothing* changes God's commitment to bring people into His kingdom. He is not willing that any person, whether urban, suburban, rural, traditional, or modern, perish (2 Pe. 3:9). He gave His only son so that **whoever** believes in Him might have eternal life (Jn. 3:16). One's faith response is critical, but one's place of residence and cultural heritage are not.

In this book we do not view the city either as inherently good or evil. Instead, we view the people who live in urban cultures as persons for whom Christ died and who should be presented the good news of the kingdom in terms that they can understand. Their social systems and physical and spiritual needs should be transformed by the renewing power of the Spirit. The gospel is the power of God for salvation for urban people today as much as much it was for the people of the cities of Rome, Jerusalem, Ephesus, Corinth, Athens, Colossae, or Antioch.

The city is, however, the scene of intense ongoing spiritual warfare until the Lord returns. Christian leaders who minimize the intensity of the present warfare do so at their peril and at the peril of the churches and communities they seek to serve. While the social structures and complexities of the city can overwhelm a person, they are not the source nor ultimate target of the warfare. The issue of spiritual warfare as it relates to cities has come more sharply into focus in the writings of such authors as Wagner, Linthicum, Dawson, McClung, Wimber, Wink, and others.

The purpose here is not to review these books, but to suggest that both the training ground and arena for ministry in the city for Christian leaders is one of spiritual conflict. Linthicum describes the urban context well in the title of his book, *City of God, City of Satan*. He writes,

> In the very name *Jerusalem* is expressed the tension of every city. It is *Je*-rusalem—the city of Yahweh, of God. It is Jeru-*salem*—the city of Baal (or Satan). Jerusalem is the city of Yahweh. Jerusalem is the city of Baal. It is a city that contains the power and influence of both forces within its walls. The very name of Israel's primary (and idealized) city expresses the foundational urban message of the Bible. Jerusalem—and every city—is the battleground between God and Satan for domination of its people and their structures.[12]

The warfare in urban areas erupts on several key fronts. We who live as Christians in cities experience it in our personal lives, bombarding our senses and sensualities to distract, dislocate, discourage, dismay, and deceive. However, the warfare has erupted in the domain of every structure affecting the city as well. Christian leaders who would serve in the theater of operations must be aware of the arena in which they serve as shepherds, stewards, and soldiers of the kingdom.

The Task

Effective leadership is always directional—it moves toward the central task for the group involved. The central task of Christian leadership is kingdom oriented. Within this kingdom orientation fall two primary mandates: an evangelistic mandate and a cultural mandate. Linthicum writes, "The kingdom is the ultimate focus of God's intentions. Like any other empire, the kingdom of God would have its political, economic, social and religious dimensions. It would be a corporate reality."[13] Christian leaders who would serve the kingdom will serve these two mandates in three dimensions or arenas. The goal clearly moves toward transformation in both mandates. Again, Linthicum writes,

> The vocation of the church in the city is to seek the city's spiritual transformation. That transformation must include (for it to be transformation) the corporate systems and structures and their principalities and powers. That can occur only as the church exposes the lies on which the city is built. It will occur only as the church so "lives and moves and has its being" in the city that it exhibits to all people and systems of the city a new creation: the kingdom of God.[14]

Evangelistic Mandate

Christian leadership in the city has a mandated task toward which its influence is to be directed. The Great Commission clearly states the task: "to make disciples" of *panta ta ethne*, "all nations," every ethnic group, every "people."

The task facing Christian leaders in cities falls clearly into that mandate. The great diversity among urban residents whether seen in different economic, ethnic, political, educational, or settlement patterns does not change the mandate. The ministry of reconciliation that aims at bringing every person and group to accept Christ as Lord does not differ, whether evangelizing the traditional nomad or subsistence farmer, the urban high rise dweller, or oppressed slum dweller. Neither the density of the population, the complexity of the social organizations, the physical environment, nor the absence or presence of technology serves to modify this mandate. God wants every person and people to come to repentance.

> LMI sees its primary task as the equipping of the Church and its Latin American leaders of every level to multiply churches first in the capital cities and then to move across the Latin American nations.
>
> The Harambee Center sees its task as leading people of the community to know the Lord in the context of local churches and to equip them to live with justice and respect in that community as Christians.

1   The Task

> It is the task of the church in the city to introduce its citizenry to God in Christ. This is its primary calling and its exclusive calling. It is not the church's only calling, but it is primary and exclusive. If the church does all the rest, but leaves this task undone, then it has been irresponsible and derelict to its unique call.[15]

This task must be understood and carried out both by means of and as a result of a second equally binding mandate to love one's neighbor. God shows His justice, mercy, and righteousness through this love. He expects the same of us, especially those of us who would be leaders.

Glasser, showing the urgency of this mandate to disciple the nations, writes,

> The evangelistic mandate, then is God's call to His people to participate with Him in this redemptive activity. "Preach the Gospel to every creature," (Mk. 16:17) "Teach all nations," (Mt. 28:19) Evangelism does not mean denouncing sin or pronouncing judgment. No words of sadness or terror. Biblical evangelism is announcing the Good News of salvation through Jesus Christ in order that by His Holy Spirit, men may come to repentance and faith.

> The Church cannot be indifferent to the manner in which it discharges the evangelistic mandate. No mere transmission of the Gospel will do; no careless tossing out to non-Christians a verbal formula with a "take it or leave it" attitude. The Gospel must be communicated in an attractive and winsome manner. It must be presented to people in a familiar and meaningful thought forms.

> By the evangelistic mandate, "the church is gathered out of the nations. Not that the church is an end in itself. It is solely God's means to the end of extending His kingdom throughout the world."[16]

Cultural Mandate

The cultural mandate on the other hand is the first obligation God placed on humankind. This mandate involves the "totality of human existence."[17] This mandate does not place one person over another, but rather places responsibility for caring for the creation on the shoulders of people. The psalmist writes,

> Yet Thou hast made him a little lower than God, and dost crown him with glory and majesty! Thou dost make him to rule over the works of Thy hands; Thou hast put all things under his feet, All sheep and oxen, and also the beasts of the field, the birds of the heavens, and the fish of the sea, whatever passes through the paths of the seas (Ps 8:5–8).

Wagner writes,

> As with any significant kingdom concept, the Cultural Mandate has its origin in God. It was given before the fall, when only Adam and Eve comprised the human race. As the creation narrative unfolds, God says, "And now we will make human beings, they will be like us and resemble us. They will have power over the fish, the birds, and all animals, domestic and wild, large and small" (Gen. 1:26, TEV). It was done, and Adam and Eve were ready to receive their first recorded divine commandment: "Have many children, so that your descendants will live all over the earth and bring it under their control. I am putting you in charge of the fish, the birds, and all the wild animals . . ." (Gen. 1:28, TEV).

> These first human beings were given what Robert Webber calls "delegated sovereignty" over God's earthly creation . . . . They were to treat creation as God himself would treat it. That was the Cultural Mandate.

> . . . Jesus not only exemplified the Cultural Mandate in his own life and ministry; he summed up the entire teaching of the law and the prophets by saying, "Love the Lord your God with all your heart, with all your soul, and with all your mind. This is the greatest and most important commandment. The second most important commandment is like it: Love your neighbor as you love yourself" (Mt. 22:37–39, TEV). No one can be a kingdom person without loving one's neighbor. No Christian can please God without fulfilling the Cultural Mandate.[18]

The concerns of the cultural mandate demand attention in the metropolitan regions of world today. The content of this mandate includes the "distribution of wealth, the balance of nature, marriage and the family, human government, keeping the peace, cultural integrity, liberation of the oppressed—these and other global responsibilities rightly fall within the Cultural Mandate."[19] God has never rescinded this mandate. It began at creation and will continue until the second coming.

The Lausanne Covenant states:

> The message of salvation implies also a message of judgment upon every form of alienation, oppression, and discrimination. And, we should not be afraid to denounce evil and injustice wherever they exist. When people receive Christ they are born again into his kingdom and must seek not only to exhibit, but also to spread its righteousness in the midst of an unrighteous world.[20]

God led the writers of Scripture to connect closely these two mandates. "Neither represents a superior form of Christian action. Both must be taken seriously if the will of God is to be accomplished."[21] Both belong to and are expected of every believer.

The working out of these two mandates into more specific objectives in a wholistic approach requires a broadening of our categories for strategic plans and job descriptions. Classic and contemporary missional concepts require a contextualized restating and redefining both in the light of Scripture and immediate urban setting to clarify the task. Any serious consideration of concepts such as presence, proclamation, persuasion, propagation, incorporation, liberation, revolution, transformation, revitalization, reconciliation, or redemption demands a theological and cultural review of the task at hand. Any one of these concepts by itself, does not present the wholeness of the task. However, when taken together they begin to give shape to it.

John Dawson, in *Taking Our Cities for God: How to Break Spiritual Strongholds*, clearly calls us to be aware of the spiritual warfare dimension of the urban ministry/leadership task. Both mandates address spiritual issues. One should not see one as spiritual and the other as secular. Both relate to the kingdom. Both relate to a spiritual struggle.

> Unless you understand biblical warfare you will be frustrated, angry, confused and ineffective in your ministry to the city. You may be attempting to coordinate Christian concerts, pioneer a church or reach businessmen. The principle is still the same: We need to bind the strong man and gain a place of authority over Satan before we will see the fruit of our labors[22].

God does not give Christian leaders the option to choose between these two mandates. Both carry important messages about the kingdom of God. The two commands while related symbiotically,[23] require contextually appropriate joint implementation. Some ministries fall into the deadly trap of focusing only on a single dimension. Urban ministries are no less susceptible to the patterns that have separated both evangelistic and developmental ministries over the past seventy-five years.[24] On the other hand, urban ministries often show how these two mandates can be joined effectively to transform not only the spiritual condition of people, but their social and physical environments as well.

Whose Task Is It?

God did not give the tasks of discipling the nations and loving one's neighbor to a small elite group of leaders only. Indeed, He gave these commands to the whole community of believers. Jesus gave the Great Commission (Mt. 28:18–20) to the eleven with a clear application to the people who would follow: ". . . teaching

> The Crenshaw Christian Center views the question, "Whose Task is it?" in terms of the whole people of God working in the community. Between forty-nine to fifty-one percent of the people who attend worship on Sundays in the Church on Brady participate in "obedience oriented" training programs during the week.

> 2   Whose Task Is It?

them to obey all I have commanded you." The mandate continued to be reinforced in the next generation of believers. The Apostle Paul wrote a blessing to the believers in Rome that they would be established in the gospel which is to be "made known to all the nations, leading to obedience of faith" (Ro. 16:25–26). Neither the blessing nor task was laid at the feet of the then existing leaders only. He also wrote to Timothy, "the things which you have heard from me in the presence of many witnesses, these entrust to faithful men, who will be able to teach others also" (2 Ti. 2:2).

The early church clearly understood that every believer is responsible. This understanding was evidenced through the wildfire growth of the church beginning in Jerusalem and spreading south to Egypt, west beyond Rome, north to the Black Sea, and east to India in the first century. Obviously, the eleven along with the apostle Paul understood the mandate as belonging to the whole community of believers. Christians today must also see these mandates as applying to every believer. Christian leaders are then expected to lead and equip the whole church in ministry.

The two mandates apply to individuals and to the corporate societies in which individuals live. Peter affirms that God is not willing for any to perish, but that He wants all to come to repentance. People who are saved are not just described individualistically in the Scriptures. "Note the broad use of corporate images to describe the saved condition—covenant people, the nation Israel, the people of God, the remnant, the kingdom of God, the church, the new Jerusalem."[25] Linthicum goes on to say, "If the church does not deal with the systems and structures in the city, then it will not effectively transform the lives of that city's individuals.[26]

Critical Traits of Urban Christian Leaders

The possession of any certain combination of traits does not guarantee that a person will be a leader. One can describe characteristics common to Christian leaders such as giftedness, social habits, initiative, or physical characteristics, but the possession of these traits does not make that person a leader.[27]

> The Church on Brady expects the emerging leaders to exhibit an unquestioned commitment to Christ and the extension of His church. Other traits such as physical attributes, educational achievements, and personality characteristics are of much less importance.

3   Leader Traits

However, one can observe traits from another perspective. For a Christian leader the absence of a few critical traits serves to predict dysfunctionality in that person's leadership. The leadership environment will condition the expression of these critical traits or characteristics, but they are nonnegotiable from a biblical perspective. Clear teachings and anecdotal evidence clearly show their importance and the results of their absence.

Love

Christian leaders must be characterized by an unfeigned love for God and other people. This deliberate good will for others must be obediently and faithfully displayed with an unquestioned integrity.

Love serves as the primary guiding and constraining value for Christian leaders. It drives one to act for another or to restrain one's use of power in a situation.

Expressions of what love is appear in 1 Corinthians 13 and Galatians 5:22–23. It is patient, kind, not insistent on its own way or jealous. It does not brag or act arrogant or unbecomingly. It is not self-seeking or easily provoked. Love does not keep a list of wrongs suffered or rejoice in unrighteousness. Rather, it believes, hopes, and endures all things. Joy, peace, patience, kindness, goodness, faithfulness, gentleness, and self-control all characterize love.

Integrity

Integrity in both the process of influencing others and followership is critically important for Christian leaders. Outstanding examples of integrity reflect God's blessings. Joseph, Esther, and Daniel exemplify God's response to integrity. King Saul, Ananias, and Sapphira provide sad examples of the result of compromised integrity. Leaders are expected to show integrity by not only being unreservedly truthful, but also by an unquestioned commitment.

Integrity provides the key component for treating the complexities of a leadership situation, whether it be mono- or multicultural.[28] Badaracco and Elsworth clearly demonstrate that a commitment to integrity is preferable to either "political" or "directive" leadership in the real world of complex leadership.[29] Bennis says, ". . . there are three essential parts of integrity: self-knowledge, candor and maturity."[30] He suggests,

> Integrity is the basis of *trust*, which is not as much an ingredient of leadership as it is a product. It is the one quality that cannot be acquired, but must be earned. It is given by co-workers and followers, and without it, the leader can't function.[31]

Integrity serves as the foundation of trustworthiness. Perceived trustworthiness, coupled with competence, results in leadership potential, whether in relation with God, other people, or the organization.

Integrity is critically important for spiritual leadership. Paul's requirement that elders, bishops, or overseers be "above reproach" is a demand for integrity (1 Ti. 3). Peter's statement about elders to the five provinces in what is now Turkey was a call for integrity (1 Pe. 5:1–3).

Critical Roles in Leadership Development

Often when we think of developing leaders, our minds immediately turn to focus on the *training* of men and women to serve. However, leadership development is broader than training.

Training is important, but it is only one of many critical elements in facilitating the emergence of a leader. Leadership development involves character, competencies, and commitments. It also involves the followers' motivations, abilities, and relationships. It also must take the leader/follower situation into account. The leadership influence process takes place in a situation of time, place, and social interaction. It occurs in a framework of shared values. The development of leadership requires more than just training because training may not adequately consider the followers, time, context, and shared values.

Leadership development can be described in terms of relational empowerment. Leadership is always based on and occurs through relationships. The power bases which provide the means of influence for a leader are either spiritual, interpersonal, or corporate. Developing leaders involves the development of these three kinds of relationships. Training often focuses on information or skills without the corresponding development relationships.

All of the equipping models cited in this study clearly differentiate between emerging leaders and existing leaders. The models which are more closely tied to local congregations (e.g., CCCMTI, Bresee, and the Church on Brady program) and more traditional Bible institutes (e.g., ABI) publicly affirm their dependence on the Holy Spirit. CEFI affirms its dependence on the Holy Spirit in a more indirect way through seeking to discern "needs" and "markets" among the churches.

4   Leadership Development Roles

Furthermore, the development of leaders often brings the leaders-in-training into focus without a close examination of at least two other critical roles, namely, the roles of the Holy Spirit and existing leaders.

Three basic, but very different critical interactive roles contribute to the intentional development of emerging spiritual leaders: 1) the superintending role of the Holy Spirit, 2) the selecting/equipping role of the existing leaders and church family,[32] and 3) the trusting/obedient role of the emerging leader. These complementary and essential roles all contribute to the emergence of new leaders. When any one is neglected, the whole leadership development process suffers.

The Holy Spirit's Role

The Holy Spirit initializes, energizes, integrates, and superintends every crucial stage of the leadership development process. He is active in all the phases—in the selection, equipping, empowering, assigning of ministries, maturing, and transitioning. He works through a person to equip others, bringing first a sense of destiny and then a sense of fulfillment as one's giftedness, maturity, status, and role converge. He works in the context and the people in that context, through the already existing leaders to facilitate, motivate, correct, and enable the new leader to grow and reproduce. The Lord works both subtly and openly in the development of the emerging leader. The Holy Spirit fills the most critical role through the whole process.

Leader Selection

God calls men and women to lead in ministry. The Lord selects a person for a specific ministry. He matches the person with the task, followers, and situation. He sovereignly selects the person to be gifted and equipped for the ministry at hand.

The Holy Spirit says, "I WANT YOU!" As the Great Recruiter, He not only calls, He provides the equipment for the job. The spiritual gifts He gives enable each believer to serve effectively. The gifts of the Spirit (1 Co. 12, Ro. 12, Eph. 4) aim at the good of others in the Church and for their equipping for service. These gifts provide the initial and ongoing empowerment of the Holy Spirit for ministry. They are the Holy Spirit's authorization to use spiritual power for God's purpose in the Church. They may be seen as part of the Spirit's legitimation of His selection process. As they are employed within the community, the gifts also contribute to the formation of a context where other people can emerge as leaders.

Gifting is under the sovereign control of the Spirit. He decides both which gifts to give and when to give them. The gifts contribute to the purpose of building the whole church, and to the individual's growth as well. The whole church experiences organic or infrastructural growth as the gifts are employed. It also experiences a deepening of spiritual growth. As these two kinds of growth emerge the extension and expansion growth can be expected to follow.

The Holy Spirit is responsible for the equipping of men and women for ministry. He superintends the whole process. He works in every situation for the good of those who love Him and are called according to His purpose (cf. Ro. 8:28ff). It is He who works to have them thoroughly fit for ministry.

Paul wrote Timothy,

> All scripture is God-breathed and is useful for teaching, rebuking, correcting
> and training in righteousness so that the man of God may be thoroughly
> equipped for every good work (2 Ti. 3:16–17).

Whatever one's developmental stage, the Scriptures provide both the contents and the standards for "teaching, rebuking, correcting and training in righteousness." Always the aim is for the disciple to be "complete," "mature," or "perfect," "thoroughly equipped" for ministry.

Word processing expresses what the old gospel preacher did in interpreting and applying the Scriptures as facts to be believed, promises to be enjoyed, commands to be obeyed, and warnings to be heeded. The Holy Spirit continues to convict of sin, righteousness, and judgment as one reads and meditates on the word (Jn. 16:7–11).

Processing the facts, promises, commands, and warnings in one's own context enables one to know, to become and to do, as the Spirit leads in a given time and place. The Spirit leads in this processing both to stimulate personal spiritual maturity and to help form one's ministry. Whether one is a Muslim student leader in the University of Djakarta, a gang member from Los Angeles, or the owner of a thriving recording business in Buenos Aires, the Holy Spirit works through the word both to convert and equip a person to become a spiritual leader. The Muslim leader is not only converted, but leads his own family and many other Muslims to acknowledge Jesus as God's Son and their Lord. As the converted gang leader learns God's mercy, grace and expected obedience, he begins leading other gang members, drug dealers, Satanists, and prostitutes to the Lord. Following the direction he received from Scripture and the Holy Spirit, the Argentinean executive becomes a key leader in the largest church in Latin America.

Leading through Others

The Holy Spirit works through the Christian community and especially through existing leaders to develop others. While the Spirit spoke to Cornelius, He led Peter to do the needed personal counseling and instruction (Ac. 10:1–48). While commissioned by the Holy Spirit, Paul spoke personally to encourage the development of men like Timothy and Titus (1 and 2 Timothy and Titus). The Spirit worked personally through Paul with a wife and husband team, Priscilla and Aquila (Ac. 18:2, 26; Ro. 16:3; 2 Ti. 4:19). Paul wrote words of encouragement under the Spirit's direction for Philemon, Phoebe, and Onesimus. Again under the direction of the Holy Spirit, Paul wrote to bring correction in the lives of the people quarreling in Philippi (Phil. 2:1–4, 14; 4:2–3). He also wrote the people who were divided over factions, spiritual gifts, moral issues and other significant problems in Corinth (1 Corinthians). The Holy Spirit works through leaders to correct other leaders. He worked through Peter to correct some early racial prejudice of the Jewish Christians (1 Corinthians) and then later through Paul to bring correction in Peter's ministry (Gal. 2:11–13). Paul, through the guidance of the Holy Spirit ,sent others on ministry as-signments, for example, Timothy and Titus (cf. ministry assignments of Timothy: Ac. 16:3, 17:14, 19:22, 20:4; 1 Co. 4:17 and Tit. 1:4, 5). The Spirit works through existing leaders to prepare the situation, select, equip and discipline the development of emerging leaders. As He leads through existing leaders, He continues to develop them.

Growth Processing

The Holy Spirit continues to direct the development process in emerging leaders through complementary ways, such as interaction with the word, or through existing leaders, contextual events, and internal reflection.[33] The Spirit even works for one's good in circumstances such as conflict, danger, isolation, suffering, and persecution. He provides both instructional and re-flective guidance. Each process can be checked against Scripture for valid-ity and reliability.

The growth processing of the Holy Spirit is evident in the person by the emergence of the fruit of the Spirit. Continued maturation moves be-yond the spiritual and character formation of the person to ministry forma-tion and the development of one's ministry philosophy. In one's ministry formation a person's giftedness and character join to allow the person to serve in a ministry particularly suited to him/her. This serving flows out of the quality of the person's life rather than just out of technical competence. This growth processing aims at moving a person to be Christlike.

One growth processing activity of the Holy Spirit can be understood in terms of the horticultural process of pruning. Pruning is "the removal of part of a plant for the benefit of all the plant. Pruning has three basic ef-fects: it directs growth, it improves health, and it increases production."[34] When understood from a horticultural perspective, pruning is a useful cy-clical process. It can help "rejuvenate an old, sparse shrub or tree"[35] or shape a young tree to its environment.

When a leader makes a transition from one role or status to another, the Holy Spirit may initiate a pruning process to insure health and vitality in the new situation. The Holy Spirit also may use the pruning process to correct or repair damage. As with a tree pruning may help insure health by removing diseased or irreparably injured parts. The Holy Spirit, a wise gardener, oversees this process. Like plants, people vary widely in their need for pruning. Some people seldom need pruning; others need it regularly. The Holy Spirit decides, based on the kind of plant, the context, and His purpose for the plant.[36]

The analogies are obvious. Most leaders need occasional correction to optimize their effectiveness. Their growth may overtax their fruit-bearing potential or it may be inappropriate for their situation. The reproving correction will not likely be for gross errors or defects, but for shaping and refining. Normally, heavy pruning occurs only when the plant has experienced serious damage or neglect.

Pruning not only affects the individual, but the context in which the individual lives.

> Pruning to direct growth is also a way to control the microclimate of your garden. The cuts you make can affect the movement of air, the degree of sunlight and shade entering a yard, air temperature—even the condition of the soil.[37]

The Holy Spirit delegates authority to leaders. This delegated authority contributes directly to the emergence of a person as a leader. As one matures spiritually, spiritual authority emerges. A follower's allocation of authority to a spiritual leader grows out of the recognition of God's working in and through the life of the leader to influence others for their good according to God's purposes. Neither delegated nor allocated spiritual authority is based on one's own status or power. Rather than emerging out of commonly expected forms of power such as expertise, information, organizational connections, personal charisma, or control of rewards and punishments, it flows out of a committed servanthood (Mt. 23:1–12) as the Holy Spirit works in the leader's life.

Summary

Spiritual leadership development is a key role of the Holy Spirit. He superintends, empowers, equips, gifts, guides, directs, disciplines, provides insight and delegates the authority to lead. It is His work. However, the Holy Spirit has chosen to use two other crucial elements in the developmental process. Without these roles new leaders will not emerge. They concern the role of the existing leader and the role of the emerging leader. The next sections will deal with these roles.

Role of Existing Leaders

Whether one is the pastor of a mega-church or a small group leader, part of the leadership portfolio is the development of others for ministry. The task does not rest solely on the theologian, college professor, or Christian education director. No single person is expected to do everything needed in the development of another person to be a leader. Instead, the entire Christian community, in particular the whole distributed leadership, is responsible for the wide variety of leadership development functions which mirror the complex work of the Holy Spirit.

Obedient Discernment

Even as a gardening staff for a nursery must understand the owner's desires for their work of preparing the soil and planting, so the existing leaders must discern God's will for leadership development.

While leadership development is the work of the Spirit, the Spirit gives the gifts of apostle, prophet, evangelist, pastor and teacher to "equip," "teach," "mature," "complete," "perfect" others for the work of ministry. Within the body, one primary leadership task is knowing the God-given purpose, goals, and objectives for that body. The purposes, goals, and objectives will be consistent with what is revealed in Scripture. The basic instructions about what leaders ought to know, be, and do are in the word. When leaders are committed to carry out these instructions, then they can cooperate in the task of leadership development.

Existing leaders are expected to be discerning in at least three ways to facilitate the development of new leaders. Obviously, the first required discernment is of God's will and guidance for the situation at hand. The Holy Spirit provides guidance through the word, the Church, and through other means the existing leaders have already learned. Certainly, Bible study, prayer, and other spiritual disciplines serve to keep discernment sensitivities attuned. Spiritual guidance is clearly culturally conditioned in terms of the forms it takes. However, it will always remain consistent with the revealed Word of God.

Spiritual guidance may occur in a variety of ways: 1) "double confirmation" in which multiple independent witnesses or circumstances attest to the same guidance, 2) words of knowledge, 3) visions and dreams which are often less accepted forms of guidance in the West, 4) new applicational insights gained in the study of God's word, or 5) through the instruction of another spiritual leader. God through His Spirit seeks to meet the need of existing leaders for obedient discernment of His will. To be able to discern the Spirit's leading the existing leader must have a strong personal relationship with the Spirit that is shown through an unwavering commitment. Existing leaders show this commitment by their trust and obedience.

Existing leaders must be careful not to impose their own personal perception of God's will for another person. The Spirit works consistently, and so what is clearly revealed in the Scriptures, confirmed by the

Christian community, and discerned by the existing leaders should be considered. Leaders do speak for, represent, and participate in the Christian communities they lead. Their role is not just personal.[38]

The second kind of discernment relates to the emerging leader—the present leader's disciple. Many issues require discernment to assure appropriate leadership and developmental direction. The disciple's goals, calling and giftedness, ability or capacity for the task at hand, his/her commitment, level of motivation, and character are only a sampling of the issues requiring discernment. To know or discern any one of these issues requires a personal relationship with one's disciple. To presume one can begin to develop another without this discernment will lead to disappointment and frustration.

This level of discernment also requires that significant amounts of time be spent together and ample conversation occur. Instant discernment is seldom reliably accurate. Time spent interacting in a variety of circumstances in which the full range of the roles of both the emerging leader and existing leader can be mutually observed will provide the primary content for discernment.

> The Church on Brady seeks to discern the needs of the emerging leader by personal interviews with each person who is being equipped and by having the emerging leader interview others about their perception of his/her giftedness.
>
> CEFI seeks to discern the needs of classes of leaders by means of "market research" which includes questionnaires and interviews of men and women among the kinds of leaders who might participate in seminars and workshops. The participants' feedback from seminars also helps provide this kind of information.

5   Discerning Emerging Leader Needs

The third kind of discernment relates to the situation in which the leader and disciple serve. Existing leaders must discern the relevant aspects of the situation which will bear on the leadership transactions and the development of their disciples' followers. From the situation one should discern such issues as values, and external constraints for either ill or good. The disciple should certainly be matched with the situation where both the disci-

> The staff of the Bresee Institute often walk the streets in the vicinity of the First Church of the Nazarene in Los Angeles and talk with people on the streets to discern the needs of the community to be addressed in the training programs.

6   Discerning Ministry Needs

ple/emerging leader and the followers will benefit. The existing leader should make the effort to discern how favorable a situation will be to the emerging leader. Favorableness is seen in terms of the emerging leader's potential for influence in that situation, the degree to which the task has been defined, and the quality of the relationship the emerging leader will have with the followers.

The critical role of existing leaders then is to discern God's will, the emerging leader's condition and the situation in which the emerging leader will serve and develop. Leadership always has three basic requirements: a leader, followers, and a situation. These elements are as essential to leadership as oxygen, fuel, and heat are to fire. If any one is removed, leadership will disappear—the fire will go out. Each is critically important. One may begin with any one of the three basal elements, but must include the other two before effective leadership can be expected to emerge. One may need to provide more heat, oxygen, or fuel to get the fire going. The existing leaders may have to give more attention to the leader, the followers, or the context to help the process of development.

Prayer

Prayer provides the base for both discernment and the empowerment of others. Leaders are responsible to pray for their followers. Every step along the way should be based on prayer. Jesus prayed before the selection of His disciples. He prayed for those who would later become His disciples and then for their disciples. The Apostle Paul wrote of his specific prayers to his disciples (cf. Co. 1:9–12). Supporting one's disciples in prayer and working through prayer to discern the Lord's leading are important parts of one's leadership. Samuel showed the importance of prayer in the midst of a serious leadership crisis and transition. Even when the people had rebelliously insisted on having a king, when Samuel would likely have been angry with the people, he prayed for them and promised to continue to pray (1 Sa. 12:1–25, especially 23).

Prayer not only provides a key to discernment both of the individual and of the context, it also unleashes God's power to move in the whole situation. Intercessory prayer focuses God's power on the emerging leaders so they can be effective in their ministries. Intercessory prayer is an important role of the *episcopos* or elder. The root meaning of *episcopos* is to "watch over" or "to cover"[39]

Responsible Flexibility

Existing leaders require flexibility to be effective in carrying out their roles in the development of new leaders. This flexibility relates to several interactive issues. Both the motivation and ability of the emerging leaders vary over time as they relate to the present ministry. Time, task structure, size, group structure and history of the group involved, relationships with and among the group members, and resources all come into the existing leaders' attention and should affect their leadership style choice.

Leader Selection

Another important role of the Holy Spirit is the selection of leaders. Existing leaders carry out their selective role in new leader discovery and recruitment. The discovery of the men and women the Lord has chosen requires discerning observation. Effective recruitment requires a knowledge of what leadership or ministry needs exist in the congregation or parachurch ministry. Existing leaders also need to acknowledge all the members of the congregation and their present and potential abilities to fill these needs. Both the discovery and recruitment processes are made effective by prayer.

ABI selects learners in cooperation with the churches. Churches recommend from their congregations emerging leaders who have completed local "Bible Academy" training. For the second level of training (the second three year program) students must have demonstrated a regular commitment in a local congregation to an identifiable ministry.

In the CCCMTI virtually anyone who seeks to serve in the church may enroll in the "Helps" ministry training program. However, for one to progress to the third year program which aims at equipping men and women for pastoral ministries, the students must be personally convinced of a call to serve and have others affirm that call on the basis of their ministries.

7   Learner Selection

The selection of leaders continues as a critical issue, whether one is selecting another to be a street evangelist, a Sunday school teacher, an elder, a pastor, a district superintendent, or a national chairperson. Selecting the right person for training is no less important. The selection of the leaders probably has as much impact on the final outcomes of a task as any other factor.

How can one validly and reliably select the right person for the task? Stogdill's list of traits[40] provides clues about the characteristics of the person. A person's adherence to a shared worldview and value base is also critical. One's "task maturity" also should play a part in the selection process. Hersey and Blanchard suggest that "task maturity" consists of competence and motivation as they relate to a particular task.[41] The selection of people for spiritual leadership also requires an assessment of the person's spiritual and ministry maturity as they relate to the immediate ministry/task. Lyle Schaller has addressed assessing a person's church planting aptitude within a middle class main stream American suburban setting. If the task and situation are similar, his list of traits is an excellent example of this approach to selecting the right kind of person for this kind of ministry.[42]

Some interrelated variables one should consider in the selection process include the following: 1) spiritual gifts or gift mix, 2) technical competence, 3) motivation, 4) spiritual maturity, 5) ministry maturity, 6) demonstrated faithfulness or trustworthiness in carrying out responsibilities, 7) the task or ministry to be done, 8) the task's structure and priority, 9) the support community where the leader will be assigned, 10) the followers' cohesiveness, 11) the followers' relationship with the leader, 12) the personal power of the leader, 13) the leader's corporate power base, 14) the leader's spiritual power, and, 15) the shared value base. While effective selection occurs frequently and in many different contexts, the risks and complexities remain evident to every person who has ever tried to select another person either to lead or to be developed as a leader. The application of "trait theory" to the selection of leaders serves well when such variables as worldview, culture, task, followers, and task structure are held constant. However, whenever these variables change either with the person being selected or in the community to be served, the required trait combinations must change as well.

Existing leaders should know the local situation and the emerging leaders well. By knowing both the situation with its needs and the emerging leaders with their capabilities, the existing leaders should be able to help match the emerging leaders and the situation.

The very process of selection contributes to the emergence of leaders because of what social psychologists call the "Pygmalion Effect." The Pygmalion Effect is based on a Greek myth about Pygmalion. Pygmalion sculpted a statue of a beautiful woman. He fell in love with the statue and

> The learner selection process of nonformal approaches such as CEFI depends much more on the community being served and the learners themselves. When a seminar is announced, church leaders who desire that particular seminar enroll.

8   Nonformal Selection Process

through the power of his love and expectations he brought the statue to life.[43] The expectations of leaders on people who respect them have a powerful molding effect for good or ill. Expectations shape the perceptions of others and influence behavior toward them. Expectations often become self-fulfilling prophecies. The trust, confidence, conviction and commitment of the existing leader in the emerging leader can result in a trustworthy, committed leader with a strong sense of direction. If we expect others to excel, they are likely to excel. If, however, we expect them to fail, they will probably not disappoint us. Doubt or any inkling of a lack of committed support from the existing leader will generate defensiveness, turf protection, and a person who leads only for personal benefits.

Selection by existing leaders requires a careful discernment of the Lord's leading. An arbitrary selection of whomever for whatever leadership role will only bring disaster for the group and for the person. One's giftedness, motivation, present level of ability or competence, and sense of calling all require careful selective discernment by the existing leaders. Only the wisdom available through the discernment of the Lord's leading can provide the essential guidance through the complexities of selection.

Recognition

As the new leaders emerge, the existing leaders must publicly recognize their development so it may be encouraged, empowered, and employed. This recognition occurs in the dynamic leadership situation where the emerging leaders' faithfulness and influence are observed over time, with the people

> One way the Church on Brady recognizes the accomplishment of emerging leaders to encourage them in their further development is by noting their successes in the leadership of small groups and by increasing their level of responsibility.

9   Accomplishment Recognition

who are being influenced. Recognition is not aimed at building an unhealthy pride, but rather a confidence and commitment toward accomplishing the task and fulfilling the ministry. Public recognition helps build the perception of trustworthiness and competence in both the immediate followers and in the broader community. Recognition then is critically important to empowerment as power comes from both the individual followers and the broader community. The existing leader who claims credit rather than giving it to others effectively destroys motivation and diminishes commitment.

Contextual Preparation

As a part of the situation existing leaders already have an influential role. They have the key responsibility to prepare the situation for the emergence of the new leader. The better prepared the situation is the greater the potential for the healthy development of a new leader. Leaders can be expected to

> The Bresee Institute sends its staff members into the community to prepare the people with whom the interns from the Institute will be working by defining what they will be doing and what their relationships will be in the community.

10 Contextual Preparation

emerge as the context stimulates them. Existing leaders serve in part by removing the obstacles which inhibit the work of the emerging leader.[44] Wise leaders recognize that long term effectiveness as transformational leaders requires as much attention to the situation as to the immediate followers.

Ideally, the initial ministry environment into which the emerging leader is placed will be characterized by a strong sense of vision or mission, not just activities or busyness. This sense of mission will provide the initial nurturing for intentional directionality that anticipates the future and moves toward it. It should be an environment where the emergent leader is given the right to do what is to be done. Callahan says, "the greater the range of [delegated] authority, the more likely the level of leadership competencies is to grow. The more fully persons are given authority, the more likely they are to develop their leadership competencies."[45] And, "it is decisively crucial to provide persons with an authority range that, at a base minimum, is commensurate with their current competencies."[46] The granting of authority—the empowerment for action—should precede the assignment of responsibility.

The context should be structured where decision making is modeled in a participatory way for accomplishing significant objectives. The environment should be characterized as coaching or encouraging context, rather than a correcting or legalistic one.

As a gardener prepares the ground for the new plants, so existing leaders prepare the situation for the new leader. The emerging leader must be given legitimate space to grow into having influence. The existing leaders must be careful to prevent others from overshadowing and stifling the emerging leader, but rather to facilitate the building of his/her credibility and legitimacy.

Existing leaders prepare the context not only for the formation of strong interpersonal relationships through which personal power is both developed and legitimized they also prepare the context so that relationships with the community structures can be developed. In this way the bases for positional power are legitimized by the community. Finally, they must work in the context to facilitate the development of the emerging leader's relationship with God so that their spiritual authority may be developed and recognized.

Existing leaders establish legitimacy for the emerging leader by showing why he/she has the right to influence or lead in that situation. Establishing the legitimacy of the new leader confirms their authority as the followers see that the right to influence is being delegated by the community. As existing leaders reflect the work of the Holy Spirit, a part of their work is to verify and affirm both the emerging leader's spiritual gifts and their appropriateness for the present ministry assignment. When the existing leaders address the recognition of legitimacy among the followers, the allocated dimension of authority, or the giving of the right to be influenced, is established.

Gardeners choose and prepare the place so the texture, the fertility, acidity, moisture, and temperature of the soil are all appropriate for the young plant. Similarly, mature leaders prepare and clarify the role, relationships, and status of the new leader, not only with the new leader, but with his/her followers in the situation. More mature leaders assure the presence of the necessary support services, encouragement, structure information, supplies, and equipment. They structure the tasks and roles to effectively utilize the personnel and other resources. The existing leaders prepare the context by addressing the group's interpersonal relations and work-related relations for cohesiveness and team work. They monitor and facilitate appropriate leader-follower relations. They prepare the context so it will stimulate growth, not just tolerate it. They prepare the followers for collaboration, that is, their laboring together.

The contextual preparation is always done with the purpose of the Church in mind to bring all peoples to Christ and then to bring them up to responsible discipleship. Contextual preparation *always* moves beyond mere involvement.

Additionally, in preparing the structural elements of the context the existing leaders should give attention to issues of support. Existing leaders can greatly facilitate the establishment of the support networks for the emerging leaders. These support networks not only facilitate the development of the new leader, they also provide both a group of potential followers and a pool of potential next-generation leaders.

The preparation of the context requires attention, whether one is involved with a new believer's first ministry or a more mature leader who moves into a new context. When preparing contexts for ministry or leadership development, attention must be given to the variety of contexts needed to stimulate development of *all* of the needed ministries in the church.

John the Baptist prepared the way for Jesus (Jn. 1:6–13; 19–34). Barnabas prepared the way for Paul in the Jerusalem church (Ac. 9:27). Paul prepared the way for Onesimus with Philemon (Philemon). Jesus prepared the way for Philip in Samaria by interactions with local people, including the woman at the well (Jn. 4:7–26), as well as miracles of healing.

In preparing the situation existing leaders set the process of a leadership transition in motion. Changes in influence begin to be anticipated. The emergent leader can seldom fulfill this role, because the existing situation is seldom immediately conducive to the planting, growth, or transplanting of a new leader.

Possible initial growth situations are as numerous as the ministries of a church. One may work with a Sunday school teacher to open a place for a junior high assistant. The person operating the sound system may prepare a role for someone to assist. An elder may be asked to apprentice a faithful Sunday school teacher to expand the eldership. The senior pastor may equip an associate who will become the senior pastor of a new congregation or succeed him. The organist may teach another to serve in that role. The person who counsels with people addicted to drugs can equip another counselor. The street evangelist can equip street evangelists. Every leader's role is to prepare each ministry to be an equipping link to the next generation of leaders, not only for the local church, but for new churches. No place exists for "dead-end links" in the church.

The preparation of the context does not require a program, but rather a perspective of the whole cadre of leaders in a community. Contextual preparation requires continuous complementary attentive action at every level of leadership.

Preparation of Followers

Even as the context must be prepared, the anticipated followers of an emerging leader should be prepared for his/her entry into leadership among them. The existing leaders' task includes the includes the initial legitimizing of the newcomer. The temporary empowerment of an introduction and commendation helps prepare the followers for the emergence of a new leader on his/her own among them.

The kind of leader the emerging leader is becoming will determine what followers the existing leaders need to prepare. The basic principle is to prepare the people who are expected to be within the initial sphere of influence. The first task is to clarify the ascribed status of the emerging leader in

> The Crenshaw Christian Center prepares the followers by introducing the emerging leaders and calling for their acceptance. It only takes a word from the senior leadership for the people to develop expectations of the new leaders.

11 Follower Preparation

the ministry context with the initial followers. The establishment of emerging leader's assigned position in the group is an important function of the existing leader. Not only do existing leaders address the question of status, they must also address the issue of the expected role for that status. What is that newly emerging leader expected to do in the new position? Leaders should clarify the followers' expectations for the appropriate level of direct or indirect ministry. Will the new leader interact with them and influence them on a face-to-face basis or indirectly through other people? Will he/she influence only two or three or indirectly influence the whole community through organizational policy making? The existing leader has the task to prepare the initial expectations of the followers for the new leader.

When the pastor recruits a new teacher for an adult Bible study group, part of his role is to prepare the group for the acceptance of the new teacher. Simply sending the new teacher to an unsuspecting group is not adequate. A transitional preparation is needed. Existing leaders can best do that. That preparation may well continue for an extended time as the new leader is getting established.

Ministry Assignment

After preparing the soil, gardeners plant the seed, expecting it to take root and grow. Existing spiritual leaders similarly place the emergent leader in a prepared ministry context and expect growth. Gardeners transplant the young plants in a suitable places which match their requirements for sunlight, temperature, moisture, and acidity. Similarly, if effective leadership is expected, the emergent leader must be placed in suitable growth environment. Fiedler suggests three things by which the situation can be judged for suitability for the leader: 1) task structure, 2) leader-follower relations, and 3) the power given to the leader.[47] Several illustrations of the appropriateness of ministry assignments which take these variables into account may be drawn from the assignments the Jerusalem church gave Barnabas or the ministry assignments Paul gave to Timothy and Titus.

> LMI/ABI begin with ministry assignments in the Bible academies in local churches.
>
> The first three years of study in ABI see students involved in voluntary low level ministry assignments. These may include part-time teaching, leading in small groups, or assisting existing leaders. During the second three-year period ministry assignments take on a more important role in the LMI/ABI programs. Students are expected to be regularly involved in significant observable ministries.
>
> The CCCMTI program expects ministry assignments to correspond with each of the three years' programs: First year students should be involved in helps ministries; second year students should be involved in Bible teaching ministries; and, third year students should be involved in roles that lead to associate positions on a church staff. Some of these roles would include assisting with youth ministries, assisting with pastoral ministries in terms of calling and counseling, and the like.

12 Ministry Assignments

The existing leader's role should, therefore, serve to define the task the emerging leader is to do in the new ministry assignment. Task structuring is critically important for the new leader whose knowledge, skills, and motivation are yet to be developed. As one matures this need not only decreases, but should be given less emphasis by the existing leader.[48]

The existing leader is probably the best person to facilitate the initial formation of the leader-follower relations in the new ministry. By giving support and encouragement these relationships may be expected to develop. Initial introductions, mediation, role differentiation, and status clarification are critical activities in transitional periods.

The empowerment of the new leader may or may not require a transfer of power from an existing leader in a new ministry assignment. More often the existing leader should focus on the development of multiple kinds of power for the emerging leader to use, including spiritual, personal, and positional power.[49] While all three forms operate in a given context, each one needs a specific developmental emphasis. The use of each kind of power is both guided and constrained by one's values.

Existing leaders also have the parallel role to legitimize the new leaders among the followers. Even as legitimation establishes the right of the emerging leader to lead among the followers, the initial ministry assignment or leadership committal serves to establish the person in the new status and role relationships. The new status and accompanying roles are entrusted to the emerging leader (cf. 2 Ti. 2:2). The newly emerging leader is given a trust for which he/she is to be accountable and which is expected to benefit the One for whom the trust is held. The basic value of servanthood runs deeply through every ministry assignment because the assignment is never to be given or accepted for personal gain (1 Pe. 5:1–4).

Initial ministry assignments are always done with hope, faith, and expectation. The more clearly the expectations are communicated to the emerging leader, the greater the potential for their realization. A respected person's expectations have a powerful motivating effect. The motivational effect can be multiplied not only by personal acceptance of the emerging leader, but by repeated public affirmation. Generating appropriate expectations among the followers also serves to strengthen potential for long term effectiveness of the emerging leader.

If the person is not yet a leader, then the most appropriate ministry assignment will be a task which will build competence, test the faithfulness of the person, and provide satisfaction in its successful completion. The assigned (ascribed) status should reflect the person's spiritual maturity. The accompanying role should be

> The Church on Brady assigns students the task of initiating new small groups. Not only is the maintenance and teaching in small groups important, the formation and coordination of small groups is important. These requirements are a part of the ministry assignments for the church on Brady's training program.

13 Manual Ministry Assignments

within the person's range of motivation, ability, and spiritual maturity. Generally, an initial status and the accompanying roles will not carry a high level of visibility. In addition to fitting the maturity of the emerging leader, it should also fit the expectations of the followers. For early effectiveness which stimulates further growth, the expectations of the leader, emerging leader and followers should correspond as much as possible.[50] Small "wins" should be expected. Existing leaders should help structure the whole situation to allow for success. Win-win situations should be structured whenever possible.

Initial ministry tasks will often be physical or manual jobs. This principle follows Jesus' statement in Luke 16:10 about granting increased responsibility on the basis of faithfulness in small things. Three other principles also may prove to be helpful: 1) Provide ministry opportunities which allow one to stretch, that is, opportunities which require growth. 2) Allow the emerging leader to take more responsibility before he/she asks for it. 3) Always give the authority to do what needs to be done in the assignment. Youssef asserts, "Leadership emerges when people receive opportunities to develop themselves . . . [And,] most leaders learn on the job."[51] This principle holds true whatever type of leader is being developed, from Type I through Type V.

The initial ministry assignment should follow close on the heels of conversion. Faithful obedience in small things contributes both to spiritual and ministry formation. Passive, unattached, uncommitted believers risk being stunted in their spiritual formation and ministry maturity. Assigning busywork just to be involved with no attendant empowering will guarantee passive uncommitted followers whose leadership potential will remain untouched. The delay of a ministry assignment remains the most common cause of inhibited growth and passive apathy in churches. Delayed development of accountability results in rebelliousness, disobedience, and selfish apathy.

Volunteerism, as it is widely known and depended upon in the church today, was not the primary way of leader-ministry assignments in the early church. Barnabas was commissioned to go to Antioch. The team was selected from the Antioch church to go to Cyprus. Ministry assignments were an important part of the ministry/leadership development of the early church.

The provision of ministry assignments continues as an important role of existing leaders. Ministry assignments should be followed by the recognition of trustworthy service and the subsequent enlargement of responsibility or the transfer to another place for continued growth. While initial ministry assignment is crucial to allow development, similar principles apply for later assignment.

The initial ministry assignment requires existing leaders to match the people and the ministry on the bases of the variables which promise the best possible fit. Normally, it only takes a brief interview to assess which ministry in the church a new person will initially fit. At that point natural talents, developed skills and a person's desire to serve ought to be considered.

The existing leaders place emerging leaders in a ministry context which matches their temperament, ability, motivation, and spiritual maturity. They are placed for *success* and *growth*, not frustration and failure. The situation into which the new leaders go must be considered in terms of its favorableness toward the new leader. Favorableness is "the degree to which the situation enables the leader to exert his influence over his group."[52] Existing leaders can and should address 1) personal relationships between the leader and members of the group, 2) the degree of structure in the task the group has to do, and 3) the power and authority the leader has in the group to carry out the task at hand.[53] The maturity of the existing leader may be judged by how well these issues are addressed. The maturity of the emerging leader may be judged by the competence and maturation he/she demonstrates related to the task at hand.

Emerging leaders are often volunteers. Their vitality is profoundly influenced by the attitudes and feelings of the older, professional church leaders. Existing leaders must keep the emerging leaders' constraints in mind. They have only a limited amount of time since they are not paid staff members. They are likely to make only temporary commitments to a given role until after they have attained a certain level of maturity. Even as they mature, the amount of time the emerging leaders can invest may be limited. The responsibility given to the emerging leader should not be so heavy that it will stunt growth or discourage. Rather, it should stimulate and encourage growth.[54]

Empowerment for Ministry

The ministry assignments given to an emerging leader should be seen in the context of empowerment. Empowerment has three key dimensions: delegated, allocated, and internal/confirmational. Each dimension directly contributes to the development of the new leader.

> Delegated empowerment is addressed by the Bresee Institute by the sending of interns into specific ministries. These interns are then given specific jobs to accomplish that are significant in that ministry area.

14 Delegated Empowerment

Three kinds of power occur in each dimension of empowerment: positional (related to one's status in an organization), personal (related to one's personal abilities and charisma), and spiritual (related to one's relationship with God).

The delegated dimension of empowerment for new spiritual leaders comes first from the Holy Spirit and then through the existing leaders in community. The Holy Spirit empowers, that is, delegates the right to use His power to influence in a variety of ways which are described in Scripture as spiritual gifts. The emerging leader is granted the authority, the right to use the Spirit's power, in evangelism, teaching, liberality, encouragement, or in many other ways. One develops these gifts through their use in ministry and in the context of the fruit of the Spirit. This empowerment may relate to one's status within the community and the legitimizing of that status and its accompanying roles. Delegated empowerment may focus more on the person's potential to influence others through interpersonal relationships. Or delegated empowerment may focus on spiritual power and issues such as spiritual gifts through which the person influences others.

Existing leaders again mirror the work of the Holy Spirit empowering new leaders by delegating authority to them to lead, and influence toward God's purposes. Empowerment is the process of enabling, equipping, and allowing people to influence significantly in a situation and the recognizing that contribution. Empowerment is also the process of establishing relationships. Since power, including spiritual power, is not a fixed commodity, but a variable potential, the empowerment of new leaders not only releases their potential for influence, but it increases the existing leaders' potential for influence with the new leaders. The more that is given, the more that remains. On the other hand, the more spiritual power is grasped, the less it becomes.

When the leader shares power with other people, those people in turn feel more strongly attached to the leader and more committed to effectively carrying out their responsibilities. They feel that a failure to carry out tasks lets them down, as well as their leader.[55] Leaders create a sense of covenant when they help others to grow and develop. When the leader is viewed as helpful, other people will more likely be committed to the leader and the organization's goals.[56] The process of empowerment contributes to higher satisfaction with one's work and is positively correlated with increased effective performance.

Rosabeth Moss Kanter suggests four ways to empower others. These four principles apply to the ministry assignments of emerging leaders:

1. Give people important work to do on critical issues.
2. Give people discretion and autonomy over their tasks and resources.
3. Give visibility to others and provide recognition for their efforts.
4. Build relationships for others, connecting them with powerful people and finding them sponsors and mentors.[57]

One empowering role of existing leaders mirrors the work of the Holy Spirit. While the Holy Spirit provides the gifting and spiritual authority, the existing leaders facilitate its implementation. Existing leaders authorize and legitimize the new leaders in status and role relationships. The initial forms of power (both personal and corporate)[58] may be in the hands of the existing leaders. However, a critical part of their role is to transfer these kinds of potential for influence to the emerging leader. Their role includes empowerment.

Public rituals to recognize and to bless the new leader facilitate empowerment. Private encouragement and personal disengagement allow the engagement of the new leader in ministry. Empowerment may also be assisted by the building of specific power

> The CCCMTI uses public rituals of empowerment to launch new leaders. They do this by publicly recognizing in ceremonies graduates and the installation of those graduates in ministry assignments.

15 Public Ritualized Empowerment

bases. An existing leader can aid in building spiritual authority by a continuing discipleship relationship focusing on spiritual and ministry growth processing. Information, expertise, referent, and connection power can all be developed through an ongoing mentoring-sponsoring relationship. Empowerment through mentoring leads then to another important role of existing leaders, that is, equipping. Barnabas' mentoring of Paul serves as a significant example.[59]

A second dimension of empowerment comes from the allocation of the right to be influenced by the followers. Authority or the right to use power does not just come from above, but is recognized and allocated to a leader from the followers. Again, the development of three kinds power (positional, personal, and spiritual) emerges.

The community, church or followers recognize the potential for influence in the emerging leader in terms of status among them, competence and commitment to them, and their shared goals and in terms of his/her relationship with God. As they recognize this potential, they allocate or grant the emerging leader the

> The Harambee Center facilitates allocated empowerment as it recognizes the acceptance and legitimacy of local emerging leaders within the community. The community around the Harambee center allocates the right to be influenced to the men, women, and young people who they equip.

16 Allocated Empowerment

right to use this authority. This allocation is a form of empowerment. Again, public rituals in which the followers participate constitute an important legitimizing function for the existing leader to plan and implement.

The empowerment of spiritual leaders flows from the Holy Spirit's working in the community, the newly emerging leader, and existing leaders to bring His influence to bear. Look, for example, at what happened with

Saul of Tarsus as he was influenced by Barnabas at Antioch and in Cyprus. It is no accident that the process of empowerment is often greatly facilitated by leaders with the gift of exhortation or encouragement. Empowering others requires working beside them without holding them back. It is the process of turning followers into leaders. Leaders are always power brokers, but they must be power brokers on behalf of the people they lead, empowering them and employing their power on their behalf.

A third dimension of empowerment is the internal/confirmational dimension. Again, the Holy Spirit is the primary agent, "bearing witness with our spirit." The Spirit confirms who we are with power so that we may serve with confidence and without fear. Internal empowerment serves to build character ("Christlikeness"), maturity, and integrity. It results in the fruit of the Spirit which allows Christians to employ their spiritual gifts with their maximal potential influence. This empowerment leads to a strength of character, but not to pride or arrogance. The internal/confirmational dimension of empowerment helps establish the emerging leader's potential for influence in positional, personal, and spiritual relationships.

The process of empowerment must be accompanied with a building of the value base which both directs and constrains the use of social and spiritual power. Without these values, based around the two great commandments to love God and love our neighbor, the misuse of power would be inevitable.

Nouwen writes,

> What makes the temptation of power so seemingly irresistible? Maybe it is that power offers an easy substitute for the hard task of love. It seems easier to be God than to love God, easier to control people than to love people, easier to own life than to love life . . . The long painful history of the Church is the history of people ever and again tempted to choose power over love, control over the cross, being a leader over being led. Those who resisted this temptation to the end and thereby give us hope are the true saints.

> One thing is clear to me: the temptation of power is greatest when intimacy is a threat. Much Christian leadership is exercised by people who do not know how to develop healthy, intimate relationships and have opted for power and control instead. Many Christian empire-builders have been people unable to give and receive love.[60]

Emerging Leaders' Roles

D. B. Towner well summarized the essential developmental elements for the emergent leader in his song, "Trust and Obey." The beginning point for effective spiritual leadership is effective followership. The Gospel accounts clearly demonstrate this. This followership or discipleship plays itself out in trust and obedience. Trust and obedience provide the essential stimulation for both spiritual and ministry maturation. A person should expect maturation to occur, but it requires active stimulation through trust and obedience. The profound irony of spiritual empowerment is its emergence through trust and obedience. God's power in us is seen when we are weak (2 Co. 12:9). Trust (faith, confidence, conviction, and commitment) in God as one obeys leads to empowerment, although the evidence of potential for influence may not appear immediately.

Trust and obedience do not come naturally. A person must learn both. If existing leaders want their disciples to have the optimum head start then their modeling trust and obedience is critical. Trust is expressed toward one's superiors, accountability group, in oneself, and/or toward one's followers. Fred Smith writes, "Leaders need to submit themselves to a stricter discipline than is expected of others. Those who are first in place must be first in merit.[61]

Kouzes and Posner assert,

> The winning strategy for fostering collaboration is to cooperate first, and then practice reciprocity. This means setting the example for the behavior that you desire in others. It requires you to demonstrate your commitment and trustworthiness before asking for the same from someone else . . . . Leaders must demonstrate their willingness to trust the members of their teams first, before the team members can wholeheartedly put their fate into the leaders' hands.[62]

The key New Testament word for follower is *disciple*. Jesus invited people to become His disciples. Disciples follow, learn, and apply what is learned to their lives in ways that others can tell whom they follow. The Greek word, *mathetes*, which is translated disciple may also be translated as pupil, apprentice, or adherent. The word occurs in both masculine and feminine forms. *Mathetes* is the "usual word for apprentice."[63] It occurs at least 250 times in the New Testament. *Mathetes* denotes the person who is attached to Jesus as Master.[64] The word leaves no question about "a personal attachment which shapes the whole life of the one described as *mathetes*, and which in its particularity leaves no doubt as to who is deploying the formative power."[65] A disciple is a follower who learns to be like the one he/she follows (cf. Lk. 6:40). A disciple, a follower, an apprentice, a learner trusts and obeys.

The disciples of Jesus had a deep personal allegiance to Jesus as a person. There is no hint that His teaching was the primary source of strength after the crucifixion or that the disciples recognized their having an important legacy in the word of Jesus.[66] Rather, they saw their relationship in personal follower perspective.

To be a leader one must first learn to be a follower. To continue to be a leader one must continue to be a follower. Followership also appears in the Scriptures as servanthood. A servant or slave, *doulos*, is utterly accountable to his master. A servant, *diakonos*, follows instructions, particularly in regard to the task at hand. The servanthood of *huperetes* particularly recognizes the authority of one's superior. The servant, *leitourgos*, recognizes the organizational structure over him.[67]

Through the gospel accounts many metaphors are used to describe the emerging leaders whom Jesus would commission "to disciple all the nations." However, these word pictures and His clear teaching demonstrate a remarkable omission. No power terms are used to refer to these disciples. None of the words like *leader* or words related to the Greek word, *arch*, such as *head* or *overseer* is used. Rather, the focus throughout the Gospels is on trust, obedience, and development as followers.

> The Church on Brady expects two things of the emerging leaders: trust and obedience. Trust is seen in the trustworthiness of the interns and trainees as they participate and lead in small groups. Obedience is seen in their accountability to the existing leaders who are supervising the small groups.
>
> **17** Trust and Obedience Expectations

Accountability is implicit in the primary New Testament pictures of leaders. Servants and stewards are accountable by definition. Shepherds are accountable because in actuality they nearly always are responsible for caring for the flocks of others. Peter focuses on this accountability in 1 Peter 5:1–3.

Trust

One essential follower response or trait is trust—trust in the Lord to influence through other leaders. The writer of Hebrews says, "Without faith it is impossible to please God, because anyone who comes to Him must believe that He exists and that He rewards those who earnestly seek Him (11:6). A follower expresses trust in confidence, conviction, and a commitment to the leaders and their vision. This trust provides stimulus for the follower's growth in influence potential. Trust is absolutely essential in the development of spiritual leaders. To be trusted either by the Lord or by people one must know how to trust. To receive commitment one must demonstrate commitment. To generate conviction one must demonstrate conviction. To receive confidence one must show confidence in others. As the emerging leader learns about trust and commitment from his/her mentors then this same trust and commitment can be modeled for his/her followers.

Trust in another person is not a blind commitment nor a means to build a hierarchical structure of domination and oppression. Rather, it should move toward reciprocal ministry as the existing leader also trusts in the emerging leader.

The process moves from being willing to listen or receive information to having one's whole worldview characterized by the new values. With this change in worldview all of the person's life is understood in the light of these new values and all of a person's actions will be based on and reflect this altered (converted, transformed) worldview.

When one looks at the lives of leaders in the Scriptures, the issue of trust (faith, faithfulness, conviction, confidence, and commitment) consistently stands out. Leaders in both the Old and New Testaments have this trait in common. The writer of Hebrews makes it plain that faith is required to please God (He. 11:6). Jesus underscored the principle of building on faithfulness when He said, "Whoever can be trusted with very little can also be trusted with much" (Lk. 16:10–12). His parables of the pounds and talents further demonstrate this same principle (Lk. 19:11–27 and Mt. 25:14–30). The beginning requirement for the developing leader is faith.

The demand of trust is *from* the emerging leader. I must learn to trust God, my leaders, and my followers before I can lead. The demand is not *to* the leader. A leader should never have to say, "Trust me." The leader's demonstration of trust should render him/her to be trustworthy.

Obedience

Faith and action cannot be separated in one's response. James declares, "I will show you my faith by what I do" (Jas. 2:18). When one looks at the emergence of the faithful leaders mentioned in Hebrews 11, their active obedience becomes obvious. The beginning activity for an emergent leader then is obedience. For one to remain as a spiritual leader, obedience continues as a key requirement. Trustworthiness appears through obedience. Trustworthiness is expected of spiritual leaders, (2 Co. 4:1–2). Trustworthiness may be seen in many contexts as integrity or character. One's trustworthiness or integrity will be tested at every ministry development stage in one way or another. In every case obedience to the word and to God's clear guidance is expected. A clear biblical principle related to obedience is found in Deuteronomy 28:1–68. God blesses obedience while He curses disobedience. The principle remains true both on the personal and the societal level. Obedience is required for God's blessing.

Obedience is closely related to accountability. The emerging leader will not only recognize his/her accountability, but will seek to be able to account for his actions, learning and attitudes. A growing accountability is expected of an emerging and later functioning leader. This accountability is seen in the words translated as *disciple* and *servant*. Again, this obedience is not aimed at the building of domineering tyrants, rather it seeks to build faithful servants. The leader is no less a servant than the one who is following. To Americans in particular the idea of being obedient in the church often raises cultural hackles, but it is none the less an expected part of one's discipleship development. The writer of Hebrews linked obedience and accountability for both leaders and followers:

> Obey your leaders and submit to their authority. They keep watch over you as men who must give an account. Obey them so that their work will be a joy, not a burden, for that would be of no advantage to you (He. 13:17 NIV).

Obedience provides a way to demonstrate love for God (1 Jn. 2:3–6). Obedience to the commands God has given, however, extends into obedience to the people God has placed in authority. No one is above submission even as Jesus Christ demonstrated. Moses was required to be obedient, and when he did not explicitly obey, he was punished.

Jude (v. 11) warns against people within the church who would fall into Korah's error (cf. Num. 16). Korah was guilty of rebellion against spiritual authority. God in judgment destroyed him, his family, his coconspirators and their families, and 16,700 people who "murmured" in agreement with him.

The command to obey is clear as is the warning about disobedience. No believer leader is exempt from the requirement to obey. This teaching is difficult for some people in the West, particularly individualistic Americans, to accept. The decline in personal obedience and accountability among Christian leaders in the US has contributed to many serious embarrassments to the Church in recent years.

The emerging leader in becoming an existing leader continues to develop. In this development spiral a person has to be careful not to *demand* the trust or obedience of others. It can only rightfully be allocated by others. It may be earned or won, but not demanded. While on the one hand, trust and obedience are required for one to develop, the paradox is that the leader who assumes, aspires, or grasps the power which would force another to comply is moving out of an obedient trusting relationship with the Lord. Allegiance is to the Lord, not just to another person. However, when properly developed our obedience often will be seen in response to God's leading through others.

Within his/her obedience the emerging leader will give time to reflect on the experience he/she has been having. Without reflection experience may be of little use.

The opportunities for growth often threaten or test the emerging leader's potential. The obedience of the moment may seem irrelevant to both the present and the future. It may be pure drudgery or seem useless. Remember the response of the fishermen as they let their net over the side one more time (Lk. 5:4–7). The tests allow the emerging leader to demonstrate the integrity of his/her commitment. Through these often very private and seemingly unimportant checks the genuineness of one's heart intent appears. These tests can be expected in both positive and negative forms. The positive forms may be seen in opportunities for service. The negative forms may be temptations. Often these temptations will arise around money, pride, or sexual issues.

The demand for obedience then must come *from* the emerging leader *toward* the person he/she is to obey. I must obey. I must obey God. I must obey the people in authority over me. The emerging leader cannot expect obedience or compliance from others if he/she is not first obedient or compliant. A leader should not then demand obedience, but rather so model obedience that others will want to obey.

Summary of Emerging Leaders' Role

The emergent leader's role then is trust and obedience. The trust and obedience is in the Lord's service, but carried out under the spiritual authority of existing leaders. The obedience begins with the level of maturity the emergent leader has as can be seen both in his/her motivation and ability. Often these two characteristics of maturity will be challenged in the spiritual task given. Even after significant formal training time for reflection and life maturity, Moses was challenged with the demands for both trust and obedience as he was called to lead.

The guided trust and obedience of David, Daniel, and Timothy illustrate the importance of these two essential principles in the formative phases of a leader's development.

As trust and obedience continue, the emerging leader's spirituality begins to mature. Within this spirituality several maturing characteristics or traits appear. Among these traits are the fruit of the Spirit: love, joy, peace, patience, kindness, goodness, faithfulness, gentleness, and self-control. Trustworthiness and integrity are repeatedly demonstrated in whatever situation arises. One's confident ability to discern the Lord's leading for oneself from a study of God's word, prayer, and interaction with other Christians will become increasingly apparent.

The growing spiritual maturation which emerges out of trust and obedience provides the basis for an emerging spiritual authority given by the Holy Spirit and effectiveness in ministry or leadership. Spiritual leadership emerges out of one's quality of life. This quality of life is first given by the Holy Spirit and then nurtured by both existing leaders and the emerging leaders themselves (1 Co. 5:17).

By trust and obedience, or responsible discipleship, emerging leaders are empowered to lead. Their initial legitimacy will be established by existing leaders while the Holy Spirit will empower their long term ministry effectiveness through the development and recognition of their spiritual authority. Emerging leaders do not passively receive this empowering, authorizing legitimacy to lead, but actively cooperate with existing leaders in serving in accordance with the gifts given by the Holy Spirit.

Summary of Three Critical Roles

The roles of the Holy Spirit, existing leaders, and emerging leaders all contribute to the development of emerging leaders. These three crucial leadership development roles continue in a local church, seminary, or church agency regardless of its size or cultural setting. The Holy Spirit guides through the word, other leaders, and increasingly in the life of the emergent leader. The existing leaders are charged with leading in ways by which the new leader will mature internally in spiritual formation and externally in ministering. Existing leaders aid in discerning the Lord's will, preparing the context, making ministry assignments, encouraging, protecting, assisting in transition, teaching and shepherding the newer leader. The emergent leader's role is to mature, grow, and develop in the context of trusting obedience.

It is the nature of the plant to grow, mature, and bear fruit for multiplication. Similarly, one should expect emerging leaders to develop and bear fruit. Spiritual leadership, or that process influencing God's people toward His purpose, should be facilitated by each of the gifts the Lord gives. That influence potential should be facilitated and expected to develop in the life of each Christian.

Non-growth in a plant indicates a pathological condition which should be addressed. The problem may be with the plant, the soil, the climate, parasites, or a host of other possibilities. Similarly, in the life of a Christian non-growth is not normal and should be addressed. Training is only one of many possible treatments. Training may increase leadership fruitfulness, but other issues (such as the context and followers) may have to be addressed first.

One can provide a stimulating external medium for growth, but growth results primarily from internal processes. It is in the new nature of a Christian to grow. Normal developmental growth should be expected, but it cannot be forced. It can only be facilitated.

As a tree is nourished by its roots in the context where it grows, so also a Christian leader develops and grows in spiritual maturity as he/she interacts within the Church. It is a transactional context in which the leader and the followers benefit from the interactions. Both one's mentors and followers provide the stimulus for continued growth and development. The nutrients for this growth come from the Holy Spirit through the word and His personal ministries.

Likewise, as a tree gives stability to the soil where it grows, so also spiritual leaders contribute to the context where they serve. Leaders will not only benefit the immediate followers, but the wider context in which they all live and serve as well.

Wise gardeners work with many kinds of plants which are at many stages of development at the same time. They will regularly plant seed and at the same time be caring for mature trees. A pastor or existing church leader similarly will continually be involved in the development of a wide variety of spiritual leaders at every stage of the process. One seldom just planting stage, but is rather involved with all of the stages simultaneously with different people in the church.

Spiritual leadership is not a narrowly limited set of functions, but is expected from every believer. Just as every person receives at least one spiritual gift, so every person is expected to use it to influence others (lead) toward God's purposes. Every person is expected then, through trust and obedience, to emerge into the role of influence God has prepared (Eph. 2:10).

Critical Christian Leadership Values

Leaders in a given cultural setting share a wide range of values which emerge out of the local culture and worldview. Christian leaders like other leaders share in the same worldview. That worldview provides the shared assumptions about causation—people-creation relations, people-people relations, and time-event relations. A Christian's worldview may change some from that of the surrounding culture, but the basic assumptions will likely remain unchanged over time.

If a Christian leader is a person with a God-given capacity and responsibility to influence a specific group of God's people toward God's purposes[68], the critical values center around those purposes. These revealed purposes or values take precedence over local cultural values and worldview assumptions, community values or organizational values. These purposes or values apply cross-culturally, across time, and in urban settings as well as non-urban settings. The Apostle Paul assumes and refers to these values in his letters to the urban churches in Rome, Corinth, Ephesus, Philippi, Athens, Jerusalem, and Colossae. The Apostle John addresses churches in seven cities in the book of Revelation using the same set of values.

Values provide the shared roadways on which Christian leaders exercise their influence and followers respond. While driving I am always aware of the road and continually correct my driving to the road. While other conditions such as the weather, traffic congestion, my own vehicle and its condition and load affect my driving, the road provides a primary set of directional constraints.

Many variables affect leadership effectiveness, yet values provide the constraints for all of them. Leadership effectiveness depends on many influences, but values provide the paths for these influences. Effective influence toward shared goals depends upon integrity to these values regarding such elements as:

- leader competencies,
- appropriate leader behavior,
- leader motivation,
- leader-follower relations,
- follower competencies,
- follower motivation,
- immediate and broader situational elements,
- task (structure, priority), and
- available influence means (personal and corporate power).

In each case shared values provide the criteria for both what ought and what ought not to be done.

Biblical values undergird selection criteria, the development processes, and the bases for evaluation of spiritual leadership. These values fit interculturally with only the specific local forms changing as the values are expressed. They serve as the criteria for judging how well or appropriately a spiritual leader functions.

Scripture writers use a variety of words to express the concepts which relate to leadership selection and development. While the contexts provide the perspectives to interpret these words, the words themselves provide useful insights into the selection and development of spiritual leaders.

Biblical "Selection" Concepts

The writers of Scripture use more than twenty words to describe the act or the process of selection for leadership. The implications of these words provide a useful range of insight to understand how spiritual leaders were selected along with some of the undergirding values for the selection. Often, the context explicitly describes the process and values, but attention to the words used adds further insight.

Selection in the Old Testament

The most frequently used word for selection in the Old Testament is the Hebrew word, *bachar*. It appears about 120 times. This word means to "choose after testing." Conventional wisdom also supports the idea that leaders should be ones chosen at least on the basis of proven competency and motivation or commitment.

Selection in the New Testament

The New Testament writers use a wider range of Greek words to describe the selection of leaders. In the English translations these words are not always distinguishable because several Greek words may be translated by the same English word or one Greek word

> The ABI in Lima will only select for the second three-year training program men and women who are actively committed in ministry and who are recommended by the churches in which they are serving.

18 Selection Values

may be translated by several English words which overlap.

The New Testament writers frequently use the word, *kaleo* (call), and a related word, *prokaleo* (call to or toward). Often this calling indicates a selection or choice. The selection contains a directionality "from" and "to" suggesting a purpose. Other choice related words include *hairetizo* (to lift), *haireomai* (lift for oneself), *eklego* (lay out), *epilego* (lay open), *stratolego* (enlist).

The importance of the selection of leaders is repeatedly underscored in Scripture. The selection process brings different elements into brighter focus as different leaders are considered. In David's selection, for example, the character of his heart was brought into focus. Jesus' selection of His disciples followed a night of prayer. The selection of Barnabas and Saul at Antioch brought together a discernment of the leading of the Holy Spirit and an affirmation of the Antioch church.

While integrity is always important, and the qualifications, commitment, situation, status, and other traits are often brought into focus, another consistent, essential component in the selection process is God's calling. God called Noah directly. Joseph received vi-

> The CCCMTI will not admit students into the third year of training unless they have a clear sense of call from the Lord and a confirmation from people who are influenced by their ministries.

19 Selection by Call

sions and dreams. David was selected from his brothers by an incredulous Samuel. God clearly called Isaiah, Daniel, Ezekiel, Jonah, Amos, Hosea, and

Nehemiah from very different situations and backgrounds of experience to very different leadership ministries.

The selection always related to a specific leadership/ministry to be done. "Generic" selection is unknown. God chooses women and men for specific ministries.

Several biblical examples of specific selection for a specific ministry could be cited. However, one will serve to illustrate how several selection variables converge. This selection of emergent leaders bring together multicultural and gender concerns in an urban setting. The issue of role differentiation lies at the heart of the issue. The specific task formed the first community-wide ministry assignment. Both social and spiritual qualification combine in the selection criteria. The positioning of these emergent leaders for future expanded ministries is borne out in later testimony. These leaders were selected from among the leaders within the group known to have a "good reputation" and to be "full of the Spirit and wisdom." The "whole congregation of the disciples" participated in the selection of these seven leaders called deacons. After their selection, they were brought before the apostles who after praying publicly, legitimized their ministries (Ac. 6:1–6).

We can see from Scripture the importance given to the selection of leaders. It was always a Spirit-led process—something in which God was actively involved. The forms of the involvement varied from a direct confrontation such as Moses had to the casting of lots with Matthias. The

> The CCCMTI, as it begins in its helps ministry training program, equips men and women for specific ministries. These ministries may include ushering, teaching classes, or a score of other ministries on the campus of CCC.

20 Selection for Specific Ministry

choice was always with a purpose. Joseph was chosen to preserve his family in Egypt. Moses was chosen to lead the Israelites to freedom. Joshua was chosen to lead the Hebrew people into Canaan and get them settled. Gideon's task was smaller, but no less demanding. The seven deacons were selected to serve tables, that is, care for the Greek widows. Saul was selected with a clear purpose to bring light to the Gentiles. Titus was selected and commissioned to serve the church in Crete.

The selection of leaders frequently involved the equipping participation of other leaders. Moses worked with Joshua. Samuel anointed Saul and later David. Elijah worked with Elisha. Jesus chose His disciples and then equipped them. The disciples then helped select others. Leaders involved in selection and equipping were occasionally surpassed by their followers. Look at Barnabas and Saul. Look at Jesus' disciples. Jesus never traveled more than beyond the narrow confines of Palestine except for a brief period as a refugee in Egypt, yet His disciples reached west beyond Rome, south to Alexandria and Ethiopia, north into Turkey and east to South India. Paul addressed the equipping of leaders to at least three generations beyond himself (cf. 2 Ti. 2:2).

New Testament Values for Leading

The primary values for Christian leadership are found in the New Testament. The key person is Jesus Himself. He taught and exemplified the ideal of what was to be expected of Christian leadership. The apostles, Peter and James, both provide case studies and teaching for developing bases for Christian leadership. The Apostle Paul, both as an example and as a teacher, provides much additional insight into the values, principles, and expectations for Christian leadership. Moving back from a Christo-centric model, the Old Testament provides an additional wealth of insight and information with both positive and negative examples.

The primary value for Christian leadership is expressed in the double-edged great commandment to love God with all of one's heart, soul, mind, and strength and to love one's neighbor as oneself (Lk. 10:27).

> Love is patient, love is kind. It does not envy, it does not boast, it is not proud. It is not rude, it is not self-seeking, it is not easily angered, it keeps no record of wrongs. Love does not delight in evil but rejoices with the truth. It always protects, always trusts, always hopes, always perseveres (1 Co. 13:4–7).

Nouwen writes,

> ... the most important quality of Christian leadership in the future ... is not a leadership of power and control, but a leadership of powerlessness and humility in which the suffering servant of God, Jesus Christ, is made manifest. I, obviously, am not speaking about a psychologically weak leadership in which the Christian leaders is simply the passive victim of the manipulations of his milieu. No, I am speaking of a leadership in which power is constantly abandoned in favor of love. It is a true spiritual leadership.[69]

The primary base for Christian leadership is servanthood. Servanthood provides a different way of looking at the concept of a "differentiated role." This theme grows out of firmly established roots in the Old Testament prophets, priests, and kings.

The serving roles of each of these key Old Testament leadership models contain a wealth of insight for reflection in and for urban ministries. Part of the range of the prophetic role can be seen in the lives of urban prophets like Jeremiah who warned, wept, and suffered in and for a city. Daniel entered the power structures of successive administrations of a city both to demonstrate integrity and speak for God in the centers of political influence. Jonah depicts some of the emotional and cross-cultural frustration of what prophets may be called to proclaim in a city.

The range of priestly functions of leaders serving in and for cities is seen across the span of Hebrew history. Abraham unsuccessfully interceded for the cities of Sodom and Gomorrah. Sam Kameleson asks whether it was because of a lack of faith that he did not plead for the saving of these cities for the sake of a single righteous family.[70] Was this series events a test of Abraham's faith in terms of cities? Was God willing to go only as far as Abraham's intercession? Does God today only go as far as our intercession? Ezra the priest led a city and nation into a profound spiritual renewal. Priests could and often did serve not only a mediation role, but an instructional one as well.

The quality of kingly service in administration and leadership can be seen in a willingness to follow detailed instructions, as exemplified by Moses or Gideon. That a servant should be serving his/her Lord and not personal interest clearly appears in the contrast between Saul's and David's encounters to calls for repentance. The impact of personal sin or personal repentance in a king on a city or even a whole nation appears again and again in their lives and the lives of their successors. The principle of a leader being held accountable as a servant cannot be missed in the chronicles of the kings.

The prophets, priests, and kings were expected to serve the one true and living God and to lead by serving. The emergence of these leaders suggests that the "leadership development programs" the Lord prepared for them required faithfulness and a willingness to serve from the outset.

The New Testament authors further develop the ideas about servanthood.[71] Within the New Testament servants are called to interpret God's message in the immediate context in view of the future (a prophetic ministry), teach and intercede for others (a priestly ministry), and to administer the ministries committed into their hands (a kingly ministry). Questions of who is Lord, faithfulness in obedience and trusting, who calls, commissions, empowers, and how one should serve/lead in hope are much are fully developed in the New Testament through the teachings and examples of Jesus, His apostles, and the others leaders in the early church.

The picture of the servant leader begins to take a clearer shape through the major prophets (Isaiah, Jeremiah, Ezekiel, and Daniel). Jesus then fills in the details of the picture through His life and teachings. Then in the early church the apostles demonstrate and amplify what it means to be a servant leader. In these Scriptures God can be seen to initiate four activities to place a person in service. He calls, cleanses, commissions, and empowers for service. God continues to reaffirm these actions and adds to them preservation and guidance in service. The servant responds simply, with humility, in faith and obedience. Finally, the Lord vindicates His servant with victory. From the calling to the vindication the authority is the Lord's, and the servant simply seeks to obey while influencing as he/she is led.[72] Through the Gospel accounts about thirty-five different images or metaphors are used to describe the disciples as emerging leaders. The focus is on their obedience, faith, and learning to follow. Significantly, terms related to power and position are not only missing, but are criticized by Jesus when brought into focus.

The New Testament writers portray rich and complex pictures of Christians in ministry as they serve and lead. Christian writers have categorized these leadership ideas as taught and demonstrated in the New Testament. One may legitimately see different types of leaders as described in this book. One may also describe leaders in terms of local (elders and deacons) or itinerant (apostles and evangelists). One may also interpret both the fruit of the Spirit and the gifts of the Spirit in terms of vocation. One only need observe how Paul defined Timothy's qualifications in his letters to Corinth or the ways he described spiritual gifts in Romans 12 and 1 Corinthians 11. The treatment of New Testament leadership in this book does not attempt to be comprehensive, but suggestive.

What does not appear in the New Testament are the sharp status and role distinctions between the clergy and laity which exist in some Christian communities today. Jesus and the eleven were all laypersons in terms of formal theological education and ordination. Only the Apostle Paul had formal theological training. However, even he had to have year of in-service training in Antioch before he could be sent out as an apprentice apostle under the supervision of Barnabas. Indeed, all of these leaders were seen as God's people (laity) and all were called (clergy) to serve. A serious risk we face today is reading back into the New Testament account our own perspectives.

The words leader and leadership do not appear in the Gospels in reference to the disciples. Bennett asks, "Why is this?" Could it be that leadership has more to do with learning to follow than learning to command, supervise, or manage? Could it be that effective leadership depends more on right attitudes than on mastery of certain skills? Could it be that it is more important for the leader to understand what he/she has in common with other followers of the Lord than to focus on what sets the leader apart from the rest?[73]

When the mother of James and John, the sons of Zebedee, came to Jesus requesting special leadership status for them, He refused. After the other ten had heard about this request, they were indignant. Jesus then spoke pointedly about their status and expected relationships with each other.

Jesus specifically prohibits the two common traits of leaders in secular situations: "lording it over others" and "exercising authority" over others. The phrase, "their great ones exercise authority over them," carries the idea of tyrannizing one's subjects.[74] This attitude toward leadership was not new with Jesus. Samuel had reprimanded Saul about his disobedience, self-seeking rebelliousness, and arrogance in leadership (1 Sa. 15:22–23).

While terms of power and authority are used to describe Jesus in the Gospels, it is important to note that these kinds of words are never used to apply to the disciples. None is called *bishop*, *lord*, *teacher*, *administrator* or *leader*. Jesus' intention for His disciples was that they be good followers. He instructed them not to apply these *power* terms to themselves (cf. Mt. 23:8; 20:25–26).

Jesus showed His disciples how to follow, how to obey, how to respond to the authority and call of God. He knew that the effective leader must first learn how to be a faithful follower. Jesus also knew how destructive the attitudes of pride and ambition could be within the community of disciples. Therefore, He taught them attitudes of humility and self-sacrifice, using the image of the servant, and He reminded them of their equal standing before God as brothers. Jesus wanted His disciples to think of themselves as "among" one another, as brothers, and "under" one another, as servants, more than "over," as those in authority.[75]

Jesus severely criticized the strict religious leaders of His day who had been deeply affected by the status seeking, hierarchical background of Hellenistic influence.[76] This criticism provides further insight into Jesus' intentions by showing what was not acceptable.

Jesus clearly exposed both the leadership styles to be avoided and by contrast pointed toward those elements of leadership which should characterize Christian leaders. Jesus thoroughly criticized leadership which moved away from a servant orientation.

> Then Jesus spoke to the multitudes and to His disciples, saying, "The scribes and the Pharisees have seated themselves in the chair of Moses; therefore all that they tell you, do and observe, but do not do according to their deeds; for they say things, and do not do them. And they tie up heavy loads, and lay them on men's shoulders; but they themselves are unwilling to move them with so much as a finger. But they do all their deeds to be noticed by men; for they broaden their phylacteries, and lengthen the tassels of their garments. And they love the place of honor at banquets, and the chief seats in the synagogues, and respectful greetings in the market places, and being called by men, Rabbi. But do not be called Rabbi; for One is your Teacher, and you are all brothers. And do not call anyone on earth your father; for One is your Father, He who is in heaven. And do not be called leaders; for One is your Leader, that is, Christ. But the greatest among you shall be your servant. And whoever exalts himself shall be humbled; and whoever humbles himself shall be exalted" (Mt. 23:1–12).

Ward observed,

> Leadership for the church is to be non-tyrannical servanthood, evaluated in the light of the teachings of our Lord. Let us therefore accept the evaluative criteria of Matthew 23:1–12. Verse 3: Let us reconcile word and deed. Verse 4: Let us not be delegative but participatory. Verse 5: Let us seek no exalted status. Verse 6: Let us accept no special privilege. Verse 7: Let us take no pride from secular recognition. Verse 8: Let us reject titles of authority, preferring instead a simple relationship as brothers. Verse 9: Let us develop *real* relationships, not artificial and titular relationships. Verse 10: Let us share with all God's people the recognition of one master. Verse 11: Let us relate as servants to the needs of others. Verse 12: Let us live in humble life-style.[77]

Summary

The leadership perspective and expectations of the Apostle Paul support both what Jesus taught and exemplified. When Paul wrote about leadership matters, he saw leadership as service, but not as related to any hierarchical status. In his own ministry he did not seek to build relationships on his own learning or religious status, but rather as one who was also seeking to serve Jesus Christ (Phil. 3:3–11). Paul cited his own example of leadership seven times and called others to emulate him as a leader.[78] In the selection of leaders he was concerned about their total behavior, experience, and ability, not their rank.

Paul emphasized a distributive leadership among the people of God based on gifts or God-given abilities rather than on an authoritarian hierarchical structure. Paul held that the various leaders are essentially equal even though their functions differ. This emphasis appears in his analogy of the church as a body with many different functioning parts (1 Co. 12:12–27). The purpose for every kind of leadership was for the building up of the church (1 Co. 12:2–7; Eph. 4:11).

Both in his own example and in his teaching, the Apostle Paul's expectations for leadership coincide with the criteria described by Jesus in Matthew 23:1–12. Paul lived as an example of what he taught (Phil. 4:8–9; Ac. 20:17–27; 1 Co. 11:1). He sought not just to tell others what to do, but to participate with them as an example (Phil. 3:17). His acceptance of Onesimus and his urging of Philemon is an example (Phl. 8–22). Paul considered leadership as that which should bind the church together in service, not as something which splits the church into status-seeking parties (1 Co. 9:13, 3:3–11). In these passages the only leader who has any higher status is Jesus Himself (v. 11). Paul did not seek or rely on the privilege of being an apostle (Ac. 20:33–35; 1 Co. 9:13–15; 1 Th. 2:9; 2 Th. 3:8). From these passages we know that he maintained a simple lifestyle. Paul did not seek either secular or religious recognition after his conversion (Phil. 3:4–11).

Several of the more important general values which undergird the concept of Christian leadership are summarized below. These values apply interculturally. While the specific applications and forms will vary from culture to culture, they may still serve both as guidelines for action and evaluative criteria for Christian leadership.

1) Christian leaders should function as servants. They are to be evaluated primarily by the criteria of the servant model of leadership lived and taught by Jesus and His apostles as the norm for Christian leaders.

2) Christian leaders should behave in ways which are above reproach in their communities.

3) Christian leaders should be distributed within the church with different persons leading according to the particular gift they may have, e.g., teaching, pastoring, or showing hospitality.

4) Christian leaders should not base their leadership on their own rank, status, or power for personal gain.

5) Christian leaders should contribute to the purpose, fullness, and functioning of the Church.

6) Christian leaders should reproduce themselves through others, by such means as contextual preparation, discipleship, empowerment, and legitimation.[79]

7) Christian leaders should be selected for a particular purpose based on the person's calling, demonstrated commitment, and competence.

8) The primary constraining and guiding value for Christian leaders is love.

Notes

[1] See Arthur Glasser's Syllabus: "Theology of Mission" (Pasadena: Fuller Theological Seminary, 1989) for a more complete treatment of these two themes. The cultural mandate relates broadly to the loving of one's neighbor and the responsibility for the stewardship of the earth and all that is in it. The evangelistic mandate relates broadly to the proclamation of the good news of the Kingdom and the discipling of the nations which are mandated in the Great Commission.

Charles Van Engen's *God's Missionary People: Rethinking the Purpose of the Local Church* (Grand Rapids: Baker Book House, 1991) also addresses this issue in a wholistic way.

David J. Bosch's *Transforming Mission: Paradigm Shifts in Theology of Mission* (Maryknoll, NY: Orbis, 1991) documents these concerns as well.

[2] Some of the more prominent authors who are writing about theological issues related to urban ministries include the following: Robert C. Linthicum, *City of God, City of Satan: A Biblical Theology of the Urban Church* (Grand Rapids: Zondervan Publishing House, 1991); John Dawson, *Taking Our Cities for God: How to Break Spiritual Strongholds* (Lake Mary, FL: Creation House, 1989); Floyd McClung, *Seeing the City with the Eyes of God* (Terrytown, NY: Chosen Books, Fleming H. Revell Company, 1991); C. Peter Wagner, ed., *Territorial Spirits* (Chichester, England: Sovereign World, Ltd., 1991); Walter Wink, *Naming the Powers: The Language of Power in the New Testament* (Philadelphia: Fortress Press, 1984).

[3] Dean S. Gilliland, ed., "Contextual Theology as Incarnational Ministry," *The Word among Us: Contextualizing Theology for Mission Today* (Dallas: Word, Inc., 1989), p. 9–31.

[4] Robert W. Ferris, *Renewal in Theological Education: Strategies for Change* (Wheaton: The Billy Graham Center, Wheaton College, 1990), p. 141.

[5] Worldview is used here to mean the undergirding assumptions which form the bases for perception, interpretation, and action.

[6] Gilliland, p. 27.

[7] Ibid., pp. 313–314.

8   Ibid., p. 315.

9   Ibid., p. 316.

10 Paul G. Hiebert, "Critical Contextualization," *International Bulletin of Missionary Research*, 11: 3 (July, 1987): 103–112.

11 Gilliland, p. 317.

12 Linthicum, p. 26.

13 Ibid., p. 98.

14 Ibid., p. 142.

15 Ibid., p. 171.

16 Arthur Glasser, "Confession, Church Growth, and Authentic Unity in Mission Strategy," *Protestant Cross-Currents in Mission*, ed. Norman Horner (Nashville: Abingdon Press, 1968), pp. 186–187.

17 Idem., Syllabus: "Theology of Mission" (Pasadena: Fuller Theological Seminary, 1989), p. 44.

18 Wagner, "A Missiological View of Relief and Development," *Christian Relief and Development: Training Workers for Effective Ministry*, ed. Edgar J. Elliston (Dallas: Word Books, 1989), pp. 119–120.

19 Ibid., p. 119.

20 International Congress on World Evangelization, *The Lausanne Covenant*, Article 5 (Lausanne, Switzerland: Lausanne Committee for World Evangelism, July 1974).

21 Arthur Glasser, "Confession, Church Growth, and Authentic Unity in Mission Strategy," p. 187.

22 Dawson, p. 70.

23 Tetsunao Yamamori, *God's New Envoys* (Portland: Multnomah Press, 1987).

24 Fred Smith, *Learning to Lead: Bringing out the Best in People* (Waco: Word Books, 1986).

25 Linthicum, p. 44.

26 Ibid., p. 47.

27 Ralph M. Stogdill changed the direction of leadership theory in the US in his classic article, "Personal Factors Associated with Leadership: A Survey of the Literature," *Journal of Psychology*, 25 (1948): 35–71. He writes,

A person does not become a leader by virtue of the possession of some combination of traits, but the pattern of personal characteristics of the leader must bear some relevant relationship to the characteristics, activities, and goals of the followers. Thus, leadership must be conceived in terms of the interaction of variables which are in constant flux and change. The factor of change is especially characteristic of the situation, which may be radically altered by the addition or loss of members, changes in interpersonal relationships, changes in goals, competition of extra group influences, and the like. The personal characteristics of the leader and of the followers are, in comparison, highly stable. The persistence of individual patterns of human behavior in the face of constant situational change appears to be a primary obstacle encountered not only in the practice of leadership, but in the selection and placement of leaders. It is not especially difficult to find persons who are leaders. It is quite another matter to place these persons in different situations where they will be able to function as leaders. It becomes clear that an adequate analysis of leadership involves not only a study of leaders, but also of situations.

The evidence suggests that leadership is a relation that exists between persons in a social situation, and that persons who are leaders in one situation may not necessarily be leaders in other situations. Must it then be assumed that leadership is entirely incidental, haphazard, and unpredictable? Not at all. The very studies which provide the strongest arguments for the situational nature of leadership also supply the strongest evidence indicating that leadership patterns as well as nonleadership patterns are persistent and relatively stable.

See Bernard Bass, ed., *Stogdill's Handbook of Leadership* (New York: The Free Press, 1981), pp. 66–67.

John Wesley Hall, Jr., "Holistic Ministry Variables in Four Latin American Cities: A Factor Analysis" (n.p., 1991) showed that no particular combination of traits related to leadership effectiveness in churches in four Latin American cities.

[28] Joseph L. Badaracco, Jr. and Richard R. Elsworth, *The Quest for Integrity in Leadership* (Boston: Harvard Business School Press, 1989).

[29] Ibid.

[30] Warren Bennis, *On Becoming a Leader* (Reading, MA: Addison-Wesley Publishing Company, 1989), p. 40.

[31] Ibid., p. 41.

[32] Existing leaders may well be family members and people in the community as well as people in the church who deliberately seek to influence the emergent leader. A person emerging as a leader will always be influenced by the community.

[33] J. Robert Clinton, *The Making of a Leader* (Colorado Springs: NavPress, 1988).

[34] Charles Deaton and Michael MacCaskey, *All about Pruning* (San Francisco: Ortho Books, 1978), p. 7.

[35] Ibid.

[36] Ibid.

[37] Ibid.

[38] The appropriate balance of the "priestly"—people's representative and intercessory role, the "prophetic"—God's spokesperson role, and the "kingly"—administrative and protective roles, must be kept when seeking to discern accurately God's will in a given situation with and for another person.

[39] Dawson, p. 108.

[40] Bass, pp. 43–96.

[41] Paul Hersey and Kenneth H. Blanchard, *Management of Organizational Behavior Utilizing Human Resources*, 5th ed. (Englewood Cliffs, NJ: Prentice Hall, 1988).

[42] Lyle Schaller, *Forty-four Questions for Church Planters* (Nashville: Abingdon Press, 1991), pp. 105–127.

[43] James M. Kouzes and Barry Z. Posner, *The Leadership Challenge: How to Get Extraordinary Things Done in Organizations* (San Francisco: Jossey-Bass Publishers, 1987), p. 242.

[44] Max De Pree, *Leadership is an Art*, (New York: Doubleday, 1989), p. xix.

[45] Kenneth L. Callahan, *Effective Church Leadership: Building on the Twelve Keys* (New York: Harper and Row, 1990), p. 154.

[46] Ibid, p. 155.

[47] Fred E. Fiedler, "The Trouble with Leadership Training is that it Doesn't Train Leaders," *Leadership and Social Change,* eds. William R. Lassey and Richard R. Fernandez (La Jolla, CA: University Associates, 1980), p. 242.

[48] For a thorough discussion of follower maturity and the ways which leaders should respond to various levels of follower maturity through different leadership styles see Hersey and Blanchard, pp. 177–183.

[49] See Gary A. Yukl, *Leadership in Organizations*, 2nd ed. (Englewood Cliffs, NJ: Prentice Hall, 1989); Hersey and Blanchard; Wink; or

Dennis H. Wrong, *Power: Its Forms, Bases and Uses* (New York: Harper and Row, 1980) for treatments of power.

50 Hersey and Blanchard, pp. 275–281.

51 Michael Youssef, *The Leadership Style of Jesus* (Wheaton: Victor Books, 1986), p. 156.

52 Fiedler, p. 242.

53 Ibid.

54 Douglas W. Johnson, *The Care and Feeding of Volunteers* (Nashville: Abingdon, 1978), p. 22–23, 41.

55 Kouzes and Posner, p. 164.

56 Ibid., p. 165.

57 Ibid., p. 175.

58 Hersey and Blanchard, pp. 275–281.

59 For a thorough treatment of spiritual mentoring see Paul Stanley and J. Robert Clinton, *Connections* (Colorado Springs: NavPress, 1991).

60 Henri J. M. Nouwen, *In the Name of Jesus: Reflections on Christian Leadership* (New York: Crossroad Publishing Company, 1989), pp. 59–60.

61 Smith, p. 45.

62 Kouzes and Posner, p. 141.

63 K. H. Rengstorf, "Mathetes," *Theological Dictionary of the New Testament*, IV, ed. Gerhard Kittel, trans. Geoffrey W. Bromiley (Grand Rapids: William B. Eerdmans Publishing Company, 1967), p. 416.

64 Ibid., p. 441.

65 Ibid.

66 Ibid., p. 446.

67 See David W. Bennett's treatment of these Greek concepts of servanthood, *Images of Emergent Leaders: An Analysis of Terms Used by Jesus to Describe the Twelve* (n.p., March, 1989).

68 J. Robert Clinton, *The Making of a Leader* (Colorado Springs: NavPress, 1988), p. 197.

69 Nouwen, p. 63.

70 Reported in Linthicum, pp. 105–108.

71 The writers of the New Testament use several Greek words which are translated as servant in English: *diakonos* is a servant viewed in relation to his work, stressing his activity particularly as in the rendering of personal service with humility and love. *Doulos* is used to focus on the relationship of the servant to his master, thus emphasizing his accountability, responsibility, obedience, and undivided allegiance. *Huperetes* focuses the servant relationship on his superior, thus emphasizing the authority he is under to carry out orders. *Leitourgos* is a servant in relation to the organization that employs him, so highlighting the administration he is part of. *Therapeia* is a servant who waits upon the master to provide personal care or assistance. *Misthios* is a temporary hired servant. Jesus contrasts the hired servant with a good shepherd's concern (Jn. 10:12–13). In Matthew 20:1–16 a landowner hires (*misthosasthai*) at different times to work. The principal point is that the reward is entirely at the discretion of the employer. *Oiketes* is a servant named for his sphere of service, that is, the household. Jesus uses this word to remind the disciples of their single source of authority and that they are members of God's household. *Pais* is a servant of the lowest status in either age or responsibility. Such a servant was not given responsibility over other people. Even though the status is low, the *pais* is still under the protection and care of the lord (cf. Philip Greenslade, *Leadership, Greatness and Servanthood* (Minneapolis: Bethany House Publishers, 1984), p. 3; and Bennett).

72 John Kirkpatrick, *A Theology of Servant Leadership* (D.Miss. dissertation, Fuller Theological Seminary, 1988), pp. 235–240.

73 Bennett, p. 1.

74 Walter Bauer, *A Greek-English Lexicon of the New Testament and Other Early Christian Literature*, trans. and adapted by William F. Arndt and F. Wilbur Gingrich (Chicago: The University of Chicago Press, 1957), p. 422.

75 Bennett, p. 85.

76 The Greek culture was deeply affecting the eastern Mediterranean area at the time of Christ. The Greek language was widely known and Greek thought permeated the learning centers of that whole area. Several key Greek concepts which conflict in some crucial ways with Hebrew values had been accepted into the synagogue and temple leadership. The Greek approach to the use of schools and schooling which grew out of the Greek social structure deeply affected the synagogue and later the church. Whereas the Hebrew idea had been that education should be holistic, centered in and through the family and essentially religious,

the Greek idea was based on schooling, hierarchy and status. These Hellenizing influences were contrary to the traditional Hebrew concepts of leadership and education. These same Greek values persist in western society today and have often been the source of church/mission or leadership tensions especially in nonwestern societies.

The Greek concept of education was largely a one-way communicative process. Some had the information or knowledge and passed it on to others. This facet of Greek thought leads to another. Social privilege was gained through educational competition. Plato's philosopher-kings were those who had progressed furthest through this educational system. The Greeks conceived of knowledge as having its own existence as a commodity. It could be acquired. Learning was seen as reaching out for that knowledge. Knowing was seen as the basis for doing. The Greek idea related the knowing with the doing.

The Hebrew concept of knowledge in contrast was a close integration of knowing and doing, and learning through doing and reflection (cf. Ted Ward, "Facing Educational Issues," *Church Leadership Development* (Glen Ellyn, IL: Scripture Press Ministries), p. 14; William Barclay, *Educational Ideals in the Ancient World* (Grand Rapids: Baker Book House, 1974).

[77] Ted Ward, "Facing Educational Issues," *Church Leadership Development* (Glen Ellyn, IL: Scripture Press Ministries, 1977), p. 22.

[78] Ac. 20:35; 1 Co. 4:16; 7:7; Phil. 3:17; 4:9; 2 Th. 3:7; 2 Ti. 1:13.

[79] Adapted from Elliston, "Biblical Criteria for Christian Leadership," *Curriculum Foundations for Leadership Education in the Samburu Christian Community* (Ph.D. dissertation, Michigan State University, 1981), pp. 187–226.

CHAPTER FOUR

CHARACTERISTICS OF THE URBAN CONTEXT WHICH AFFECT EQUIPPING

This chapter identifies significant educational issues which undergird the intentional development of leaders for urban ministries. These issues range from educational philosophy to specific curricular and instructional decisions and the administration of these decisions. Again, educational values come into view, i.e., what decisions should be made regarding the "why," "what," "how," "where," "how much," and "who."

The contexts where the emerging leaders will be equipped "do more than any other thing to determine the form and shape of instructional and administrative models which supplement the curriculum design."[1] Understanding the contextual characteristics, then, forms one of the critical foundations of any curriculum design.

The significant contextual characteristics may be expected to include the impact of each of the following arenas: politics, economics, spirituality, religion, culture, social networks and institutions, geography and environment, education, demographics (population density and distributions), and technology. The complexities of these arenas are multiplied in metropolitan areas beyond what is present in nonurbanized areas.

Traditional Christian leadership development programs have emerged in much less urbanized contexts. They were developed in either agrarian or industrial social settings. Now, however, the contexts have changed and are continuing to change rapidly. This chapter seeks to alert the reader to some of these shifts which should affect leadership development.

The differences between urban or metropolitan areas and rural or traditional regions are documented and described in virtually every sociology textbook. Any difference can be expected to influence the design of a training program. This chapter seeks to identify some of these more significant characteristics. No two cities will exhibit the same configuration of these characteristics. The uniqueness of each city or subculture within a city requires an examination of its characteristics so the equipping of leaders may be tailored to that situation.

If a person wants to purchase a high quality suit that fits well and matches his/her purpose for the suit, he/she will look for a particular fabric, color, size, and style. To find that distinctive suit one must go to the clothiers who make and tailor that kind of suit, whether it be a western business suit, an Indian *sari*, a military uniform, or a pressurized diving suit. When a particular suit has been selected, normally some minor tailoring adjustments need to be made. If no suitable garment is found, one may have to have it custom designed. When shopping, one is often influenced by the range of designs available.

In a similar way an equipping model needs to be both designed and then specifically tailored for a situation. Some "off-the-shelf-models" may approximate what is needed, but they will seldom fit precisely. Some tailoring will be required. In some cases a "custom design" is much more in order. In either case the style, dimensions, fabric, and color will all have to fit the characteristics of the community and purpose for which the model is being designed.

The characteristics of metropolitan areas described in this chapter are like people who come in many different sizes, shapes, and with differing tastes. This chapter will provide a wide range of contexts and characteristics into which different cities may or may not fit exactly. However, with appropriate alterations, or tailoring, they should fit comfortably.

The Church and the City

Stephen Neill's assessment of the church's past failure to make significant inroads into urban culture challenges the Church today as it attempts to reach into and evangelize the city. What he wrote in 1964 remains true today with only a few notable exceptions:[2]

> No Church has yet succeeded, on any large scale, in holding its own in . . . [an urban] society, in making the Gospel, seem relevant to it, or in finding the new vessels into which the wine of the Gospel can be poured. The greater part of what is commonly called evangelism either takes place within the boundaries of the Church or is no more than a series of forays outside it; no Church in the world can claim that it has made of the industrial world a successful mission field.[3]

Jacques Ellul seems to extend this negative view to the city itself. He is the spokesman for many Christians when he characterizes the biblical reference to the founding of cities as being the result of sin and its resultant separation from God.[4] Many Christians still see the city as being evil.

Yet, Donald A. McGavran, the founder of the church growth movement, and very perceptive to church growth potential, has said that many conditions in the city are conducive to church growth.[5] His observations bring him to the conclusion that the church is already in the city. Its task now is to bring "the urban multitudes to faith and obedience."[6] It is in this context that we are asking the question, "Which characteristics of the city are conducive or harmful to developing leaders in this context?"

Let's face it, the city is a tough nut to crack, but by no means impossible. Just the attempt to define the city has, to date, frustrated scholars. If one struggles with a definition for the city, one also would find it difficult to determine how to equip urban Christian leaders. Add to this the deep-seated belief that cities are evil. Denominations and mission agencies alike share an anti-city bias. This aversion is driven by several perceptions. First, urban ministry is thought to be inner-city relief and a financial "black hole." Secondly, true biblical faith is pictured as being connected to rural life and the city as being its antithesis. Thirdly, because of the first two reasons, any ministry is perceived as being "dead-in-the-water."

Robert Linthicum has greatly helped the contemporary Christian community to see the city's domination of biblical text and to view the city in a more favorable light. The world of Moses, David, Daniel, and Jesus was decisively more urban than was the world of 1000 A.D.

The world in which the Bible was written was a world dominated by its cities. By 2000 B.C.E., Abraham's city of Ur numbered 250,000. Ancient Nineveh was so large that it took three days to cross it on foot (Jon. 3:3 NRSV). Babylon at the time of Nebuchadnezzar was an amazing city with eleven miles of walls and a water and irrigation system (perhaps even including flush toilets) not equaled again until the end of the nineteenth century. In New Testament times Ephesus had street lighting along its famed Arcadius Street, of which Ammianus writes, "The brilliancy of the lamps at night often equaled the light of day." Antioch had sixteen miles of colonnaded streets. And Rome? Well, there was no city to equal Rome.

The Rome of the apostle Paul's day numbered more than one million people—the first city in human history to exceed that number. Its streets were so crowded that wheeled traffic had to be banned from its center during the day. The rich lived in large, private mansions, the middle class in sophisticated apartment buildings. But the poor—the great mass of the residents of Rome—lived in 46,000 tenement houses, many eight to ten stories high. The first high-rise apartments buildings were built not in Chicago, but in ancient Rome nearly two thousand years ago![7]

The biblical people of God were themselves urban people. David was king of Jerusalem as well as an empire. Isaiah and Jeremiah were both prophets committed to Jerusalem. Daniel was appointed mayor of the city of Babylon by King Nebuchadnezzar. Nehemiah was a city planner, a community organizer and governor over Jerusalem.

Paul was Christianity's premier evangelist to the major cities of the Roman Empire. John could only envision God's ultimate intentions for humanity as an indescribably beautiful city. Jesus' redemptive act of crucifixion could only have happened in a city where the political power of Rome and the religious influence of the Jewish priesthood could act in concert to kill the Son of God.

Most of Paul's letters were written to city churches giving instructions on how the church can minister effectively in a city. The Psalter is filled with city psalms; note how often they speak of Jerusalem or Mount Zion (Mount Zion, incidentally, is not some rural snow-capped peak; it's the hill upon which Jerusalem was built!). Paul's doctrine of the principalities and powers opens one up to an understanding of the nature and power in the city . . .

The Bible was written in an urban Near East, but the main theological formulations of the faith of the church developed in a rural Europe.[8]

The Church's attitude toward the city often has been characterized by two attitudes. Either it shies away from the city because it views the city as being evil, or it is intimidated by the city's pluralism, the high cost of ministry in that context, or a lack of theological perspective concerning how to approach evangelizing a totally different cultural milieu. To see ministry to the city as central to God's original intentions is liberating and propels us into the heart of what God is doing in our world today.

Characteristics of the City

What are the characteristics of the city as it now exists and as it will become? The question facing Christian leaders as they equip others to be leaders is, "What are the implications of these characteristics for the equipping of Christian leaders who will be called to serve in this urban world?" As noted earlier in this book, cities consist of complex interlocking systems. These systems tend to generate the surface level characteristics so apparent today. These surface level issues include individualism, immigration, pluralism, technological change, educational challenges, alienation, anonymity, dysfunctionality, poverty, and significant differences between the traditional and rural.

Linthicum describes these primary systems as

. . . the economic, political, and religious institutions. These systems constantly interact and cooperate with one another, thereby forming either holy alliances or an unholy trinity. The systems have the potential to work for justice and economic equality for the people and wise stewardship of a city's resources if their functioning is based on both corporate and individual relationship with god. But systems can be demonic as well, enhancing the economic privilege of a few while exploiting the poor and powerless, using the political order to further such exploitation while maintaining a city's order, and turning faith commitment into formalized religion that legitimizes "the powers that be" while benefiting from the powers' largess.[9]

Scripture writers attribute

the perversion of these systems to "principalities and powers." An understanding of these "principalities and powers" and their potentials for corruption will help emerging Christian leaders discern the scope and complexity of the warfare in the city.[10] (See the end notes for a brief description of these terms.)

... the principalities and powers are the spiritual forces that work through the structures and systems of the city, nation, or universe. Such forces may be celestial (1 Pe. 3:22). But the principalities and powers can also be godly or satanic forces that are solely terrestrial and earthly (Ps. 8), or both celestial and terrestrial at the same time (Ps. 103:13–22; Co. 1:15–20).[11]

It is critically important to understand these dark forces in order to hasten the assured victory in the warfare in which we are engage—and to minimize the present causalities. Both evangelical and ecumenical Christians in the West must take care not to dismiss "... the biblical witness about the phenomenon of angels because it does not fit into a secular and scientific world perspective."[12]

Individualism

One of the most marked attributes connected to city life is that of individualism. Pluralism, freedom from certain restraints, and other traits of life in the city, tend to foster and allow for the development of individualism. Individualism is one of the most revered values in the culture of the United States. Elsewhere in the world, a more balanced view of individualism versus social responsibility is commonly held.

When individualism is taken to its logical end, no one would be responsible to or for anyone else. This outcome would precipitate not only the total breakdown of a sense of community, but it would also mean the total isolation of the individual from others. In this light, it is possible to understand how an individual can feel totally alone in a large crowd. Individual rights, when played out to the extreme, often issue into the tyranny of a vocal and well organized minority, the powerful or the unscrupulous. Untold suffering and feelings of total isolation loom large on the horizon of rampant individualism.

It is into this kind of a vacuum of isolation and anchorless *angst* that the Christian Church can provide a real sense of belonging and safety, and lead the way in forming proper attitudes within the household of faith.

Immigration

The greatest migration of people in the history of the world is in progress. Including population explosion figures, Barrett projects two items of great interest to the Christian world: 1) between 1990 and 2050 A.D. the world's urban population will grow from 45.7 percent to 79 percent respectively, and 2) the Christian urban influence in that time period, in terms of Christian population, will decline from 45 percent to 38 percent.[13] Even though the bulk of the world's movement to the cities is located mostly within the Two-Thirds World regions, the changes that cities go through are not only confined to numerical growth.

In the United States for example, the cities on the east and west coasts are growing mainly by immigration. Estimates are that 600,000 immigrants are entering our country each year legally and 400,000 illegally. The vast bulk of the immigrants settle in cities. The overwhelming majority of the growth in these communities then will continue to be non-English speakers. Culturally diverse neighborhoods, non-English speaking neighbors, and many other realities will face United States citizens. However, it is more than just cultural differences an increasingly diverse society faces. Something else has been smuggled in. There seems to be the belief among some that "morality itself is culture bound and, therefore, in an increasingly pluralistic society, wholly malleable."[14] Gabler suggests, that "this time, multiculturalism stealthily slid into moral relativism without anyone paying much attention to the confusion between the anthropological and moral realms."[15]

Training Christian leaders in an increasingly ethnic diverse city context must include plans for the inclusion of planting churches and equipping leaders within as many of these different immigrant groups as possible. In addition, curricula and resources must help train the traditional ministry base to become more comfortable and effective when ministering in diverse cultural communities.

Already, the religions of the world are establishing their presence in our cities. The Hindus in New England have consecrated a Temple to the goddess Lakshmi in Boston; Muslims are erecting a mosque (one of one thousand in the US) in Toledo, Ohio cornfields; the American flag flies over the Hsi Lai Buddhist temple in Hacienda Heights east of Los Angeles; in Quincy, Massachusetts, a mosque has been built not far from the birthplace of John Quincy Adams.[16]

Islam is now an American religion. Today there are more Muslims in the United States than there are Congregationalists or Episcopalians.[17]

If the Church, particularly in the United States, continues to minister to its traditional constituency, it will, over time in many parts of the city and the country, become a minority religion. Churches will close while mosques, temples and other places of worship will take their place as the spiritual and value change agents in our urban societies.

Pluralism

The range of differences among the people who live in cities continues to widen. The range of ethnicity challenges virtually every major city. The Los Angeles school district must address about one hundred twenty languages for its incoming students. This language diversity does not reflect the further ranges of ethnicity, national origin, religious background, or socioeconomic status.

This kind of pluralism is not limited to the West or to those who are not yet Christians. In a class of fifty I taught recently in Jos, Nigeria, thirteen first languages and twenty denominations were represented. Some of the students walked to class because they lacked bus fare. Others arrived in chauffeured Mercedes.

The impact of the pluralistic ages of the city's dwellers is increasingly being felt. Mexico City for example has more inhabitants under fourteen years than the entire population of New York City.

Technological Change

As we have already seen, the northern hemisphere is already highly urbanized. Rapid technological change in the cities heightens the impact of the cities on the overall society. Change in itself can be both constructive and destructive.[18] Slow change can be positive. However, the more rapid it becomes, the greater becomes

> CEFI is seeking to employ modern technologies both in the research and development and in the delivery systems of its programming. The intent to have access without limitation to time and venue to critical information is shaping present and future delivery systems.

21 Technological Change

the potential for disorientation and negative counteractions. Nevertheless, the continuing development of technologies enables a deepening and more rapid exchange of information and knowledge. This trend is already changing the ways we live and learn in the city,[19] and it will continue.

Because of these realities, we can safely assert that good news can provide an anchor in a sea of disorientation if presented in a way the peoples of the city can understand. This hope places the importance of equipping discerning urban Christian leaders who can distinguish when and how such dynamics are at work and provide relevant solutions, both practical and structural.

Educational Challenges

The continued success of any city depends, as it has in the past, on the ability of that city to educate each successive generation. This includes the knowledge necessary to maintain and extend not only its knowledge base, but also its value systems and infrastructural integrity. Education which achieves these goals is becoming increasingly difficult to sustain. Many obstacles must first be overcome. Changes in technology make curriculum adaptation necessary at some levels of education. Dysfunctionality of families and students in the classroom also affects the educational atmosphere. The management of knowledge and its development, transmission, and utilization must also be mastered. Innovation must be encouraged. Resources must be directed, and often redirected, towards strategic priorities.

When developing Christian leaders in the city, particular attention needs to be given to their ability to adapt to differing educational needs. Teaching urban leaders may differ widely depending on their backgrounds. The full implications of these discrepancies begin with the curricular priorities inherent, for example, in a traditional seminary education. In the city a high degree of non-formal and informal teaching methods are indicated to cope with the rapid change. Many seminaries, however, continue to educate their graduates almost exclusively in traditional formal training methods. Classroom theory needs to be equally balanced with hands-on training. Seminary professors need to participate in urban ministries in order to have first hand experience from which to reflect and teach.

Alienation, Anonymity, and Dysfunctionality

While cities are characterized by heavy population densities and highly complex social networks individual people are often alienated and outside of meaningful supporting networks. The urban poor are often among those who are pushed outside of these net-

The Bresee Institute sends its students almost daily onto the streets to build relationships, to address the issues of alienation, anonymity, and anomie.

22 Building Relationships to Prevent Alienation and Anomie

works. The urban poor comprise seventeen percent of the world's population. The unknown people of the city are the poor. They often are the dispossessed. They are alienated from each other, from the environment, and from the church.

Given the fragile economic and political situations in many parts of the world, people live on the brink of poverty. The loss of the pay check, a sickness, a storm, a temporarily debilitating accident will put a person onto the streets outside of his or her home. In the not distant past the homeless of the cities were older men who were stereotypically alcoholics or drug abusers. However, the streets are now populated by young people, families, mothers with children, and discouraged immigrants.

By stereotype they are alienated from the people who have the power and potential to help. They remain anonymous—without names, without identity, without self-esteem, and without hope. The hopelessness leads to a profound sense of dysfunctionality.

The theological educator must help the learner to break through the alienation to build relationships, to recognize the identity of the people in the city, and to communicate the good news of hope.

Poverty

The majority of the world's population live in cities. Dawson says that by 2010 three out of four people on earth will live in cities.[20] Most of these people are unreached by the gospel. And most of them are poor.

Poverty, partially defined in terms of economics, is only a symptom of a deeper condition. Middle and upper class people often accuse the poor of laziness, weakness, indolence, or addictive behaviors as the causes of poverty. Certainly, these factors are present, but oppressive structures, injustice, greed, and a thirst for more power on the part of the powerful also significantly contribute to poverty as well.

Powerlessness in the physical realm (economics), in the social realm (politics), and in the spiritual realm (enslavement to sin) is the key characteristic of poverty. The poor of the cities are impaired in all three realms.

Linthicum provides some additional helpful insight about the nature of poverty as seen in the Old Testament.

> The Old Testament analysis of poverty is stated succinctly in Amos 2:6–7: "For three sins of Israel, even for four, I will not turn back my wrath. They sell . . . the needy [*ebyon*] for a pair of sandals. They trample on the heads of the poor [*dallim*] . . . and deny justice to the oppressed [*anawim*]."
>
> In this passage, three different types of poverty are identified by the prophet. The *ebyon* are people totally dependent on others, those who are utterly destitute and must beg in order to survive. Those who are *dallim* are the physically weak and materially poor—they simply have neither the capital nor the strength

to make it financially in life. Finally, there are the *anawim*—those who know themselves to be of no account, the people broken under their weight of poverty so that they are entirely dependent on others for their survival. Today we would call the *ebyon* the exploited, the *dallim* the impoverished, and the *anawim* the oppressed.

What is significant in this passage is not the analysis it contains about the Israelites' understanding of the nature of poverty, however. The significance is that God condemns Israel for allowing some of its people to be exploited, impoverished, or oppressed.[21]

Differences between Rural and Urban

In the past, the differences between rural and urban were marked. We are, however, becoming more and more aware that the distinction between urban and rural, urban and suburban, metropolitan and nonmetropolitan, is fading and will become increasingly difficult to delineate.[22]

> World Impact consciously orients Midwestern rural and small town young adults to the urban culture of west central Los Angeles through hands-on experience and reflection.
>
> **23** Rural/Urban Differences

The arrival of cable television, the domination of urban banking in rural areas, the advancement of gangs and illegal substances into the small towns of America, the slow agonizing death of the small family farm, the migration of young people to the city and their influence back home, are just a few things which bring these changes into focus. "Increasingly, urban-nonurban differences are differences that have ceased to make a difference."[23]

Does the vanishing gulf between rural and urban mean that leadership training in the Christian sector can continue to be supported by traditional training methods? The answer is no! In fact, the opposite is true. With the continued advance of the ideological pluralism and the ethnic diversity in all of society, it is becoming increasingly necessary to develop curricula and training methods which include dealing with issues relevant to the problems found in the city. Literature for urban youth, for example, which does not reflect a Christian view of ethnicity, or confront head-on issues which help the youth to find their way as Christians in a cultural milieu and a value system which is, at best, alien to Christianity, will result in the youth deciding that Christ is not relevant to their lives. The equipping of leaders to deal with drugs, the occult and gangs is no longer the concern of the Two-Thirds World trainer; it demands equipping attention in virtually every city in the world.

Organizations within the City

Within the city the wide variety of organizations ranges from informal associations to highly complex institutions. These organizations, many of which function as subcultures, affect all of the people who live in the city.

Associations

Traditionally it has been thought that kinship ties of the tribal and peasant societies in the city tend to break down, and associations tend to replace them. Some of these associations are informal and others are formalized with legal and multigenerational implications. More recently, research-

> The Harambee Center provides a new relational center for the community. The educational content addresses the development of social skills from family functions to community building and economic development.
>
> **2 4** Associations

ers are discovering that urban migrants often establish the location of relatives or fellow villagers before they come to the city, and then move in with them. For example, life in squatter villages in Mexico City doesn't always suffer from disorganization. Small groups continue in extended families and in the neighborhoods. Family networks and religious commitment remain strong.[24]

Friendship groups play an important role in all societies, but in the city they often do replace kinship ties as the closest relationships people have. Sports clubs, bar friendships, and bowling teams are all examples of such friendship groups.

Gender based associations may continue to exist (e.g., certain men's clubs, women's auxiliaries), but are now being challenged from both sides. Even though these clubs are no longer gender exclusive, some of the most significant business and political deals, social belonging, and much more are brokered in such clubs.

Age based associations such as gangs, AARP, and senior citizen church groups are likely to become more prominent and may be expected to carry many of the functions that were previously the domain of either the nuclear or extended family. Many of these groups also express the human need for predictability and safety in the midst of disorienting change. For example, a nonprofit organization in Los Angeles helps senior citizens who have no one at home to find roommates as an alternative to selling the home and going to a senior residence.

Secret societies such as the Masons or the Ku Klux Klan often assume quasi-governmental functions if they become strong. They often take on racial or religious overtones in unsettled social settings.

Prestige associations such as country clubs, spas, elite business clubs, and airline clubs provide people with opportunities to demonstrate their status and traffic with people who have influence. Again, much business and political maneuvering occurs in such settings. In the information age, a new and perhaps more powerful kind of association is emerging—temporary and voluntary networks which are formed in synergistic ways to accomplish together what neither could have done alone.

Special interest associations in urban settings are based on common interests of their members. Such groups are Parent Teacher Associations, chess clubs, lobbies, neighborhood associations, Alcoholics Anonymous, Tough Love, and others. The greater the needs which bring these groups together are felt, the more likely they can be expected to multiply.

This brings us to one of the most significant social phenomena which can be observed in urban society. It is the inception and rapid growth of groups which seem to capture an idea and/or meet a need. These groups seem to spring up overnight and become nation wide in a very few years. Urban Christians could make significant inroads into urban society by finding such needs and meeting them. Every Christian leader must have training in convening and leading small groups.

Institutions

Associations that develop formal patterns of organization, maintain stability over time and acquire property are often referred to as *institutions*.[25] This would make institutions such as churches or denominations subcultural. The characteristics of an institution or subculture will generally include the following:

> Both LMI and the Church on Brady equip people to establish new institutions. LMI helps form local congregations, associations of congregations, and Bible Institutes in its design. The Church on Brady helps form new congregations from small groups.

25 Institutions

1. All institutions have an **identity**. Their identity will usually be based on: a) their function—what they do, b) their cultural ethos—who they are, and c) their distinctive—what they stand for.

2. Another characteristic which almost all institutions have is **membership**. They develop sets of statuses and roles within that insti-

tution which are occupied by people who belong to the institution. Some of the roles in a church include: pastor, ushers, board members, janitors, and the like. A structure is developed which allows these people to carry out their functions. Recruitment of members, initiation rites, and socialization procedures are also usually a vital part of an institution. If functions change with time, the structure needs to be changed.

3. The ownership of **property** and separate legal status are among the characteristics of an institution.

4. **Culture** plays an important part in the development of institutions. The previous three attributes work together to create an atmosphere within which systems of shared beliefs, norms, systems of authority and leadership, social organization, hierarchy, and symbols are developed.[26]

Denominations, lodges, various rights groups, and other institutions constitute subcultures within the dominant culture. Yet they all exert their own influence on that dominant culture and ultimately shape it into something it never would have been without that subculture.

Jesus spoke of the Church as being leaven, light and salt. Another way of saying it is that the Church should be equipping its leaders to be change agents. The Church accomplishes this task by, first of all, simply being who it is[27] and, secondly, by working actively to influence the dominant culture and shape it into that which it never would have been without the Church. It is because the Church sometimes overlooks this authority that it fails to speak to and challenge structural evil in the city in all of its forms. In many ways, this is just as essential as confronting personal sins in the lives of individuals.

Institutionalization is the process by which an institution comes into being, grows, matures, and finally ages. The first generation of founders have strong convictions about the institution and a strong commitment to its ideal. The second generation is usually

> A major contribution of CEFI is the equipping of Types III, IV, and V church leaders to continue to overcome problems involved in the predictable stages of the institutional growth of the Church.

26 Institutionalization

caught up in its elders' enthusiasm, but retains less of the commitment, and remains members because of devotion to its elders. The third and following generations may resort to rules and regulations to shore up flagging zeal. The size of the institution has also grown to make it possible for individuals to make a living within the organization. At this point, a shift in motivation for membership also precipitates a shift in motivation for its preservation.

This previously mentioned process helps explain the different stages of institutional development: 1) the reasons and motivation for fellowship, 2) the qualifications and style of leadership, 3) the development of formalization of the structure, 4) the integration of the group into a cohesive—perhaps even exclusive unit, and 5) the understanding and living out of the original vision.

"Old First Churches" often fall very neatly into this category. The same could be said for other organizations which can look back on an illustrious, yet fading history. There is a need for renewal and attendant structural change, possibly even a reexamination of and return to the original vision.

Coping in the Urban Social Environment

Another very real aspect of the city within which all people move is called the social environment. Different cultures cope in various ways with an urban environment. Questions of how to deal with strangers, how to behave, and how one defines community are of paramount importance when one equips emerging leaders.

Strangers—How Do We Deal with Them?

Strangers can be very threatening, and in a large city, we know very few people. How do we manage? How do we find people we can risk being comfortable with? Lyn Lofland has offered that we cope by identifying strangers on the basis of their appearance and their spatial location in the city.[28] For example, in China the emperor wore yellow; today college professors wear tweed jackets, nurses wear white uniforms, business executives wear dark suits.

Where we see people in the city is a help in identifying strangers. Young people on a campus are assumed to be students, middle-aged conservatively dressed people in an office district are assumed to be business people. People who use airports are considered to be higher status than those one finds in a bus station. When conversing with someone, one asks a social class question: "What do you do for a living?" or "Where do you go to school?"

While skills in addressing strangers can be helpful in averting danger or alleviating fear, the Christian needs to be cautious in its use. Such skill can also lead to the formation of stereotypes and prejudices which will shut out the very people emerging Christian leaders are hoping to reach.

What is a Community?

Just as with the term *urban*, the term *community* has never been defined uniformly to everyone's satisfaction. There is no current consensus on the significance of community in the modern social life of the city. Suzanne Keller and Claude Fischer propose that the neighborhood serves only minimal functions.[29] Weber submits that modern urbanites can have "community without propinquity" or nearness.

During the Los Angeles riots, it was possible to note several different reactions on a community basis which illustrate varying degrees of commitment to community. Some people defended their communities. They barricaded the streets and held watch. The local residents felt threatened by external change, and saw this defense as the only way they could feel safe and secure. These groups are proceeding to build security fences.

There are communities that emphasize the voluntary and limited involvement of residents in the local community to maintain the identity and boundaries of their community. Generally, all towns and cities, like Los Angeles, fall into this category. Local organizations and particularly the local community press have a vested interest in maintaining the identity and boundaries of the area. They have, for example, worked hard to restore faith in the viability of Los Angeles as a tourist city.

Then an even more diffuse community description like "The Valley," or "Northside," will be used. "The disruptions even reached in the Valleys."

Finally, there are intentional, brand new communities which are usually built from the ground up. They can be as diverse as Irvine (a planned city south of Los Angeles in Orange county), or Jordan Downs (a government project in South Central Los Angeles). These new communities tend to be more homogeneous, ethnically and financially.

Trends Affecting Leadership Development Strategy

Several trends occurring in our global community affect how the Church approaches leadership development. Only a few are suggested here to note the profound changes occurring in urban areas today. Any one of these trends requires significant changes in existing leadership development structures.

Deconcentration of Cities

Many cities no longer have a single nucleus. The geography and size of the population bring strains on the transportation, trade, communications, and other systems of cities. The cost of maintaining large operations downtown, where costs are high, makes decentralization attractive. Technology has helped to overcome any spatial barriers. Costs are lowered, and a qualified work force is more accessible.

Los Angeles, for example, is expected to become ten to twenty times its present size. In that context, businesses can be expected to continue to build satellite offices, set up employees with computer terminals and modems on Local Access Networks (LANs) at home, or even building satellite plants in the suburbs instead of expanding

> LMI is facing deconcentration by a focus on both Bible Academies in local churches and Bible institutes placed in each metropolitan area.
>
> CCCMTI has instituted an extension and continuing education program which positions it to face this issue.

27 Deconcentration

in downtown Los Angeles. Los Angeles is no different from many other cities both in the developing world and the more developed regions. This trend only accentuates the reason for defining *urban* more broadly.

A Movement away from Hierarchical Systems

Alienation, frustration, loneliness, and fear are often problems the urban pastor encounters. One of the coping strategies that a pastor sometimes turns to is an authoritarian style of leadership. Seminaries teach competition for grades. Some denominations continue to encourage competition for

> The Crenshaw Christian Center offers a "full service" church program including day care, day school, a three level ministry equipping program, and an in-service nonformal training for upgrading pastors' effectiveness.

28 Self-contained Wholism

the "better" and the "larger" churches. A casual or naive reading of management literature and some church growth literature may lead pastors to believe that strong leadership can be equated with authoritarian hierarchical leadership.

Bakke writes:

> The slide into authoritarian styles can be seen among the Christian leaders in any major city. The styles have little to do with the gospel but reveal a lot about the way urbanization affects our personalities. Authoritarianism ministers to the

needs of the pastor to be important and decisively in charge. Pastors may no longer gain personal satisfaction, growth, and meaning in small communities of primary relationships, so they steadily alter their styles and goals in authoritarian directions as ways of coping with the erosion of their power and status in their communities.[30]

In the past the industrial cities were product-oriented and company-oriented. Clear trends show changes in the direction of in-house, company-run day care centers; leisure centers; continuing education opportunity; and reduction of assembly line human automatons. High priority will be given to amenity-rich work environments. Large investments of time and money are made so that highly educated people working in knowledge and information-intensive jobs will stay with the company.

Futurists point to the need for and the trend toward a "service," "people," or "relational" orientation of businesses. This shift affects what people will accept in terms of timing and space limitations for the church and for equipping programs. It affects the structures and functions of associations and institutions, including churches and urban missions.

When training Christian leaders for ministry in the city, the church is going to have to abandon assembly-line, denomination-oriented, systems-associated methods. A new focus will be placed on short- and long-term cooperative coalitions, avoidance of duplication of efforts through the use of service networks, understanding that once the job is done (first generation) all parties are free to search out new partners for a new and different task. The flexibility and freshness such structures afford in a rapidly changing environment cannot be underestimated. Local church as well as denominational cooperation without the surrender of distinctives is going to be a new and dynamic direction for ministry. This also has the advantage of presenting a united front to those who would take issue with a divided Church.

People- and task-orientation, rather than institution-orientation, will have to carry the day, if the Church wants to make inroads into the culture of the city.

Relocation

Some Midwest industrial cities are being revived as they shift their emphasis from heavy to light industry and service industry. However, many American sociologists are suggesting that it is futile to revive all of these cities. They suggest, rather, that money for renewal should be spent on retraining and relocating families to cities which have the appropriate jobs. Such obsolete areas, they advise, should be allowed to shrink to viable sizes.

Relocation has long been a formative characteristic of cities. Now the relocation of businesses and urban centers has gone far beyond the individualistic relocating effects of individuals and families. In some cases the relocation of even capital cities, as in Brazil and the coming move in Nigeria, has brought profound changes on the leadership development context.

Systems

Urban systems are also being transformed by the new technologies. For example, medical services and health care systems have traditionally been urban based and urban driven. Rural people had to go to the city to get specialized care. Previous attempts to decentralize health care with the rationale that everyone should have access to good health care failed. Now a rural doctor whose clinic is wired for conference communications can consult simultaneously with specialists in several cities. Closed circuit cable TV channels allow for direct conversations and diagnostics.

There are two ways this could be interpreted. The first is that the city is intruding further into the rural lifestyle. Secondly, it could also be said that if a dichotomy between urban and rural ever really existed, it exists no longer.

Other Trends

In addition to the above challenges, several other results of the Information Revolution may be expected to impact how the Church does business in the future.

Automated assembly lines are transforming not only the speed and quality of many different products, they are also creating long unemployment lines in the large industrial cities which were built on the backs of blue collar workers. Change has overtaken and devastated many people. One implication for individual families and the society as a whole is that retraining will be necessary. The jury is still out on what the ultimate implications will be. The Church has a great deal of ministry potential resulting from this revolution, and the training of leaders in this context will be crucial to ministry success.

Growth of the working poor by the inclusion of the blue-collar worker could be the result of the shift to high technology. Good paying jobs require ever higher levels of education and training. Even traditional blue-collar wages will be earned in data entry and the service industry, far from traditional blue-collar skills. Unless there are massive retraining programs in new vocations which are compatible to the new technologies, this segment of society will continue to lose ground to the middle class. The call of God and training to minister to the needs of these newly poor are be significant.

Home businesses are on the rise. There are books which explain the what, how, where, and why of operating a business at home. Exhibitions can be attended in which home businesses are featured. These possibilities are made viable through computer technology, modems, and Local Access Networks (LANs). People can work at home and deliver their products anywhere in the world. Mothers and fathers can now have a good paying job and be with their families. The Church may be able to tap into the possibilities and trigger a new emphasis on small family businesses. The potential and logistics of evangelism and leadership development by the use of telephone, modem, fax, and other new technologies need to be explored more fully.

Individualized entertainment may also further isolate people from each other and internalize and personalize human emotion. Again, this is not necessarily an urban phenomenon, but it will be primarily found in the city. Such trends will have to be monitored, because they will have profound and as yet unknown effects, both positive and negative, on evangelism. In addition, it may have an impact on the development of leaders who can relate in meaningful ways with other people.

Dysfunctionality is another issue which is affecting development of leadership. In a conversation with the national director of InterVarsity, the greatest problem this organization faces in its attempt to develop leaders is dysfunctionality. Without getting technical, dysfunctionality is the inability to form meaningful and long-term relationships with other people. There are many sources for and many varying degrees of this problem. The main sources are the lack of proper role models in increasingly fragmented family structures, and substance abuse. Will the Church also have difficulty in finding and training future leaders?

The **globalization** of business is one of the reasons for explosive world urbanization. When a major European, American, or Japanese manufacturer opens an affiliate in a major Two-Thirds World city, there are ten people who are willing to move to the city for every resulting job opening. What we are observing are conditions, comparable both in terms of opportunity and human suffering, to that of seventeenth and eighteenth century Europe during the Industrial Revolution. Robert Reich, a Harvard economics professor, writes about a new global economy based on cooperation between companies located in different nations.[31] IBM has recently joined forces with major companies in Europe and Japan to produce a super computer chip. This allows these companies together to achieve that which no one of them can do together.

With such synergy generating incredible achievement in the business world, it is possible to imagine denominations beginning to cooperate with each other in similar ways. The task of providing leadership for the cities of the world is so colossal, that the kingdom of God can only begin to approach the possibility of success by pooling resources in collaboration with one another. Together, the Church of Jesus Christ can do that which denominations alone could never even attempt.

Summary

The increasing ethnicity, the growing gulf between the classes, deteriorating moral dynamics, the increase of isolation and insulation, the escalating cost of living, the increase of the urban poor, and much more, are characteristics of the modern city around the world. The Church must meet these issues head-on and find answers as to how to effectively minister in the midst of them. The elements of equipping Christian leaders for ministry will also have to be measured against these and other urban concerns, if they are to be appropriate in the urban context. With God's help, new methods and structures can be found to meet these immense challenges.

Notes

1 LeRoy Ford, "A Manual for Designing Theological Education" (n.p., 1989), p. 262.

2 The impact of such churches as the Yoido Full Gospel Church in Seoul, Korea, the Vision of the Future Church in Argentina, the Willow Creek Church in Chicago, the Saddleback Church in San Diego, the Hope of Bangkok Church, the Crenshaw Christian Center in South Central Los Angeles and a number of other churches would challenge Neill's statement. However, these churches are rare exceptions.

3 Stephen Neill, *A History of Christian Missions* (New York: Penguin Books, 1964), pp. 569–570.

4 Jacques Ellul, *The Meaning of the City*, trans. Dennis Pardee (Grand Rapids: William B. Eerdmans Publishing Company, 1970).

5 Donald A. McGavran, *Understanding Church Growth* (Grand Rapids: William B. Eerdmans Publishing Company, 1980), p. 318.

6 Ibid.

7 Robert C. Linthicum, *City of God, City of Satan: A Biblical Theology of the Urban Church* (Grand Rapids: Zondervan Publishing House, 1991), p. 21.

8 Ibid., p. 22.

9 Ibid., pp. 62–63.

10 Ibid., p. 67. Linthicum defines the primary terms the Apostle Paul uses to describe the spiritual forces with whom we as Christians are engaged in spiritual warfare as follows:

Throne— The throne is the institution of power in a state, city, or economic body. Although today the throne of a country is found in its legislative, judicial, and executive systems, the throne of Paul's day was a literal chair of authority on a raised dais, symbolizing the "seat" of authority.

Dominion— A dominion is the territory influenced or ruled by the throne; it is the sphere of formal influence of that structure of power. Thus the dominion of the United States is its fifty states and possessions and territories.

Principality— The principality or prince is the specific person who currently occupies the throne. It can be the major of a city, president of a country, or chairman of an economic institution's board. The prince, or specific person, can and will change, but the throne continues as long as that institution continues . . .

Power—   The power of a throne comprises the rules, legalities, traditions, and sanctions that legitimize the throne's rule over that dominion and provides the authority by which the principality occupies that throne. Thus the powers that legitimize General Motors include its papers of incorporation, the bylaws according to which it structures its activities, its products, and its relationship with its customers. Removal of any of these powers would seriously curtail the capacity of General Motors to continue business (Ibid., p. 67).

Linthicum describes four basic assertions which Paul makes about principalities and powers:

1. The principalities and powers have been created by Christ, who is supreme over them . . .

2. . . . the principalities and powers have been captured by Satan and are now used by him for his nefarious work . . .

3. Christ has come to conquer the sin of the powers and to set them free from their own bondage . . .

4. The church is called to respond to the principalities and powers . . . In Ephesians 3:8–11, Paul makes this remarkable statement: . . . His intent was that now, through the church, the manifold wisdom of God should be made known to the rulers and authorities in heavenly realms, according to his eternal purpose which he accomplished in Christ Jesus our Lord (Ibid., p. 71).

[11] Ibid., p. 68

[12] Ibid., p. 73.

[13] David Barrett, *World-Class Cities and World Evangelization* (Birmingham, AL: New Hope, 1985), p. 16.

[14] Neal Gabler, "Moral Relativism? You Don't Get It," *Los Angeles Times* (June 14, 1992): M1.

[15] Ibid.

16 Diana L. Eck, "True Liberty Cherishes Difference," *Los Angeles Times* (July 5, 1992): M5.

17 Ibid.

18 Charles Kraft, *Christianity and Culture* (Maryknoll, NY: Orbis, 1979), p. 247.

19 Just a sampling of these advances are: video, fax, prodigy, ATM cards, overnight deliveries, assembly lines, the cashless society, home businesses, biogenetic manipulation, individualized entertainment, and the globalization of businesses.

20 John Dawson, *Taking Our Cities for God: How to Break Spiritual Strongholds* (Lake Mary, FL: Creation House, 1989), p. 34.

21 Linthicum, p. 91.

22 John J. Palen, *The Urban World* (New York: McGraw Hill, 1987), p. 426.

23 Ibid.

24 Ibid., p. 46–47. For a more detailed summary, see Ulf Hannerz, *Exploring the City: Inquiries toward Urban Anthropology* (New York: Columbia University Press, 1980), pp. 59–72.

25 Paul G. Hiebert, "Critical Contextualization," *International Bulletin of Missionary Research*, 11: 3 (July, 1987), 103–112.

26 Ibid., pp. 37–38.

27 By the word *being* is meant an identification with and a life which reflects the life and love of Jesus Christ.

28 Lyn Lofland, *A World of Strangers* (New York: Basic Books, 1973), p. 45.

29 Suzanne Keller, *The Urban Neighborhood* (New York: Random House, 1968); and Claude Fischer, *The Urban Experience* (New York: Harcourt, Brace and Jovanovich, 1976).

30 Raymond J. Bakke, *The Urban Christian: Effective Ministry in Today's Urban World* (Downers Grove, IL: InterVarsity Press, 1987), p. 54.

31 Robert Reich, *The Work of Nations* (New York: Alfred A. Knopf, 1991), pp. 81ff.

CHAPTER FIVE

EDUCATIONAL FOUNDATIONS FOR DEVELOPING LEADERS FOR URBAN MINISTRIES

Introduction

Without significant change traditional seminaries will not be able to meet the leadership development needs of churches in the next century. Just as new forms of church structures are emerging to serve postindustrial societies, so also new educational forms are needed to equip their leaders. The traditional dominant theological education structures are simply not designed to effectively equip the diverse range of urban leaders needed by the Church. The equipping of men and women to serve effectively in the diverse ministries needed in our urbanizing world requires reform, renewal, and the formation of new forms of theological education. The traditional Western worldview dominance is being powerfully challenged. The alumni produced by so many seminaries and Christian colleges are often ill equipped either to understand or minister in the cities of the world. Cities are often conglomerated of minority peoples. Pannell asserts, "I have concluded that evangelical schools as they now exist are inadequate to train minority leaders effectively."[1] His assertion is taken even farther by others to apply outside the minority communities.[2] The church's potential to influence cities depends largely on the leaders who are equipping and how they are equipped.

Greenway writes,

> Cities, seminaries, and Christian colleges have been living apart for too long, and it's a broken relationship that urgently needs to be repaired. In North America school after school has left the city in favor of the more plush and racially homogeneous suburbs. As a result, our schools produce thousands of graduates each year who know little or nothing about cities. They've spent their lives and received all their education in the cushioned middle class world of antiseptic isolation from harsh urban realities. As a consequence, they are unprepared to minister in cities. They are bewildered by them and avoid them. The

world on one hand has been urbanizing, but we've gone the opposite direction. Now we're faced with the dilemma that the world to which Christ sends us to be ambassadors, servants, and transformers lies mainly in the cities, and we're outside. And the schools where we train our leaders and workers are as non-urban as our churches.[3]

A recent survey of seminaries in the US[4] reveals the ambiguity of American seminaries' response to the contemporary American church context. Often neither the mission nor the message is clear. Responses to contemporary issues such as the status and role of people in ministry, women in ministry, the recruitment of new candidates for full-time ministry, the goal of ministry, homosexuality, abortion, and basic theological is-

> The Bresee Institute provides ministry experience within the community being served as a critical integrated part of the learning experience of the emerging leaders.
>
> ABI, CCCMTI, and the Harambee Institute all are integrally related with local ministry settings so that ministry experience is a critical part of the over all educational experience.

29 Ministry Experience for Learning

sues remain in dispute. While the picture is not entirely bleak, many American seminaries' response to the cities of the world almost guarantees that the people who live there will not hear the gospel from their graduates.

> Christian education, particularly at the level where leaders are trained, needs to be urbanized in a number of ways. An urban agenda for a school might begin with location. Wherever feasible students and faculty members should be encouraged to live in the city, attend city churches, and become involved with the issues affecting urban people . . . .
>
> Second on the agenda is the content of the curriculum. Future church leaders in an urban world need to be exposed to urban sociology in sizable doses. They need to know about the history of cities and of great urban ministries. They need to know ethnodemographics. In the religion departments they must look at God's dealing with cities in the Bible and ethical questions relating to justice, oppression, the poor, and the powerless surface over and over again. In ethics they must learn what loving your neighbor means in a crowded tenement, a sprawling third-world slum, and in neighborhoods where crime and poverty are as thick as flies on the garbage.
>
> Beyond school catalogs lie the deeper goals which Christian academics seek to pursue. They spring from the gospel itself, of Christ's saviorhood and lordship, and they wait to be applied to the varied contexts of the human race.[5]

Graduates from traditional theological education institutions often lack relevant urban ministry experience. This lack leaves them deficient to begin ministry with competence upon graduation. Dayton and Nelson write,

> Seminary students . . . need broader experience. Aristotle doubted whether moral philosophy could be taught to the young, because they lack the one indispensable ingredient—sustained experience of life. There is a similar problem in theological education.[6]

The problem extends to the whole range of seminary students. A major evangelical seminary as recently as 1990 downgraded its commitment to "field education" thus effectively reducing the urban/metro ministry experience of its students.

The plight of urban churches on the one hand and the dearth of churches in urban centers on the other points to the need for profound change in theological education. Only a minority of forward-looking seminaries and Christian colleges have taken significant steps to equip lay people with theological education.

Rooy writes,

> Theological education cannot be limited to the professional clergy. "Ministry" is the task given to the whole church to bring the Gospel to bear on all of human life. No discipline or profession remains outside its scope. For that reason the distinction commonly made between Christian education and theological education implies a dichotomy between the laity and the clergy that is unacceptable in biblical theology. Theological education is certainly Christian (though it may be sub-Christian in both methodology and content), just as Christian education is theological (though it is sometimes moralistic and lacking in theological roots).[7]

Great numbers of urban churches (though by no means all) range from steady maintenance to a precipitous decline. Urban churches that are growing and significantly influencing their communities remain a small minority. The attrition rate of Bible college and seminary graduates from a committed full-time ministry in urban churches is alarmingly high. "Christian colleges as much as seminaries need to urbanize. Or else we run the risk of highly educating, superbly training, kingdom servants for yesterday's world."[8]

The concern for developing Christian leaders who will serve effectively in their contexts is not only an evangelical quest. The World Council of Churches also has a long history of concern for developing leaders in context—both rural and urban. In the late sixties and early seventies the Theological Education Fund (TEF) assisted greatly in the development of Theological Education by Extension (TEE) and its spread throughout the world both in rural and urban areas. In 1977 when the Programme on Theological Education (PTE) was created to carry on the work of the TEF across six continents, the broad mandate continued to be "ministerial formation." Kinsler writes explaining the position of PTE that

> theological education is not an end itself, that it is not simply an academic or professional enterprise, that it is not even bound to institutions. Ministerial

formation is as concerned with personal growth and maturity as it is with theological knowledge, with spiritual gifts and commitment for service as well as pastoral skills. These qualities and aspects of leadership can perhaps be identified and fostered within the practice of ministry in congregations and communities . . . One of the enigmas we face is that theological education along with other kinds of education leads to privilege and power, whereas ministerial formation is fundamentally concerned with servanthood.[9]

TEE in the late sixties and early seventies was promoted worldwide as a renewal movement in theological education. It offered great promise for multiplying effective leaders at every level as they served in ministry. Associations for TEE were established in many regions and countries of the world. Even in the

> The current use of TEE in LMI related churches in Lima, Peru shows the philosophy of ministry and education among these churches by equipping of local leaders-in-ministry. The focus moves from a clergy-dominated and passive laity to an active leadership among the laity of small groups.

30 Philosophy of Education in TEE

nineties TEE continues to have many, many students worldwide. However, the current impact in the nineties of TEE on theological education is very limited. The potential has been subverted by a number of factors. TEE was seen as largely nonformal. It had a base of education that was planned, but out of school. It was aimed at the practice of ministry. The learners were not credentialed or they were not given the same credentials as learners in formal institutions. It was closely linked with one particular educational technology, that is, programmed instruction. Programmed instruction, while a powerful and useful educational technology, is not always applicable because of differences of learning styles or educational levels. Over time people connected with formal theological institutions have criticized TEE, saying that students who learn in nonformal ways such as through TEE do not receive the equivalence of a seminary education. As a result of this criticism, TEE programs, on the one hand, began to be relegated to the education of lower level leaders. On the other hand, TEE programs were increasingly formalized and structured. These two tendencies worked against each other and subverted the whole TEE movement.

The philosophy of education and values which undergirded the original formation often was not shared by the those designed and implemented TEE programs in other places. The focus again moved from praxis to content, from learner ministry to teacher direction, from lay ministry to clergy ministry, from learning what is needed for ministry to what is specified in the curriculum. A study of the decline of TEE and its impact would provide a useful study for people who would bring renewal in theological education for urban leaders. It might also provide insight about what not to do in the design of new and creative urban leadership development programs.

Ford offers a simple description of the elements in an effective design:

Somebody (the learner) is learning . . .
Something (the source) is . . .

in . . .

Someway (the methodology and the instructional and administrative models)
Somewhere (the multiple contexts)

for . . .

Some Purpose (the educational goals and objectives).[10]

Both the need for new forms of theological education for the cities and a promise of renewal are once again arising from local churches. Many local churches are forming church-based training programs aimed at developing the full range of leadership for local churches. The training programs of the Church on Brady and the Crenshaw Christian Center only serve to illustrate what has once again become a movement to develop home grown leaders. This movement has arisen in part because of a perceived lack of relevance of traditional graduate level theological education to the current needs of metropolitan churches. These metropolitan churches are both in the suburbs and in the inner-cities. These new church based leadership development programs are not limited by denomination or ethnicity.

Two educational perspectives (philosophies) undergird much post-secondary education in the USA. Varied forms of these approaches are employed worldwide. The classical university model forms its programs around humanities and philosophy. Many seminaries fit well into this model where church history focuses on Europe and America. Systematic theology addresses the issues of the Hellenized educated, upper-middle class student. Logic, homiletics, and hermeneutics flow from classic Greek ways of thinking. Much of the classical approach focuses on remaining true to the past.

A second educational perspective followed by the land-grant colleges and universities addresses education in terms of local community needs. Typically, the land-grant institutions address local economic issues, whether they are agriculture, fishing, forestry, mining, or whatever. Research is aimed at practical applications such as improving wheat or dairy production or conservation. These institutions have sought to combine the best of the classical university along with both the social and "hard" sciences to provide sound, but contemporary theory for a changing world.

Some theological education has followed this second perspective. The focus has been more on action research and equipping for ministry than found in the traditional seminaries. The School of World Mission at Fuller Theological Seminary, the Church on Brady, and the Alliance Bible

Institute in Lima, Peru demonstrate this kind of perspective on three different educational levels and in formal and nonformal modes of education.

Classical educators have often criticized this approach to education as being shallow, not academic, not equivalent, or too pragmatic. Because of the political, economic, and institutional power

> The CCCMTI brings a theological dimension to the equipping of every type of church leader including ushers, parking lot attendants and others who serve in "Helps" ministries.

leave licensure, and ordination these nontraditional forms of education often been considered as a second-class approach to education and unworthy of economic or ecclesial support.

However, to equip effective leaders for urban ministries new wineskins, new delivery systems, new contextualized approaches to addressing curricular issues are required. The traditional means simply cannot cope with the new realities.

The disaffection of mega-churches with contemporary seminaries, the formation of a plethora of new church-based training programs, the ineffectiveness of so many seminary graduates in urban areas all press seminaries to consider something new.

Seminaries with their rich resources in faculties well-trained in biblical studies, theology, history, ethics, and now sociology, psychology, anthropology, and other disciplines have the opportunity to do research in every area of resource and strength to provide both theologically sound and culturally appropriate instruction for urban ministries. If they only follow the classical model, their alumni will likely become increasingly irrelevant. If they will learn from the land-grant model, their potential contribution is yet to be estimated.

Before offering any recommendations or suggestions about the design of specific components in a leadership development program, the educational foundations should be further established. This chapter will then address the question of foundational education issues. Two major sections follow. The first reviews the major suggestions offered in "The Manifesto for the Renewal of Theological Education," as prepared by the International Council for Accrediting Agencies (ICAA). This manifesto grew out of the struggles of international evangelical theological educators to address the equipping of Christians for ministry in greatly divergent cultural contexts around the globe. The concerns, while applicable to traditional and rural settings, are particularly relevant for the renewal, reformation, or perhaps new formation of urban leadership development programs for the church.

Just as theological values shape, constrain, and guide theological education, so also these complementary educational values should further shape, constrain, and guide theological education. Following the primary values identified from the ICAA manifesto, the question of balance among educational modes is raised to further focus the design towards a holistic and balanced approach which is contextually appropriate for the purpose at hand. The following concerns from the ICAA manifesto serve to focus our attention on key value issues.

Contextualization

Theological education should be designed with "deliberate reference to the context" in which it is to be employed. The importation of training programs from outside of the context seldom works. The ICAA Manifesto suggests,

> The Harambee Center seeks to address leadership development that is appropriate in the community where the center works. Community leaders are brought into the center for regular seminars and people are given training for marketable skills in that community. The training is done in the community by people who understand the community, many of whom who live in the community.

31 Contextualized Learning

Indeed, not only what is taught but also in structure and operation our theological programs must demonstrate that they exist in and for their own specific context; in government and administration, in staffing and finance, in teaching styles and class assignments, in library resources and student services.[11]

Both the biblical and theological concerns must be addressed within the local context where the learners are to be serving.

Churchward Orientation

Theological education should not only serve the church, but it should be closely related to the church. The ICAA Manifesto states, "Our theological programs must become manifestly of the

> LMI supported equipping aims specifically at the equipping of leaders for churches in ways that will multiply growing churches.

32 Churchward Orientation

church, through the church and for the church."[12] To design urban training programs out of urban anthropology, urban sociology, a rural perspective, a traditional theological education perspective, or any other perspective that does not include a high level of participation with the church in the urban setting that is to be served will likely fail.

Strategic Flexibility

The ICAA manifesto suggests three issues around which strategic flexibility ought to be designed. First is the range of leadership roles that are to be equipped. The second is the range of academic levels. And third is the range of educational modes. These ranges need to be considered together in their interactive ways so as to equip men and women in ministry who fit that context. The range of leadership roles and different kinds of status is treated elsewhere in this text. The range of academic levels may spread from non-literate to postgraduate. This range may occur in the same community, in the same church, in the same training program. The balance of educational modes is treated in more detail in a later section in this chapter.

> CEFI maintains a position of strategic flexibility and market sensitivity by continuing to study the churches and the needs they are willing to invest time and money to address. The seminars and consultations regularly focus on a range of leaders both as the targeted audiences and as content in the seminars. The church on Brady and the Bresee Institute offer training in the nonformal undergraduate and graduate levels for Types I through IV leaders.

33 Strategic Flexibility

Theological Grounding

Every educational enterprise has at its core a set of values. The purpose of education is to operationalize or put these values into action, both in knowledge, skills, attitudes, and in the case of spiritual leaders, spiritual formation. Theological education is no different from any other form of education in this way. It too has a value base. The equipping of Christian leaders for urban ministries must have undergirding it a value base. The issue is not to objectively present all sides of theological issues, but to present with conviction what an urban leader needs to know, do, and be out of the revealed value base from which he or she works. The ICAA manifesto states,

> The theological orientation for people involved in ministry at every level begins with the "Helps" training program at CCCMTI. The philosophy of ministry which brings servanthood into focus applies both to the custodian as well as to a person in a pastoral ministry.

34 Theological Orientation

> We must come to perceive our task in even these basic points of reference within the larger setting of God's total truth and God's total plan. Such a shared

theological perception is largely absent from our midst. We must together take immediate and urgent steps to elaborate and possess a biblically informed theological basis for our calling in theological education and allow every aspect of our service to become rooted and nurtured in this soil.[13]

The explicit identification of values is an important part of the formation of a leadership development program. It is from these explicit statements of values that all of the program can then be judged.

Continuous Evaluation

After the purpose has been set and initial goals and objectives identified, the process needs to be assessed and then weighed against the goals, objectives, and purpose to provide an ongoing evaluation. The results of the evaluation

> CEFI's continuous evaluation of response to its workshops and seminars allows it to remain on "the cutting edge" and keep average seminar enrollments above 185.

35 Continuous Evaluation

should then be fed back into the process to improve what is being taught in terms of content, method, and implementation. As the outcomes are assessed and weighed against the purpose, new goals and new objectives should then be set. An early and firm commitment to the process of evaluation is very important for the effectiveness of the program. Evaluation should not be seen as something to be done just after the fact if there are time and resources left over, but rather evaluation should be seen as a critical means by which useful information is provided in every step of decision making in the educational process. The evaluation will be based on assessments weighed against the values.[14]

Seminaries, Christian colleges, and Christian universities which declare a commitment to equipping leaders for urban ministries could not only assure continued relevance, but improve effectiveness by regularly evaluating four sets of issues and then feeding the results back through the whole decision-making system. By looking at the context, the relevance of the goals and objectives could be improved. By looking at the resources, the structures could be adjusted for both effectiveness and efficiencies. By evaluating the educational processes, the quality control and implementation could be improved. Finally, by observing the results—both graduates and dropouts—in the light of the objectives, recycling decisions about continuance, modification, or termination of programs could be improved.

Community Life

A tragic irony in urban life is the
breakdown of community. Many
more people live side-by-side.
Many more networks of relationships emerge, but deep relational
communities often suffer. Whatever the form of the development
or training program, it should be

> The Harambee Center functions as part of
> the community. It was designed to be a
> place of choice where young people would
> feel free to come both to "hang out" and to
> build community.

36 Community Building

structured so that the learners and the communities in which they are serving are building deeper level relationships.

Integrated Program

Regardless of the emerging leader's educational background, spiritual maturity, kind of ministry
that is to be done, general context
in which this emerging leader is
to function, or the leaders with
whom he/she is to have influence,
any leadership development pro-

> The Church on Brady seeks to integrate all
> the parts of its training programs around
> its central purpose. If components emerge
> which do not integrate well, they are either
> modified or dropped.

37 Integration of Equipping

gram should be wholistic and integrated. It should aim to bring together
the spiritual formation, the practical ministry skills, and the information
that one must know. The following African Pot analogy draws these com-

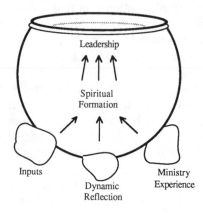

FIGURE THREE
AFRICAN POT ANALOGY

ponents together to show how each part contributes to the formation of the person in a wholistic integrated interactive way so that as the person is formed, leadership emerges.

This figure suggests a dynamic interaction among the instructional inputs, the contemporary ministry experience, and dynamic reflection. In reflection the student will raise the questions: "What does this instruction mean for my ministry?" "What should I be learning in the classroom for my ministry given this experience?" These three elements together should contribute to the ongoing spiritual formation of the emerging leader. As a person's spirituality is formed, a trustworthy and competent person emerges as a leader.

Servant Molding

The equipping of Christian leaders in a city to be servants seems strange indeed. The concept of servanthood in the late twentieth century is even more strange for leadership than in the first century. Concepts of servanthood in the first century were well-developed. Many different words were employed in the Greek language to express different dimensions of servanthood or kinds of servants. Some people were household servants. Some were servants by their own choice. There were servants whose focus was on the task. In some cases servanthood was described in terms of being under authority. In each of these cases, different words were used in Greek and yet translated by the same word in English.[15] The ICAA manifesto suggests that we should promote biblical forms of servanthood among emerging leaders by "modeling by the staff and through active encouragement, practical exposition, and deliberate reinforcement."[16]

Instructional Variety

Urban leadership development programs must "vigorously pursue the use of a variety of educational teaching methodologies, evaluated and promoted in terms of their demonstrated effectiveness, especially with respect to the particular cultural context."[17] This ICAA value underscores the need for variety. Variety aids in building motivation, maintaining attention, and certainly increasing learning through different though informationally redundant ways. By varying the learning experiences the same information, skills, and attitudes may be reinforced in a variety of different ways to fill out concepts, skills, and attitudes being developed. Whenever the method being used is entirely predictable, it will have no impact and very little information can be communicated. New skills will not be learned nor will attitudes be changed. Variety is indeed "the spice of life" for education.

Variety may be employed differently in each of the basic modes of education (formal, non-formal, and informal). A wide range of educational technologies may be used to facilitate learning. These technologies range from virtually no cost to very expensive. However, the cost of the technology may have little correlation with its potential for life changing influence. One may classify these technologies in terms of the uses of the senses and their combinations. The more effective technologies employ more sensory and emotional participation. Passive

> The CCCMTI deliberately sets out to form a servant attitude among all of the students. It does this through a variety of means which include strict discipline, ministry assignments, and chapel services which bring the issue into focus. Faithfulness in ministry for both CCCMTI and ABI in Lima is a requirement for continuation in the training programs. Demonstrated commitment and evidence of having formed functioning small groups are required by the Church on Brady before a new church is formed. The Church on Brady expects church planters to support themselves thus demonstrating a servant attitude in an unlimited reproducible model for church planting in an urban setting.

38 Formation of Servant Attitude

listening to lecture, radio, or audio tapes with no accountability for what is heard is probably the least effective. Active multiple sensory participatory technologies are much more effective. Drama, simulations, demonstrations, realistic practice with reflective feedback rate high in terms of effective technologies. High technologies such as teleconferencing, interactive video, computer simulations may be used if the resources are available and are appropriate to the learners' learning styles. However, on site demonstrations, field trips, social system simulations, role plays, learner action-reflection, student produced videos, debates, and the like cost little to plan or implement. The use of multi-sensory participatory instructional media which engage the learner's purpose and emotions may be adapted culturally to the local context and greatly enhance learning.

> The programs cited vary in their instructional methods from a heavy emphasis on experiential learning as seen in the Church on Brady programs to classroom experiences in the Bresee Institute. Ministry assignments in "real life situations" are part of the expectations of several of the programs (LMI/ABI, Bresee, Church on Brady, and CCCMTI) while specific skill formation with on the job training is used at Harambee, World Impact and other programs. Videos, books, audio cassettes, papers, articles, journals, lectures, panels, interviews, and informal conversations provide some examples of the range of means of providing information in these equipping programs.

39 Instructional Variety

Educational technologies should be selected with a few basic criteria in mind. They should be appropriate for the following issues: the learner's worldview, learning style and present level of maturity (motivation, educa-

tional level, spiritual/ministry maturity and experience), available resources within the community being served, the purpose of the learning
(cognitive, affective, skill, spiritual), instructor's competence, the content
to be taught, and timing constraints. The preferred technologies will provide for 1) the use of multiple sensory channels, 2) the immediate use of
the proposed learning in analogous or equivalent ways in which immediate
feedback is provided, 3) active rather than passive participation by the
learner, 4) opportunity for the learner to experience and personally discover what is to be learned.

A Christian Mind

The worldview of the developers
of leadership training programs is
indelibly imprinted on the curriculum, the structures, the relationships, and the teaching methods.
While I would not suggest that a
single Christian worldview exists,
I would strongly advocate that
whatever one's worldview, it must
be converted and transformed by
Christian faith and a strong commitment to Jesus Christ.

> The Harambee program demonstrates a
> Christian perspective of justice in action.
> The spoken word is present, but even
> more important is the demonstrated, lived-
> out actions toward the unemployed single
> women parents and the teenagers who are
> attracted to a the gangs of the area.

40 Justice in Training

Curricular Issues for Developing Urban Christian Leaders

Often when we think of developing leaders, our minds immediately focus
on training. However, leadership development is broader than training.

Training is important, but it is only one of many critical elements in
facilitating the emergence of a leader. Leadership development involves
character, competencies, and commitments of the leaders. It also involves
the followers' motivations, abilities, and relationships. The leadership influence process takes place in a situation of time, place, and social interaction. It occurs in a framework of shared values. The development of leadership requires more than just training because training may not adequately
take into account the followers, time, context, and shared values.

Designing a leadership development curriculum for urban Christian
leaders requires contextual adjustments among a critical set of curricular
issues. Without the local contextualization of the overall design, one can be
assured of dysfunctional leaders. Contextual readjustments are required
whenever changes occur in any one of the variables described in this

section. Several of the variables will change simply with the passage of time, so what fits well today will not fit so well the next year.

The following variables need to be addressed in the designing of a Christian urban leadership development curriculum: purpose, content, control, selection of learners, timing, costs, resources, venue, delivery system, spiritual formation, selection of instructors, and evaluation. While the beginning point is the purpose, one may then turn to any one of the other variable to continue the process. However, before the designing process is completed each of these variables must be addressed to assure a local fit.

In any given city, whether a mega-city such as Mexico City with thirty million people or a smaller urban center of thirty thousand, the final curricular design[18] may appropriately differ in a myriad of ways depending on how this set of variables is interactively addressed.

Purpose

The primary variable, purpose, serves as the basic constraining guide around which the other variables cluster and interact. None of the variables including the purpose should be seen as strictly independent. Rather, the variables

> The Church on Brady states as its purpose the intent "to become a spiritual reference point east of downtown Los Angeles and a sending base to the ends of the earth."

41 Purpose

are all interdependent and interactive. A limitation with one may be met by a shift in another. A strength in any one will compensate for a weakness or allow or flexibility in the others.

The "mission statement," the "purpose," the primary "aim," or the "cause" should be the primary driving or energizing variable. It is the base on which all else is built. It provides the starting point and it defines the end in view. It serves as the center around which all else revolves. Whatever metaphor is used the purpose is the first issue to be settled and the most important issue to keep in mind through the whole process of planning, implementation, evaluation, and reform.

Control

Who makes the decisions? How are the decisions affecting the training to be made? Do the learners, the community being served, the teachers, outside planners, or others make key decisions about key variables and the implementation of the program?

"Governance," "structure," or "control" is a key variable in the contextualizing of a leadership development program. Even if outsiders make all the right decisions, the fact that outsiders made them will likely lead to difficulty.

A key value in considering control is participation or a "sharing with" the learners and the community to be served. Even among the most depressed, least educated, or ⹁most oppressed urban slum dwellers, the people will be able to contribute significantly to the program. As they partici-

> The control of CEFI is closely related to the needs of the churches and what their leaders are willing to invest in terms of time and money. The control of ABI, on the other hand, is more closely tied to the institution and the way it perceives the future needs of the churches.

42 Formal/Nonformal Control

pate even their involvement will be developmental. The consideration and implementation of decisions about every variable becomes a critical part of the content of the overall training program.

Formal educational programs are controlled from outside of the learning community. They are structured around policies established by boards of trustees. The trustees often do not represent the communities being served. Often, they are not well acquainted with either the learners or instructors. Trustees are often selected on the bases of technical, administrative, financial, or power brokerage they can bring to the instruction. All of these characteristics mean they are not among the uneducated, the oppressed, the poor, or the alienated who would be the targets or subjects of ministry for the learners.

Nonformal educational approaches, however, are heavily influenced by both the community being served and by the learners. Nonformal programs generally involve a high level of community or learner participation in decision making at every stage of the curricular process. The com-

> Control for both the Harambee Center and the Bresee Institute is linked closely to the daily life and struggles of the communities where they live and work. The staff and students are living and walking in the community, daily listening to the local people speak of their need.

43 Control from Community

munity controls the questions to be addressed and the means for answering them. They also determine whether or not these questions have been answered satisfactorily.

Control or accountability is difficult to assess in informal education. One may see social control and the influence of relationships, but structured control of learning moves it out of the informal realm. Local cultural attitudes and worldview perspectives provide the control in informal education.

The Content

The content is the information, skills, attitudes, or basic spirituality that comprise the **subject matter** of what is to be learned. It may relate to the neighborhood, the particular skills related to ministry, Scriptural knowledge, or the way one should relate to the local people. The content may relate to what is needed to help shape one's character to move

> CEFI's focus on content is based on the perceived needs of the churches who are participating in the training seminars. The theory which is presented is intended to help explain the phenomena which are being experienced in the participants' churches, to help them predict what is likely to occur, and to provide reliable and valid courses of action in their ministries.

44 Content

more effectively into ministry. The content is a critical variable to mix in the pot. It should be initially selected on the basis of the purpose, but will be shaped by the difference between the entry level knowledge, skills, attitudes, and spiritual maturity of the learner and the required minimal entry level for the targeted ministry.

The content should be appropriate and adequate to enable the learner to begin the targeted ministry and with practice to become thoroughly proficient in that ministry. Content which does not lead to this initial minimal ministry competence in the four major content areas (information, skills, attitudes, spiritual formation) should be discarded from the training program.

The content should provide an adequate and appropriate theoretical base for the ministry. The theory should enable the learner to explain both accurately and validly the data related to his ministry. Similarly the theory should provide a reliable means of prediction of outcomes. It should also produce a reliable path of action. The level and amount of theory needed vary with the complexity of the context and the maturity of the learners.

Selection of Learners

The selection of the learners will condition the outcome as much as any other variable. Who should they be? Are the learners predetermined in the ministry context? What is their preferred learning style? What is their educational level? How mature are they in

> The Bresee Institute selects its learners in a formal way. Since it is linked with Azusa Pacific University, students must meet certain academic prerequisites to enter the program.

45 Selection for Formal Programs

terms of the ministry for which they are being equipped—do they have the knowledge, skills, attitudes, and required spiritual maturity for that ministry?

The selection of the learners will affect all of the other variables. One can, if given a choice, optimize the potential to accomplish the purpose by choosing the most appropriate learners. One important value then is that learners should be selected on the basis of the primary purpose rather than one of the following typical criteria: 1) ability to pay, 2) availability to participate at the time and place of convenience to the trainer, and 3) compatibility of worldview and learning styles with the trainer's worldview and teaching style.

The selection of learners varies greatly among leadership training programs. Formal training programs typically select learners on the bases of academic achievements, the ability to pay for the instruction, and a commitment to a specific academic program.

Nonformal programs generally do not select their own students. Rather, learners or the community to be served selects the

> CEFI selects its students by applications to advertised seminars. Only interested people apply. The classes then tend to have a homogenous feeling of need even though the individual learners may differ widely in terms of denominational or educational background.
>
> Students from the community are selected by members of the community or simply volunteer to participate in the Harambee Center training programs.

46 Nonformal Learner Selection

program. The training program is selected on the basis of how it can help bring a desired change in the community or learners. The selection of learners from the perspective of the training program is done by focusing the program on the felt needs or market potential of a specific audience.

Timing

When should the training be given in terms of the learner's career, annual, monthly, weekly, and daily cycles? How long should the training be in terms of the whole program and each segment? Timing relates to the learner's learning style, accessibility for the learner, the content, the delivery system, costs, a given point in the learner's career cycle (e.g., pre-service, initial-service, in-service, mid-career, interrupted service, or retirement), and other variables. Timing concerns are often determined at the convenience of the trainer or training institution. However, to optimize effectiveness the designer should ask, "How can the timing be adjusted to best accomplish the purpose, given the constraints of these other variables?

Flexibility in timing within educational programs reflects a contemporary value which affects virtually every dimension of modern life. Events and processes are timed for the convenience or benefit of the consumer—not the producer. Extension programs abound. Video tapes allow one to view movies according to personal convenience. ATMs (automated teller machines) allow banks to serve at any time.

Formal educational programs typically have the least flexibility in timing. Schedules are designed to fit the institution and so have little flexibility. Formal timing constraints affect many other variables such as learner selection because many learners can only attend at certain times which may or may not be convenient for the formal institution. Universities

> The Crenshaw Christian Center School delivers its Helps program over a period of one year.
>
> The Alliance Bible Institute times its program to fit in-service volunteers in ministry by having classes three nights a week for six years.
>
> The Church on Brady is flexible in its timing, recognizing it takes some people longer to learn how to plant and organize churches in some communities than in other communities.
>
> The Harambee Center offers training that is not career timed.
>
> CEFI offers primarily mid-career in-service seminars, workshops, and consulting.

47 Timing

and seminaries are able to make some significant timing adjustments such as the offering of courses on a once-a-week basis in the evenings or Saturdays. Occasionally intensive courses are offered in one to five week blocks. Timing constraints also affect costs, the amount of content in a given segment, instructor selection, delivery system, evaluation, and spiritual formation.

Nonformal education typically is more flexible and shorter in terms of individual learning segments. It often fits better with in-service training.

Costs

Costs provide a double-edged constraint in an urban setting. High costs in a leadership development program will restrict access to the learners who might profit the most. On the other hand, costs that are perceived to be too low will cause the community to be served to assign a low value to the program.

> ABI and CCCMTI charge tuition and supplement the total costs through church contributors.
>
> CEFI charges fees which, if not adequate for a given event, will lead to a cancellation of that event.

48 Costs

One principle which is employed throughout the cases cited is that the learners should be responsible for a significant part of the costs of the program. Subsidies from the community being served may supplement the costs.

Another cost principle employed by the programs cited is the containment of the costs by restricting the structure so the students and the community being served can afford the program. Most of the non-Christians of the world are poor and live in urban areas. Most could not even if they so desired, enroll in a seminary because the cost is far too high. Urban pastors in Central Nigeria, for example, receive as an annual salary the equivalent of the tuition required for one urban course at Fuller Theological Seminary in Pasadena, CA.

Resources

The available resources provide the constraints for the design or structure of the delivery system. Resources include the people, facilities, teaching materials, time, and finances.

Outside subsidies may be seen as useful for research and development, but provide a significant risk for ongoing program support.

A critical resource question is "What resources ought to be used?" or "What resources ought

> ABI limits enrollment to match its resources including facilities, faculty, and finances.
>
> The Harambee Center has structured its programs to fit the resources available in northwest Pasadena.
>
> The Church on Brady has chosen not to subsidize students to encourage and equip self-supporting church planters, and to keep the training reproducible.

49 Resources

not to be used?" Frequently, resources are available which if used would work counter to the purpose and against the development of the people concerned. Jesus could have performed other miracles. Perhaps He could have made it easier for the disciples. The Apostle Paul, however, wrote that He did not grasp His status, power or resources.

The selection of resources should be constrained or guided by at least three key values: 1) The choice of resources should serve to meet the long term purpose. 2) The resources selected should serve to enhance local resources from the community being served rather than deplete or depress them. 3) The selection of resources should not move the community being served into a long term dependency on outsiders.

Venue

The place of the training is critically important. The leadership environment is one-third of the basal element trilogy (leader-follower-situation) without which leadership will not occur. The obvious place of choice for leadership development is in the environment where the leadership will occur and with the people whom the emerging leader will be seeking to influence. In other words, the place of choice for the training for urban ministry is "on the streets." While logistics, resources, timing, or other variables may present constraints, the general principle is that the venue should be as similar to the projected ministry environment as possible and with the people to be served, if possible.

The place of ministry, while being the ideal venue even as Jesus demonstrated, does not generally fit preferred patterns. Libraries, academic communities, and facilities designed for instruction are often located outside or at a distance from the ideal loca-

> The Bresee Institute recognizes that the venue is an integral part of the learning experience, so both a central location with classrooms and on-site learning are employed.

50 Venue

tion. Reflection and the abstracting of experience into theory that applies broadly would ideally be done in the ministry setting, but logistics and the press of time often inhibit it.

Place always conditions the local culture. Culture may in fact be seen in one light as an established contextualized coping strategy for a given environment for a group of people. To equip people as leaders for a particular situation requires that they must either be in the situation or in a situation that closely simulates it. Equipping for metro-ministries is difficult in a small town. The learned coping strategies just do not work.

World Impact brings young adults from Midwestern towns and cities to a downtown gang infested area in Los Angeles to teach them how to both survive and lead in redemptive ways. The profound cultural adjustments which must be made to cope provide a set of learning experiences which contribute to their equipping.

After working among the urban poor in Los Angeles, learners are better equipped to work in similar settings in São Paulo, St. Paul, or Amsterdam. All of these settings are more similar to each other than any rural areas are to the cities.

A significant educational trend which reflects a service trend in business is delivering the educational package in the place where it has the greatest impact and acceptance.[19]

Delivery System

The delivery system constitutes the *means* of an administrative model.[20] Administrative models lay out the whole plan for bringing the curriculum design and learners together to accomplish the objectives of the design and to implement an instructional model.[21] Instructional models or delivery systems provide the approaches for implementation.[22] The delivery system combines all of the means by which the learner is brought into contact with the potential learning environment.

The delivery system should exhibit a balance within and among two important domains: educational modes and critical components. The two domains interact in a delivery system to affect its overall effectiveness. The delivery system itself with its policies, procedures, structures, and organizational culture should be seen as an important component providing a critical influence on how what is taught will be learned. All of the peripheral activities such as admissions, financial matters, housing, provision of meals, transportation, and so on may critically impact the delivery system.

Education or leadership development is delivered in some combination of three different modes: formal, nonformal, or informal education. Formal education is normally associated with schooling. It tends to follow long

The Alliance Bible Institute in Lima seeks to balance the formal dimension (classroom, certificate oriented) with the informal dimension (unplanned, relational) by not providing any dormitory space and by facilitating ministry relationships. It has structured its delivery system over a period of six years in an evening program. It is structured to have an increasing amount of ministry experience expected alongside the formal parts of the program.

The Harambee Center's program facilitates informal, relational values building in its delivery system. It also provides workshops, seminars, and training for specific skills.

The Bresee Institute provides both classroom and library learning experiences alongside working on the streets. It has structured its delivery systems in a different way as it has linked into institutions in the area, working on a nonacademic and undergraduate and graduate level. Its delivery systems are linked into and through the sister organizations and churches with whom it works.

51 Delivery Systems

cycles, is much more resource intensive, theoretical, and future oriented. It aims toward recognized certification, a diploma, or a degree. Nonformal education is planned out-of-school learning such as workshops or seminars and generally is not degree oriented. Nonformal education typically follows short cycles and is immediately functional. Informal education is not planned or deliberately structured. Informal education occurs in relational encounters. For example, virtually every person learns his/her first language and worldview informally. Informal education serves an enculturating function. For optimal effectiveness these three modes need to be balanced to fit the local context. Each of the other variables listed allows for different responses in each of these three types of education.

The balance among these three modes should be guided by the purpose of the training. When the intent is clear, the decisions related to each of these curricular variables are easier to make. The balance, however, will be affected by constraints with any one of these curricular variables mentioned above.[23]

An audit of the delivery system should begin with the purpose and the move to examine the balance among the formal, nonformal, and informal components. An effective educational delivery system will almost always involve elements from all three modes. The specific appropriate balance will be influenced by each of the other curricular variables mentioned in this section. The primary guiding variable, however, is the purpose. One should take care not to assign cognitive development to formal education, skill development to nonformal education, and attitude development or spiritual formation to informal education. Any of the three may be effectively employed to address these basic components. However, an appropriate balance will greatly enhance both the efficiency and transforming impact of the learning.

When evaluating a delivery system, the whole environment must be considered. If the housing, child care, financial support, food service, or other support services are dysfunctional, the system may fail. The informal and attitudinal components are critically important in recruitment, retention, and for ongoing commitment in ministry.

Tom Peters in *Thriving on Chaos*[24] provides several sets of critically important prescriptions which apply to an educational delivery system. One key idea is to keep on facilitating small improvements in every department which contribute to the overall purpose. These small improvements are best discovered and implemented by the people teaching.

One may use several metaphors to describe an educational delivery system (e.g., a plant, a

> The Alliance Bible Institute in Lima seeks to balance the formal dimension (classroom, certificate oriented) with the informal dimension (unplanned, relational) by not providing any dormitory space and by facilitating ministry relationships. It has structured its delivery system over a period of six years in an evening program. It is structured to have an increasing amount of ministry experience expected alongside the formal parts of the program.
>
> The Harambee Center's program facilitates informal, relational values building in its delivery system. It also provides workshops, seminars, and training for specific skills.
>
> The Bresee Institute provides both classroom and library learning experiences alongside working on the streets. It has structured its delivery systems in a different way as it has linked into institutions in the area, working on a nonacademic and undergraduate and graduate level. Its delivery systems are linked into and through the sister organizations and churches with whom it works.

51 Delivery Systems

body, a machine, a factory, or a subculture). In every case many parts must fit together to function for the same purpose. A malfunction in even a tiny part may lead to a major dysfunction, so every part should be viewed from a systems perspective.

Spiritual Formation

"The single most crucial element in successful urban evangelism has to be *spiritual* development of that human instrument which God has always used to incarnate Himself in the midst of people."[25] Effective ministry emerges out of the quality of character—not out of technical competence. Maturity in ministry includes not only the technical abilities, the abilities to do the tasks at hand, but also the appropriately developed spiritual gifts which are employed through the fruit of the Spirit. Spiritual formation helps move one's ministry maturation process beyond a focus on skills and knowledge bases to a being base. Until the Lord has shaped the vessel, it will not serve His purpose.

Since spiritual formation is seen to emerge out of a context of modeling and personal spiritual disciplines, CCCMTI insists on a high standard of modeling among its faculty and discipline among its students. The results are evident even among the first contacts one may have with its graduates—whether they be the engaging and committed security guards who serve as tour guides while giving personal testimonies, or senior pastoral staff caring for a homeless child.

World Impact and the Bresee Institute focus on spiritual formation because they have both seen that a transformed life has spiritual power to lead others out of drugs, gangs, and Satanism.

52 Spiritual Formation

Spiritual formation for Christians is the process of maturing toward Christlikeness and the showing of the fruit of the Spirit in one's life. Samaan defines spiritual formation as

> a process initiated by God, through the Holy Spirit, who convicts people of their sin and the need for Christ's atoning power in their life. Spiritual formation begins at the point when a person responds to this urging by giving his/her allegiance to Christ through faith, and it continues until the believer enters his/her glorified state.[26]

She writes, "the broadest and most comprehensive definition of spiritual formation is learning to live one's life in Christ."[27] Samaan further defines spiritual formation, as "a process by which believers learn to live their life in Christ. This is [a] holistic process which includes the knowing, being, doing, relational, attitudinal and values formation aspects"[28] Roberta Hestenes defines spiritual formation as "the process by which God reshapes persons into newness and fullness of His intention for them and towards Christlikeness"[29]

Clinton describes spiritual formation as the

development of the inner-life of a person of God so that the person experiences
more of the life of Christ, reflects more Christ-like characteristics in personality
and in everyday relationships, and increasingly knows the power and presence
of Christ in ministry.[30]

Spiritual formation relates directly to a leader's power base for influencing.
Power base refers to the source of credibility which enables a leader to have authority to influence followers. Spiritual authority is that source of credibility
perceived as from God which permits leaders to influence followers. Spiritual
authority characteristics presuppose spiritual formation. While there are other
power bases which are legitimate for a Christian leader, spiritual authority is
foundational and should be the central means of power for influencing
followers.[31]

Clinton describes ministry formation as

the development of ministry skills and knowledge, which are reflected by a
leader's growth in experiential understanding of leadership concepts, growing
sensitivity to God's purposes in terms of the leadership basal elements (leader,
follower, and situation), identification and development of gifts and skills and
their use with increasing effectiveness with followers, [and] ability to motivate
followers toward beneficial changes which will harmonize with God's
purposes.[32]

Clinton describes strategic formation as

an overall ministry perspective, a ministry philosophy, which emerges from a
lifetime of formational thrusts and interweaves lessons learned into an increasingly clear ministry framework that gives direction and focus and ultimate purpose to a leader's life."[33]

Christian leaders, looking back over their lives, perceive that God has worked
to develop and bring about their leadership. Incidents stand out in which they
sense the involvement of God either directly or indirectly. The cumulative effect
of these incidents over a lifetime indicates the integrative working of God to
shape the leader for His purposes. Comparative study of many lives makes
even more evident this involvement by God. It is a long-term process. Each of
the incidents, big or small, fits as part of the process of this lifetime of shaping.
The set of concepts categorizing and describing this "processing" by God make
up the processing variable.[34]

Clinton describes process items as anything in the life history of a person which God uses to indicate leadership potential, to train a person for
leadership, to confirm his or her appointment to a role/task/responsibility,
and to bring the leader along into God's continued appointed ministry for
him or her.[35] Process items are "learning experiences" which God provides
for the person to emerge as a leader. These learning experiences over a life

time show three distinct characteristics: They show continuity; that is, re-curring themes reinforce the learning opportunities. Secondly, sequence occurs as the leader develops. Progress may be observed. There is an or-dered progression within or among the learning experiences. Thirdly, there is integration. The learning experiences fit together into overall pat-terns which relate to a person's giftedness and calling.

Spiritual formation ("growth in holiness," "sanctification") provides the character base on which spiritual authority rests. One critical dimension of a Christian leader's empowerment to lead comes through spiritual for-mation. The delegated dimension of spiritual authority or the right to use spiritual power comes from the Holy Spirit as one is faithful and begins to bear the fruit of the Spirit. Followers grant the allocated dimension of spir-itual authority, allowing the emerging leader to influence them as they rec-ognize qualities they value in a leader. The third dimension of spiritual au-thority, the internal confirmation, emerges as one becomes increasingly confident of both the Spirit's direction and the followers' following, and the Spirit's "bearing witness" that he/she is a child of God. Spiritual forma-tion is the process of maturation guided by the Holy Spirit to bring the per-son toward Christlikeness in order to serve Him. This service will influ-ence other people toward God's purpose. While spiritual formation is Spirit guided, existing leaders/trainers should be expected to encourage, fa-cilitate, and expect it, both in the lives of the learners and in their own lives and ministries. Samuel James writes, "The single most crucial element in successful urban evangelism has to be **spiritual** development of that hu-man instrument which God has always used to incarnate Himself in the midst of people."[36]

To address spiritual formation intentionally requires an active com-mitment on the parts of both the learner and instructor. Instruction in personal and corporate spiritual disciplines will help with the content. Re-flection about the ongoing experience will aid the process. A primary re-quirement is the committed obedience of the learner.[37]

Selection of Instructors

When learners have been fully taught they will be like their teachers (cf. Lk. 6:40). Teachers not only teach the content of the syllabus, they teach attitudes and values. Students learn to emulate their teachers; in fact, they become like their teachers. This resemblance is often described even in secular settings by saying, "He is that person's disciple," meaning, "He is like that person."

The teacher who does not respect his/her students will teach them to disrespect their students. The teacher who shows compassionate concern out of the classroom will develop compassionate students. Teachers who praise will have students who praise. Teachers who are just committed to "ivory tower" academics will produce "ivory tower" academicians. Teachers who are committed to the practice of ministry will produce ministering graduates.

> The Harambee Center prominently features John Perkins who models for the African-American community how one can rise above injustice and have a profound impact on a community for the gospel and for justice.
>
> Faculty members of the Bresee Institute and the ABI are actively engaged in church related ministries. The active "doers" are the teachers.
>
> The CCCMTI and Church on Brady use pastoral staff members as key faculty to teach by modeling as well as in the classroom.

53 Instructor Selection

The purpose of the program should provide a clear guide for the selection of faculty. If the purpose of the urban training program is to graduate urban church planters, then urban church planters must feature prominently among the faculty. If the graduates are expected to have effective developmental ministries among the urban poor, then the faculty must have had experience and be committed to these same ministries.

Evaluation

The curricular development and implementation processes involve a long series of decisions about the learners, goals, objectives, educational structures, learning experiences, processes of education, recycling, and other issues. To make wise and appropriate value based decisions which undergird the whole educational enterprise, useful information is required all along the way. The process of securing, analyzing, and presenting this information in the light of key values is all part of evaluation.

Evaluation is often seen as something to do after the educational program has been completed, if there are resources left and if anyone is interested to know about the results. The word *evaluation* often provokes a defensive hostility from the educators who could profit most from it. This unfortunate view of evaluation, along with the threatening identification of evaluation with grading, has pushed many otherwise responsible educators into making ill-informed decisions based on inadequate information.

Evaluation is a cyclical process which provides useful information for decision making based on a set of values which define merit or worth. It emerges from an assessment of the critical issues at hand in the light of the established values.

Most curriculum related decisions may be aided through the process of evaluation. As one recognizes the decisions to be made, the process of evaluation may serve to provide the essential valued based information.

Curricular problems in theological education arise regardless of the wisdom of the developers or their commitment to design and implement appropriate curricula. The successful curriculum developer is one who recognizes these problems and works through them with the communities involved by making and implementing appropriate decisions.

If no change is implemented in the curriculum, the students and communities being served will soon suffer from growing irrelevance in the training. If appropriate changes are introduced in a timely way, some resistance to the changes may be expected, but there will be few disabling problems.

However, if evaluation is irregular or infrequent, the implementation of even small changes may generate significant resistance. Once curricula have been established and formally institutionalized through multiple administrative levels, they often suffer from a hardening of the categories. Inflexible curricula drift into irrelevance. The complaint of an educator may in fact be realized: "the wrong people teach the wrong learners in the wrong way in the wrong structure at the wrong time to do the wrong things wrongly." Eye-clouding inflexibility often blinds the educator's use of evaluation.

Theological educators often develop patterns of thinking and habits of design which mirror the educational programs in which they were trained. Theological educators are no less affected by ethnocentrism than other people. One tends to assign value to his/her own perspectives and experience. Without seeking to depreciate another's point of view, this ethnocentrism may lead into many kinds of problems. One could cite problems in the selection of purposes, content, learning experiences, instructional styles, and others which can be predicted in the ongoing development and implementation of the curricula process.

A set of key tasks then for the theological educator is to be able to predict and identify problems as well as work with the communities involved in problem avoidance and solution. The identification of problems is another way of considering needs.

While specific outcomes in the communities being served cannot be fully predicted, general kinds of problems can be anticipated from development theory and its focus on relationships. Some modes of education carry certain predictable outcomes when done well and other outcomes when done poorly. Evaluation may assist informing decision making about the balance at every stage of the instructional process.

One may be able to categorize curricular decisions into four general types: 1) purpose, goal, and objective related, 2) structural design, 3) process, and 4) recycling problems which relate to program change, termination, or continuance. Stufflebeam[38] using these four major categories of decisions develops a corresponding set of four variables which provide the critical information for the decisions.

Evaluation of the context to be served can help provide the needed information for setting purposes, goals, and objectives. An evaluation of the resources available can help one decide about appropriate structures. An evaluation of the process provides useful information about implementation and quality control. An evaluation of the results or the products of the educational program can be very helpful in making decisions that relate to recycling. These decisions may lead into modification of the program, termination of the program, or continuation of the program as it is.

> CEFI maintains an ongoing evaluation process. It could be seen as a marketing perspective. Ongoing contextual evaluation provides insights about trends and felt needs which serve to shape training objectives. Resource and outcome evaluation provide critical information about which conferences or seminars to continue, where to hold them, and when to discontinue them. Process evaluation provides critical information about the implementation of technologies and the balance of the modes of education in the delivery system.
>
> **54** Evaluation

Stufflebeam defines evaluation as

> The (1. Process) of (2. Delineating), (3. Obtaining), and (4. Providing) (5. Useful) (6. Information) for (7. Judging) (8. Decision alternatives).[39]

Evaluation may serve the development of urban leaders as decisions are made at every stage of their development and for every type of leader, regardless of the nature of the institution responsible for the development. Decisions about goals and objectives, structuring the delivery systems, implementation, and dealing with outcomes arise in every leadership development program. Whether the leaders being equipped serve house churches in a poverty-ridden area or are being groomed as denominational leaders, evaluation can serve to inform the decision making. Whether the development program is sponsored by a house church with limited resources or a well endowed graduate seminary, informed decision making remains an essential component to effective leadership development.

Delineation of Problem and Evaluation

Two kinds of information need to be delineated before the evaluation process can begin. First the values related to the enterprise need to be identified. The issues related to the setting of values must be treated, but are outside of the evaluation process. These values may come from theology, leadership theory, educational theory, development theory, the community being served, or other domains. Since the establishment of values and their relationship to the evaluation process can only be understood as the different kinds of evaluation are understood, they will be described more after the overall design of evaluation is described. Values provide the criteria for judging validity of the data to be obtained and the worth or merit of the outcomes or assessed data.

The second kind of information which needs to be delineated before the appropriate evaluation can be done is the kinds of decisions which have to be made. Once the decisions to be made are clearly in mind, then the appropriate evaluation research can be designed.

Obtaining Data for Evaluation

After the priority decision and its related values have been identified, then an appropriate kind of research methodology can be initiated. The second stage in the evaluation process is obtaining the data. As one considers a design for obtaining the data, the questions of validity and reliability must be raised. Validity concerns relate to asking the appropriate questions and collecting data relevant to the stated values. Reliability issues relate to the consistency of the results of the research.

Research methods available for obtaining evaluative data span the whole gamut of methods from historical to descriptive, to experimental. Typically, for an urban ministry setting the research must be multi-disciplinary. The particular design will be conditioned by the kinds of information needed, the community being researched, the resources available, and the skills of the researcher.

Providing

The third step for the evaluator is to provide the information in a usable form to the decision makers. One needs to present the data which are relevant to the problem at hand in a form which is appropriate both to the context and for the decision makers. Raw data are seldom useful for decisions makers. They must be assessed, analyzed, and summarized in a valid way. The provision of useful information depends on the relating of the assessment to the values.

Common Constraints to Evaluation

Several constraints may inhibit the benefits gained from the process of evaluation. Some people misunderstand the purpose of evaluation. Others do not have clear values on which to make judgments. In other cases, measurements which are invalid may be brought to bear on the context.

Evaluation Misconceptions

Unfortunately, many theological educators see evaluation as an extension of the grading process. While grades may well be useful in evaluation, they provide only a small piece of the picture and may seriously threaten the evaluation process if that is the only piece of the picture the educator sees. The educator involved is often the administrator. He/she does not want an outsider to come in and to say that this plan is good, this program is bad, this result shows where you have failed, or this program should be changed.

This problem of the misconception of evaluation may be treated by looking again at the purpose of evaluation, at the process of evaluation, and the people who should participate in the evaluation. If one looks at the purpose of evaluation he/she can see that it is to provide useful information for decision making. If the educator has decisions in mind that need to be made, then evaluation can fit directly into those decisions. If he/she participates in the evaluation, in the delineation of the problem or perhaps in the obtaining of the data, the threat will be diminished. If the educator participates in the assignment of values and then brings this evaluation to bear in the decision making, then this the threat of being graded can be overcome and the evaluative process enhanced.

Sometimes evaluation is requested when the values which are to be employed are unclear. If the values are unclear then it is not possible to assign a valuation to the assessed data for decision making. The establishment of values is generally not the task of the evaluator, but rather the task of the administrator or the community. These values must be established in advance of the description/delineation of the decisions and certainly before data are collected.

Invalid Research Methodology

Another set of problems which constrains evaluation centers around an invalid research methodology. In the first place, the problem may not be well defined. If one does not know where he/she is going, anywhere will do. The problem must be described; the purpose of the evaluation, its goal, and its specific objectives need to be described so that the evaluation can be done in an appropriate way. The purpose of the evaluation should relate directly to the decisions which are to be made.

The questions raised to collect data to address the problem must be the right questions. They must be appropriate. If, for example, one is to judge the effectiveness of a theological training program, it may be less important to know the number of graduates than it is to know the number of graduates who are indeed functioning as the kind of church leaders that they were intended to be. If an institution has five hundred graduates and four hundred fifty of them have entered government service as clerks and only fifty remain as part-time leaders and part-time taxi drivers, the question of how many graduates the program has would not be as important as what are the graduates doing. How are they serving the churches? It is crucial that the right questions be asked.

Not every evaluation problem requires a high level of sophistication in research techniques and the application of sophisticated statistical measures. However, the design must be appropriate for the questions being asked and the problems being addressed.

Obstacles to Evaluation

When the community being evaluated, the decision makers or the evaluators themselves misunderstand the purpose of the evaluation, the whole process is hindered. Some of the obstacles that contribute to this state include:

- Fear.
- Satisfaction with the status quo.
- Evaluation done only by outsiders who lack inside critical knowledge or information.
- Evaluation done only by insiders who lack perspective and objectivity.
- Results of evaluation often not provided to the people who could/ should make the appropriate decisions.
- Inappropriate (invalid or unreliable) research methods.

Evaluation may provide a means of identifying the pressures which lead to an unhealthy and inappropriate professionalization of the ministry. As the values from the key domains are employed in the assessing of the process-related, structure-related, and product-related data, essential information for decision making in these key domains can be provided.

Evaluation may serve at any stage of the curricular process to provide useful information for the learner, the instructor, the administrator, and the community being served. The kinds of decisions and kinds of evaluation will vary, but in each case the community being served, whether it be students, administrators, instructors, or the wider community, can benefit from the process. The evaluation process is much broader and more useful than just the tests and grading in a school context.

The process of evaluation can serve in the planning, implementation, and recycling stages of a training situation. Because of the complexities of the variables involved, evaluation has become a critical part of the whole process. Again, the purpose serves as a key value guide and constraint. Effective evaluation cannot occur without a clear set of values which focus around a central purpose.

The Selection of the Situation

Even as the selection of learners and instructors is important, so also is the selection of the learning situation. The situation should be compatible with the emerging leader's personality. Is the emerging leader more task-oriented? Or a more relationally-oriented person? Fiedler suggests that a person is likely to be one or the

CEFI gives attention to the immediate learning situation. The physical arrangements, accessibility, pleasantness of the surroundings, and general professional appearance of the situation are all important. The focus of the selection is less on the physical arrangements than on the social context for the Church on Brady.

55 Selection of Learning Situation

other and that the situation should be selected with the greatest degree of match possible. The potential degree of favorableness toward the new leader needs to be evaluated in terms of task clarity or structure, leader-follower relations, and the potential power that the emerging leader will have in that situation.[40]

The learning situation should be selected to allow realistic and relevant practice of the intended learning. The practice may be equivalent to or the same as the intended learning or it may be analogous to it. Analogous learning often takes the shape of case studies and related problem solving for leadership development. Simulations including role plays, social system simulations, and learning games may also be employed. The situation should be selected so that distributed or spaced practice with immediate feedback about the appropriateness of the learners responses can be given. In selecting and structuring the learning situation, the planners should keep in mind that it is what the learners do that they learn, not what is done to, for, or in front of them. The instructor's performance is not what counts; the learners' performance is what is important.

Developing the Venue

Leadership development concerns go well beyond the emerging leaders to the context in which they will be leading. The venue (learning context or leadership context) is another critical component to consider in leadership development. Both the selection and development of the context carry long term implications for leadership effectiveness.[41] This context is not only the context for leading, but the context for emergence

> The public recommendation of Fredrick K. C. Price of the Crenshaw Christian Center of a new pastor-in-training assures an open opportunity to begin to lead in that context.
>
> Before assigning a student in one of the many short term ministry positions open to the Bresee Institute, a staff member will meet with the people in the situation to discuss the candidate and how he/she may be able to fit effectively in that situation.

5 6 Context Preparation

as leaders. Existing leaders should give attention to the context with the clear purpose of preparing it for the emergence of these leaders. They should focus on the orientation toward the new leader, the empowerment of the new leader, and the facilitation group's acceptance of the new person so that the new leader may in fact "hit the ground running."

The clear purpose for addressing the context and the people in the context should be the "equipping" (contextually outfitting, *katartidzo*) of the emerging leaders. The goal is to facilitate the building of relationships in the context. Some issues then within the learning or "leading" context need developmental or curricular attention. Many different avenues remain open for the preparation of the context. Again, one must remember the primary active agent is the Holy Spirit. He goes before to prepare the way today even as He did with Cyrus (cf. Isa. 45) before Cyrus knew Him. Modern societies do not publicize the ancient functions of a herald who prepares the way for a leader, but the means of increasing influence potential by generating expectations and establishing legitimacy is important. John the Baptist prepared the way for Jesus through preaching. Jesus prepared the way for the disciples through acts of power and teaching. Barnabas prepared the way for Saul of Tarsus through standing up for him. Paul prepared the way for Timothy, Titus, and others through the writing of letters. The preparation of the context through the shaping of expectations, status and role clarification, and legitimation can significantly accelerate the empowerment and formation of new leaders.

A leadership development approach that does not take the emergence context seriously is unlikely to produce effective leaders. The emergence context, the venue, can nearly always be developed to improve leadership emergence by increasing its favorability.[42]

Wise leaders will give long term and continuous attention to the shaping of the situation so it will be optimally favorable for the emerging leaders. Wise leaders aim at transforming their situations, not just eliciting compliance from their followers.

The Orientation about the New Leader

The people who would be followers in the situation need to be oriented about the new leader. They need to know the leader's gifts, abilities, goals, calling, level of spiritual maturation, commitment, and perhaps enough information about the leader to know him/her as a person. Many biblical examples could be cited to show the orientation given to prepare a situation for the new leader. John the

> The Bresee Institute does not wait for allocated authority or legitimacy to be developed by the emerging leader, but rather it takes initiative to legitimize the emerging leader in the context by introductions and general orientation about the new person. The legitimacy of the newcomer by those people who are already known and trusted positions the emerging leader to begin to serve much sooner.

57 Orientation about New Leader

Baptist had as his primary mission the preparation of the situation for the coming of Jesus. Barnabas, in his role with the church in Jerusalem, instructed them, and oriented them about the emerging Apostle Paul. Paul, writing to younger churches, on several occasions made comments about the expected arrival of Timothy and Titus, as well as others. He prepared them by telling them characteristics of these men, why they were being sent, something about their abilities, and something about how they could be of benefit in that situation.

Clarification of Purpose and Goals

Existing leaders can assist greatly by working with the people in the situation, prior to the emerging leader's arrival, in helping them to clarify the purpose and the goals toward which the new leader will be moving. The intent of the clarification is not to usurp the new leader's role, but rather to prepare the people for the new leader's joining with them and being legitimized in the situation with them toward the same set of intents.

> As new churches are being organized in Lima with leadership from LMI/ABI, existing leaders from both existing churches and from the Bible institute will clarify the purpose and goals for the new congregation. The new emerging leaders who will come into these congregations can then expect that the people will have heard some orientation already about purpose, goals, and primary strategies.

58 Clarification of Purpose and Goals

Clarification of Status and Role

One of the more important educational roles of the existing leader
in the context is the clarification
of the status and role of the new
leader. The intent is to assure the
congruence of the status that is
expected from the outside leadership with the expectations of the
people within the group. The same
thing has to do with role. The ex-
pectations for what the leader is to do should be the same from the leadership outside the group as well as the members of the group.

> CEFI's individualized consulting with
> congregations and denominations has a
> heavy focus on status and role clarifica-
> tions. The repositioning of a leader and the
> redefinition of what the leader is to do in a
> congregation often frees that congregation
> for significant growth.
>
> **59** Clarification of Status and Role

Orientation to Empowerment

The formation of the emerging
leader's potential for influence
with the group must be the focus
of the existing leader in orientation among the potential followers. They should understand what
they can do to empower the newly
emerging leader. The potential for
influence can be increased in at
least three ways: through the
emerging leader's growing spiritual authority, through the emerging leader's positional or organizational status, and through the leader's relationships or personal potential for influence within the group. Each of these
kinds of potential for influence requires a somewhat different set of activities for development. In every case the biblical principle of faithfulness in
small things being required before larger assignments are given ought to be
employed. (See Kanter's suggestions for empowerment which must be understood by the followers as well as those who are existing leaders).[43]

> CEFI consults with local congregations.
> An important component of the consulta-
> tion is the orientation of the followers of
> "lower level" leaders in the congregation to
> the empowerment of the next level leaders.
> The generation of expectations about the
> leader which will benefit the whole group
> is a part of the instruction.
>
> **60** Orientation to Empowerment

Orientation Toward Balance—Developmental Components

The intentional development of a spiritual leader normally requires the following four component parts: 1) structured input (information or skills),
2) ministry experience, 3) spiritual development, and 4) regular reflection about how each component contributes to the others within the context.

Some orientation should be given
about how each of these component parts will be met within that
context and how they will be balanced for the optimal development of the new leader. When all
of the major constituencies—
church, training institution, and
learners—understand the impor-

> The Bresee Institute recognizes the value
> of explicitly addressing the issues of input
> ministry experience spiritual formation and
> reflection. Learners are oriented toward the
> balance of these components from the out-
> set of the training programs.

61 Balance of Developmental
       Components

tant parts of the learning environment, then each can better contribute to
the overall leadership formation goal.

Summary

One very real risk for both existing leaders and emerging leaders is the
preemptive potential of the existing leaders. They often face the prospect of
disengaging from a previous leadership status and role in the situation in
which "holding on to the old reins of power" remains a temptation; or they
see the potential for "enlarging the borders" of their influence by restricting the empowerment of the new leaders. As a new leader is being brought
into a situation, there may well be a leadership vacuum into which others in
that situation will be moving. The existing leader needs to be aware of
these constraints.

When considering the orientation of the followers, one does not want
to assume the expected status or role of the emerging leader. The focus is
toward the new leader, the new leader's empowerment, the facilitation of
the new leader in that situation, and, in fact, a restriction against others
moving into that leader's status and role. The clear purpose remains the development of the new leader as a leader in that situation.

The expectation of the development of servant-leaders must be pre-
ceded by the modeling of meek (purposeful, self-controlled) servant-leaders. This modeling does not grasp at power, but rather demonstrates purposeful obedience without regard to one's own advantage or rights (cf.
Phil. 2:5–8).

The fitting of a leadership development program to a given urban
situation requires a carefully crafted design. The design will show the continuity of purpose throughout. The purpose ought to be clear from every
component part and from the way every key variable is addressed. Every
variable should reinforce the purpose. The design should also demonstrate
sequence among its parts. The orderly progression over time and from one
segment to another should fit the local learning styles in terms of logic and

TABLE TWO
DEVELOPMENT DISTINCTIVES BY LEADER TYPE

Development Issue	Type I & Type II	Type III	Type IV
Purpose	Small group leadership	Small congregation leadership	Large congregation leadership or small Christian agency leadership
Control	Largely controlled by the learners	Partly external to the learner	Increasingly self-selected
Content	Specific skills and limited knowledge	Generalizable skills and knowledge, management skills	Knowledge of theories and theory construction
Timing	Short cycle, at the convenience of the learner	Long cycle, at the convenience of the institution	Short cycle, at the convenience of the learner
Resources	Limited amount needed, usually available from the learner and the community being served	Resource intensive, many resources needed, often outside subsidies are needed	Moderate resources needed
Costs	Minimal	High	Moderate
Delivery System	Informal, nonformal modeling, apprenticeships	Formal, highly structured	More nonformal, less structured
Spiritual Formation	Focus on foundations and on doing	Focus moving from doing to being	Focus on converging status, role, and giftedness
Venue	On site preferable, largely informal setting with peers	On site with opportunity to reflect with peers	On site and may be in more formal setting for theory and reflection
Selection of Instructors	Select on the basis of continued leadership in small groups	Select on the basis of experience in ministry as a Type III leader and as a teacher	Select on basis of continued experience and theoretical understandings needed for Type IV leaders

size of the steps. As the diverse components are considered, a wholistic integrated perspective ought to emerge with each component not only filling its unique niche, but fitting with the others to provide a harmonious well balanced whole.

Attention to the individual learner as well as to the situation is required if the leadership development curriculum is to be contextually appropriate.

The previous table serves to summarize the typical way the major curricular issues should be addressed for Types I–IV leaders.

Notes

1 William E. Pannell, "Developing Evangelical Minority Leadership," *The Urban Mission: Essays on the Building of a Comprehensive Model for Evangelical Urban Ministry*, ed. Craig W. Ellison (Washington, D.C.: University Press of America, Inc., 1983), p. 126.

2 Roger Greenway, "Goals of Ethnic Evangelism," *Cities, Missions' New Frontier*, eds. Roger Greenway and Timothy Monsma (Grand Rapids: Baker Book House, 1989), p. 87.

3 Idem., "Cities, Seminaries, and Christian Colleges," *Urban Mission*, 3: 1 (September 1985): 3.

4 Robert W. Ferris, *Renewal in Theological Education: Strategies for Change* (Wheaton: The Billy Graham Center, Wheaton College, 1990), pp. 45–126.

5 Greenway, "Cities, Seminaries, and Christian Colleges," p. 4.

6 Donald W. Dayton and F. Burton Nelson, "The Theological Seminary and the City," *The Urban Mission: Essays on the Building of a Comprehensive Model for Evangelical Urban Ministry*, ed. Craig W. Ellison (Washington, D.C.: University Press of America, Inc., 1983), pp. 114–121.

7 Sidney H. Rooy, "Theological Education for Urban Mission," *Discipling the City: Theological Reflections on Urban Missions*, ed. Roger S. Greenway (Grand Rapids: Baker Book House, 1979), p. 190.

8 Greenway, "Cities, Seminaries, and Christian Colleges," p. 6.

9 F. Ross Kinsler, ed., *Ministry by the People* (Maryknoll: Orbis Books, 1983), p. 6.

10 LeRoy Ford, *A Curriculum Design Manual for Theological Education* (Nashville: Broadman Press, 1991), p. xxi.

11 Ferris, p. 141.

12 Ibid.

13 Ibid., 143.

14 Dettoni's four step process evaluation with description, measurement, assessment, and evaluation, and the values outside of that, as seen in Ted Ward and John Dettoni, "Increasing Learning Effectiveness through Evaluation," *Effective Learning in Non-Formal Education*,

eds. Ted W. Ward and William A. Herzog, Jr. (East Lansing: Michigan State University, 1977), pp. 198–288.

[15] David W. Bennett, "Images of Emergent Leaders: An Analysis of Terms Used by Jesus to Describe the Twelve" (n.p., March, 1990).

[16] Ferris, p. 145.

[17] Ibid.

[18] A curriculum design is "a statement and elaboration of the institutional purpose, educational goals and objectives for learners, scope, contexts, methodology and instructional and administrative models considered by an institution in developing its approach to doing its work." Ford, p. 295.

[19] Stanley Davis, *Future Perfect* (Reading, MA: Addison-Wesley Publishing Company, 1987), and Peter Drucker, *The New Realities: In Government and Politics/In Economics and Business/In Society and World View* (New York: Harper and Row, Publishers, 1989).

[20] Ford, p. 294.

[21] Ibid.

[22] Ibid., p. 296.

[23] For a discussion of the balance of these educational modes in designing an educational program for development see Edgar J. Elliston, ed., *Christian Relief and Development: Training Leaders for Effective Ministry* (Dallas: Word Books, 1989), pp. 200–250.

[24] Tom Peters, *Thriving on Chaos: Handbook for a Management Revolution* (New York: Alfred A. Knopf, 1988).

[25] Samuel M. James, "Training for Urban Evangelization," *An Urban World: Churches Face the Future*, eds. Larry Rose and C. Kirk Hadaway (Nashville: Broadman Press, 1984), pp. 189–206.

[26] Lynn Elizabeth Samaan, *Images of Missionary Spirituality: A Study of Spiritual Formation* (M.A. thesis, Fuller Theological Seminary, 1990), p. 9.

[27] Ibid., p. 155.

[28] Ibid., p. 172.

[29] Ibid., p. 9.

[30] J. Robert Clinton, *Leadership Emergence Theory: A Self-Study Manual for Analyzing the Development of a Christian Leader* (Altadena, CA: Barnabas Resources, 1989), p. 72.

[31] Ibid.

[32] Ibid., p. 73.

[33] Ibid., p. 74.

[34] Ibid., p. 79.

[35] Ibid., p. 81.

[36] James, pp. 189–206.

[37] Clinton, p. 313, presents the following useful perspective:

Generalized Time-Line

Phase I	Phase II	Phase III	Phase IV	Phase V	Phase VI
Sovereign Foundations	Inner Life Growth	Ministry Maturing	Life Maturing	Convergence	Afterglow

Summary of Phases and Tasks

Sovereign Foundations
- laying of foundations in the life including leadership potential
- respond positively
- take advantage of these foundations

Inner-Life Growth
- identification of leadership potential
- formation of basal leadership character through testing
- respond positively to testing
- be prepared for expansion after test

Ministry Maturing
- initial identification: gifts and skills for ministry
- release of leader to increasingly use and develop gifts and skills
- teaching relationship lessons
- unfold ministry philosophy
- recognition of gifts and skills
- take steps to use and develop gifts
- learn and use lesson of submission and authority
- catch the vision

Life Maturing
- deepened understanding of God
- develop intimacy with God
- focus on relationship with God as primary responsibility, not success
- respond positively to deep processing
- deepened communion
- recognize ministry flows from being

Convergence
- guidance of leader into role and place of maximum contribution
- trust and rest and wait
- make decisions toward convergence

Afterglow
- bring glory to God for a lifetime of leadership
- honor God's faithfulness

38 Daniel L. Stufflebeam, "Educational Evaluation and Decision Making," *Educational Evaluation: Theory and Practice*, eds. Blaine R. Worthen and James R. Sanders (Worthington, OH: Charles A. Jones Publishing Company, 1973), p. 129.

39 Ibid.

Key Terms:	Evaluation
Process	The particular, continuing, and cyclical activity subsuming many methods and involving a number of steps or operations.
Delineating	Focusing information requirements to be served by evaluation through such steps as specifying, defining, and explicating.
Obtaining	Making available through such processes as collecting, organizing, and analyzing, and through such formal means as statistics and measurement.
Providing	Fitting together into systems or subsystems that best serve the needs or purposes of the evaluation.
Useful	Appropriate to predetermined criteria evolved through the interaction of the evaluator and the client.
Information	Descriptive or interpretive data about entities (tangible or intangible) and their relationships.
Judging	Assigning weights in accordance with a specified value framework, criteria derived therefrom, and information which relates criteria to each entity being judged.

Decision　　A set of optional responses to a specified decision
Alternatives question.

[40] Fred E. Fiedler, "The Trouble with Leadership Training is that it Doesn't Train Leaders," *Leadership and Social Change*, eds. William R. Lassey and Richard R. Fernandez (La Jolla, CA: University Associates, 1980), pp. 236–248.

[41] Gary A. Yukl, *Leadership in Organizations*, 2nd ed. (Englewood Cliffs, NJ: Prentice Hall, 1989).

[42] See Fred E. Fiedler, *A Theory of Leadership Effectiveness* (New York: McGraw Hill, 1967), and "The Trouble with Leadership Training is that it Doesn't Train Leaders."

[43] James M. Kouzes and Barry Z. Posner, *The Leadership Challenge: How to Get Extraordinary Things Done in Organizations* (San Francisco: Jossey-Bass Publishers, 1987), p. 175.

CHAPTER SIX

ADDRESSING NEEDS

This chapter seeks to provide a perspective on needs and how needs should affect the design of curricula for equipping Christian leaders for urban ministries. A focus on needs often forms the base on which leadership equipping programs are built. "They need more churches." "They need a clinic." "They need food and clothes." "They need a school." "They need some kind of appropriate technology to begin some income producing activity." "They need to be relieved of substance abuse." The statement, "They need . . . ," is often the beginning point for ministry and frequently sets the patterns for relationships in of urban ministry activities.

Some may have come to a "more enlightened" view by saying, "Their *'felt needs'* are for a school, clinic, pure water supply, a mother-child care program." While it is crucial to consider needs, an inappropriate view of needs often clouds the issues of relationships and inhibits effective ministries both in development and evangelism. A primary question to be addressed related to needs is that of relationships. Our relationship with God, our relationship with the client population, and their relationship with God are three key sets of relationships which must be considered as we begin to look at needs.

Ward warns of reducing ministry to simply meeting needs. This reductionist approach poses a grave danger, because it tends to facilitate the design of projects which have very short term purposes and little sense of accountability for the longer term development of a people. Only emptiness and bitterness remain when the approach is to "love 'em and leave 'em."[1]

Inappropriate Needs-Based Developmental Approaches

Bringing change without concern for the needs of the people as if local needs do not matter is as inappropriate as simply projecting one's own view of needs on a local community. This approach is often seen in development projects where the developers initiate programs in the community based on their own desires and purposes without seriously listening or observing the community.

The introduction of change based on the outsider's views of the needs of the people is often dysfunctional. Urban missions have often fallen into this trap. Certainly, every person "needs" to come to God through Christ. However, projecting needs beyond reconciliation with God is operating on shaky ground without the insiders' participation. To project a need and then to follow it with development programs way may well be more disruptive, both to evangelism and to development in the long run, than doing nothing. Identifying the needs of a people must come through cooperative participative involvement. The outside may play a prophetic role, but the insiders will need to identify the application of any insight in that society. If we can avoid inappropriate approaches to development, then we may be ready to move on to understand needs and how needs should be related to wholistic ministries.

Needs—Understanding the Concept

The concept of needs varies from one community to another and among men and women who would serve in those communities. An initial understanding of needs requires a differentiation between "needs" and "wants." Certainly not every want is a need, although that is what contemporary advertising would have us believe. One might want new clothes, but not need them. A need in this context is some psychological, emotional, physical, or spiritual condition which, if not fulfilled, will in some way be detrimental to the person, community, or society. Needs and wants will in some ways be differentiated within the community by community-based distinctions.

Intrinsic/Innate Needs Versus Acquired/Extrinsic Needs

Innate needs come from human nature. A person needs a minimal amount of food, water, clothing, shelter, love, and social interaction. Spiritual needs which relate to one's relationship with God may also be considered among the primary, intrinsic, or innate needs.

Acquired needs, however, come from one's lifestyle. Acquired needs often have their base in greed. They emerge out of the society. For example, when my family moved to Southern California, I was told on many occasions that "You need to have two cars." That acquired need was pressed upon us so much that we began to believe that we needed a second car.

Functional Needs Versus Felt Needs

A functional need is a need which is projected by an outsider to be essential for the insider to function in the given context. Sometimes a functional need is described as a "projected need." A felt need is simply a need an insider feels. There may be a functional need for a road and a felt need for a car. The contrast between functional and felt needs is inherently an insider-outsider perspective. If an insider perceives a need, it will be a felt need. The functional need is a need that the insider has not perceived or felt yet. From the outsider's point of view one could argue it would be foolish to meet the felt need first for fear of frustrating the insider.

The problem with this pair of views about needs is that, while outsiders often have a broader wisdom, that kind of viewpoint can become the source of oppression. To forcibly project one's own view of needs on people at best inhibits or damages relationships. It may seriously frustrate the people who are concerned. It may result in the outsider's caricaturing the people he/she is to work with as "stupid" or "inept."

It may be both necessary and wise to begin with felt needs to facilitate the local people's growth in their understanding of needs and issues which they may reasonably address. However, due to a history of oppression, a lack of hope, a heightened sense of risk, or a lack of confidence, expressed felt needs are often very limited and will not, if satisfied, go very far in the development of the people. Felt needs, however, must be considered.

Classifications of Needs

Needs are classified in a variety of ways. Maslow suggests a hierarchy of needs[2] in which each succeeding level is based on the fulfillment of the preceding level. Others would describe needs in terms of "basic," "social," and "spiritual." Basic needs are generally described as survival and security requirements. One must:

- Have enough food, water and sustenance
- Have protection against the wild
- Have protection against the weather
- Have a degree of security that allows one to relax from anxiety.

Social needs require satisfactions from others and for others. One has a need to build community through giving and receiving. People in every society recognize that it is not good for a person to be alone.

"Self-actualizing" needs as described by Maslow emerge from a highly Western individualistic perspective. This type of need relates to that part of the person that seeks to be expressive, to initiate, to create, to build, to make something, but it is generally expressed in terms of a Western individualism. While the theory suggests that these needs do not appear until the basic and social needs are met at an adequate level, it is also true that the basic and social needs do not have to be fully met before these needs begin to come into focus. The degree of creative expression in a people depends largely on the degree to which that people and the society have found ways to meet their basic and social needs. Adequacy for basic and social needs is culturally defined. What may appear to be inadequate for an outsider may be satisfying for the insider. On the other hand, what may appear to be adequate or superfluous to the outsider may in some cases appear to be inadequate to the insider. People who would be considered as "underdeveloped," "traditional," or "primitive" (in terms of technology) may well be operating at a self-actualizing level. The self-actualization which is understood in a Western context may be entirely inappropriate in less individualistic cultures. Because of the alienating and individualizing influence of the city, this model may be expected to be dysfunctional.

Spiritual needs form another major set of concerns. In the West, worldview perspectives frequently relegate the importance of spiritual concerns to a minor role. While the relative importance of spiritual needs may be debated in the West, the Two-Thirds World is deeply concerned about issues of spiritual power and spiritual needs. How one relates to and with the spirit world and how one deals with the issue of spiritual power are extremely important in many parts of the world. Too often the person from West simply relegates these spiritual concerns to psychological categories and fails to understand the people with whom he/she is serving.

Therefore, the Christian should not presuppose that one must always begin with Maslow's perspective of basic needs in order to relate to people. This mistake is made often by many evangelical church/mission agencies as they engage in more social ministries. The view is that because people have unmet needs (as seen from the outside) in health, nutrition, safety, social organization, that one should begin with the very basic physical and social needs while delaying attending to spiritual needs. Often, however, spiritual issues form the roots of complex physical and social problems. Without addressing these spiritual needs, other attempts to help are profoundly frustrated. Jesus addressed multiple levels of needs at the same time. The primary values must also be addressed. As Christians we are commanded to love. That command is other-directed and leads to the formation of family and community rather than self-actualization.

Viewpoints in Perceiving Needs

The one who looks ... may often project into the needs of the community his/her own views and perceive them as the expressions of the community.

> ... projection refers to the process by which people read into a situation things that really are not there ... projection refers ... to the situation in which we attribute to others attitudes and feelings that they do not in fact have but that would, if they did have them, legitimize our own feelings toward them.[3]

The variations are along the axis of wide experience and empathy versus narrow experience with ethnocentrism.

<--->

Wide	Narrow
Experience	Experience
Empathetic	Ethnocentric/
	Egocentric

FIGURE FOUR
EXPERIENCE CONTINUUM

The outsider is not necessarily looking wrongly. However, outsiders cannot altogether trust what they think they see. If one has wide experience and empathy, he/she may indeed have a useful vision of the needs of the people. However, if the one looking has had only narrow experience and is unaware of his/her own ethnocentrism, that person will probably have a viewpoint that is very much out of tune with the needs the people themselves sense.[4] The ethnocentric person sees needs in others as a projection of himself/herself.

The ones who feels ... is the insider and will have a viewpoint that ranges on an axis from oppressed to liberated.

<--->

Liberated   Oppressed

FIGURE FIVE
LIBERATION-OPPRESSION CONTINUUM

Oppressed people are apt to feel their needs in very narrow terms. Sometimes, in fact, oppressed people cannot even identify needs because they are so far from fulfillment that they have suppressed the very idea of needs. Paulo Freire suggests that questions like, "What are your needs?" or

"What needs do you feel?" are not good questions to ask an oppressed people. Oppressed people often repress their sense of need as a means to cope with hopelessness. A liberated person—even an underdeveloped liberated person—can describe not only his need, but something of an agenda of needs, or a sense of a priority of needs.

In some parts of a city oppression and powerlessness are not only a present way of life, they may well have been the experience of generations before. Minority ethnic groups often find themselves the object of discriminatory oppression. Over time, while anger may continue, the ability to discern and describe their needs or what will free them to become all that God would have them be is greatly diminished.

The one who feels needs may not be able to fully diagnose the causes of the needs or what will best treat them. Felt needs are generally expressed in terms of two sets of constraints: hope and risk. The degree to which the person who feels the need has hope in the listener or potential helper will determine the degree to which that person's needs are expressed. However, the expression of one's needs is constrained by one's concept of risk. What will it cost the person to express the need? With a high degree of risk and lack of hope a person's expression of felt needs can be expected to be surface level or seemingly trivial to an outsider who is marginally acquainted with the insider's plight.

Ted Ward has proposed another outsider's perspective which describes three contrasting levels of needs.

Developmental Conflicts as Needs

Eric Erickson suggests another way of looking at developmental needs in his eight stages of human development.[5] These eight stages of human development are defined not in terms of needs, but in terms of conflicts/tensions that must be reduced or met in order that the person can get on with further development. These developmental conflicts apply in metro-ministries among the urban poor, the suburban executives, the "over-privileged" and the "under-privileged" youth and other population sectors such as immigrants.

These eight conflicts were developed by Erickson to describe the development of a person from infancy through adulthood. While one cannot apply these issues in precisely the same ways to a society, these conflicts do suggest human patterns of development which occur in social settings as well.

> 1. ***Trust versus mistrust.*** Ordinarily this is a childhood experience, however it can recur as an adult experience. This conflict

TABLE THREE
NEEDS CONTRASTS

Definition	Fixation	Valuation	Operation
Level One Needs are understood to be things to be acquired, a gap to be filled.	The content of substance of that which will meet the needs. Doing things to or for people. Basically, an unproductive level. What do I have to offer.	What makes needs important is that there are those who lack.	To give, to meet needs of those who lack.
Level Two Needs are things to be resolved, conditions to be set right. Not goods any longer, but things to be set right or imbalances to be corrected. This level may involve some acquiring, but needs are not defined in terms to be acquired.	The fixation is no longer on the content or the substances, but on the *needs*. People in level one quite often do not even talk about needs. They talk about the "thing" they are bringing to bear. People in level two talk all the time about the needs of people.	The valuation is on those things which can be changed. Not on those who lack, but on something that can be changed.	To make people more able; to act as facilitators.

(CONTINUED ON NEXT PAGE)

TABLE THREE
NEEDS CONTRASTS
(CONT.)

Level Three			
Needs are dynamic life processes; needs are life itself. The issue is not to get away from needs, to fill those gaps, to get it all straightened out, but to understand that life is for all of us a continuing process of meeting needs.	The emphasis is now on the needs themselves and not on the content though those issues are still part of the picture. The fixation is on the dynamics of the situation. We seek to be in a relationship that allows us to get into the whole life processes with the people with whom we work and be a part of the action. We see people in this viewpoint as ones who are engaged in or who have been stalemated in normal life processes. The fixation is not on things to be added or people/situations to be changed, but people who are stalemated, inhibited in developing.	The primary value is seen in participation with, sharing live experiences with the people with whom one is working.	To reestablish, to reopen and then maintain life processes. Note the emphasis on "**re-**" The assumption is that one is not starting from the beginning. One sees himself as a "sharer in a walk." Jesus invited men to walk with Him. He said, "Follow me."[6]

dominates until it is met. If this one is unresolved (i.e., if people continue without trust) development is stalemated at that point. One of the most severe problems in many cities is a fundamental mistrust of people for each other and especially of oppressed people for the people in the dominant society. The problem of trust/mistrust is a key problem in cities.

2. *Autonomy/self-initiative versus a fundamental shame or doubt about oneself.* This developmental conflict can be seen in small children. This problem is also common among non-literate adults in developing societies. It may also be observed in oppressed areas in many urban settings.

3. *Initiative versus guilt.* Initiative relates to the kind of resolution that goes beyond the possibility of making a mistake and acts anyway. If one is so afraid of the guilt which will follow from an action that he/she cannot act, he/she has no initiative. That is a resolution that each person must make in life at some point, that it's possible to act beyond our sense of guilt. Right or wrong here is my answer—right or wrong here is my act—right or wrong here is what I believe—right or wrong here is what I will do.

4. *Industry versus inferiority.* Productiveness is the capacity to make something of one's time, to convert one's efforts into something that has value. It is in conflict with that sense of inferiority that is a problem for virtually everyone, that causes a person to assume that his product would not be worthy. This is not the same thing as guilt. Beyond guilt the initiative is there, but effort and industry are not there. The person is not willing to work hard because he/she has this feeling that whatever he/she produces will not have value. This conflict accounts for a lot of academic failure.

5. *Identity versus role diffusion.* There may be confusion over one's identity. This confusion may begin at adolescence and continue through adulthood. This problem may occur in developing countries whose people for years have seen themselves as inferior, performing menial roles, subordinate to others. Now they find themselves in positions of responsibility in a role they haven't yet clarified. Immigrant communities often face serious identity crises in the new metropolitan area where they have settled. This kind of conflict also occurs within the Christian community as people come to Christ and find a new identity in Christ. That conflict must be reduced.

6. *Intimacy versus isolation.* Needs of a person to be part of a community and to be intimate in that community—in family and in larger units—have to be addressed or the person finds himself or herself isolated. This problem is often seen in a person who has lost a spouse, or a person who has never married, or someone who has gone far from home. A person who has many experiences with people, but none at any deep level and is, therefore deprived of intimacy, isolated and tends to operate as an isolated person. This problem was addressed by the first deacons. A case of isolation existed in the early church and it went far deeper than the question of hunger. It concerned widows and orphans, those who felt isolated and needed fellowship with others. Isolation in cities forms one of the more critical ongoing tensions.

7. *Creativity versus stagnation.* This tension is often regarded as a problem of middle-life, when a person has learned to do something fairly well and he continues to do it, and yet he feels he is getting nowhere, nothing is changing. Life seems mechanical; he is stagnating. He is standing like the calm pool of water attracting mosquitoes. This conflict must be resolved as it emerges in a person's life so that he or she can see he or she is generating something which is fulfilling both individually and in the community. Oppressed segments of a community face this tension across generations.

8. *Ego integrity versus despair.* Ego integrity involves a sense of worth that is life-long; it is knowing that I as a person am worthwhile and that my worthwhileness is enduring. Despair is often a problem of old age because one's sense of worth leaves with retirement.

Summary

These developmental conflicts may fit in either levels II or III of needs as described by Ward above. They may or may not be perceived as felt needs. They do, however, provide constraints to be addressed in urban ministries as well as life processes to be shared with the people in the city. These normal life processes may be more often stalemated among the urban poor, the migrants, the homeless, the emigrants, and those entrapped by alcoholism or other substance abuse than people who live in the suburbs who have more support, services, stronger families, and more churches. These developmental conflicts or needs do not lend themselves to easy or "quick fix" solutions. These conflicts tend to be recurring and cyclical, particularly where there is spiritual, economic, or political oppression. They tend to be worsened in contexts of alienation and isolation. These conflicts can generate an ever deepening spiral of despair, hopelessness, and moral and social degeneration.

The needs of the people with whom we work provide not only direction and motivation for growth related projects and activities, but they provide opportunities for ministry to bring hope and the message of Good News. Beginning with projected needs was seen to be often counterproductive. Beginning with felt needs provides a better starting point, but generally initial felt needs do not serve well as guiding directions for development. The needs to be addressed in the long term are deep and can only be discovered in praxeological interaction or an incarnational ministry approach. The discovery and meeting of needs must be done in the context of building relationships in each of the key areas—with God, among people, and with creation.

> **Recommendation: Equip emerging leaders to identify and address the real needs of people.**

Notes

[1] Ted Ward, "The Church and Development," lecture series at Daystar University, Nairobi, Kenya, 1979.

[2] Abraham Maslow, *Motivation and Personality*, 2nd ed. (New York: Harper and Row Publishers, 1970).

[3] Ward Hunt Goodenough, *Cooperation in Change: An Anthropological Approach to Community Development* (New York: John Wiley and Sons, Inc., 1966), p. 123.

[4] Ethnocentrism is the tendency to assume that whatever was/is believed or done in one's own culture is the way it ought to be everywhere.

[5] Eric Erickson, *Childhood and Society* (New York: N. W. Norton and Company, Inc., 1950).

[6] Ward.

CHAPTER SEVEN

PLANNING THE DESIGN

This chapter describes a simple process for the designing of an approach to equip urban leaders. The issues raised in the previous chapters serve as bases for the design or redesign process described in this chapter.

Often the first question related to leadership development is, "How can they be trained?" When looking at case studies, frequently the first issue in focus is the methodology for training. What do the trainers do? **How** do they equip the emerging leaders? How do they train men and women to become leaders? Another initial focus is often on the content of the training. Giving these questions priority leads to the first serious mistake many people make when designing training programs. It's the mistake of patterning a new training model on an existing training model, either in methodology or content. One can look at a variety of successful and effective equipping models, any one of which fits its purpose and setting. However, to design a new model by taking without modification what is used in some other place will guarantee disappointment.

In this book several instructional models have been introduced. Each of these models is effective in a particular context and for a particular purpose. However, none of these models would be effective if taken as is and transplanted in another situation. Each one of these models would likely fail there. No method or training model is universally applicable. The design of an effective equipping curriculum requires attention to each of the issues raised in the previous chapter, including the questions that relate to purpose, the selection of the learners, the place where they will be learning, the timing issues, the contents, the delivery system, and the other issues that were mentioned. After the decisions have been made that relate to each of these issues as they interact with each other, then a person is ready to begin selecting the content and the design of the method for equipping leaders in an urban context.

The design of an effective equipping model requires attention to several components. It is assumed at this point that the curricular issues mentioned above have already been addressed. With the information and perspectives in mind from the interaction of these issues, one may then move

toward the design of an equipping model. Three major concerns will contribute to the formation of an effective model: 1) the selection of learning
experiences, 2) the organization of these learning experiences, and 3) the
overall balance, not only of the learning experiences, but of the whole infrastructure and delivery system.

Selecting the Learning Experiences[1]

Learning experiences are the experiences that the learner has
which stimulate cognitive, skill,
affective, and spiritual development. Learning experiences may
arise from events, relational interactions, reflections, or "process items" which provide the
content or stimulation for learning attitudes, skills, or information. Any kind of experience may
in fact be a learning experience.
What is done intentionally to provide learning experiences may
have the same range of variety as
what occurs in normal life experience. Learning experiences need
not be limited to lectures, films,
reading, panel discussions, and
drama. Only a limited amount of
creativity is needed to extend the
variety of potential learning experiences for any given set of objectives. Learning experiences may

Since the learning goal for the Church on
Brady, the Alliance Bible Institute, the
Bresee Institute, and the CCCMTI is
equipped leaders for urban ministries, each
of the training models provides a complex
set of learning experiences with an equally
complex set of expectations. The required
ministry experience is integrated with mentoring and class room experience in each
case to provide a balanced set of learning
experiences. The learners discover in the
lab of ministry what is needed to be
learned and can discover in the content
what is needed for application in the lab of
ministry. In the ministry experience there
is opportunity for the active use of the intended learning in each of these cases.

Each training model expects the set of
learning experiences provided to shape the
learner's worldview, develop specific ministries skills, and set the learner on a path
of spiritual formation that will lead to ministry maturation.

62 Expectations of Learning
     Experiences

be self-initiated or initiated, selected or designed by other people. The role
of the Holy Spirit should never be neglected in considering learning experiences. He seeks in every experience of life to bring good to Christ's followers (cf. Ro. 8:28).

The bases for selecting learning experiences have been treated earlier.
The primary base for selection is the purpose, and what follows from the
purpose are the goal and specific objectives. The question is, "What should
the learner learn, in terms of attitudes, information, and skills? What is the
purpose? Other foundational bases include: 1) available resources, 2) intended content, 3) the learner's educational, spiritual, and ministry matu-

rity levels, 4) the learner's preferred learning style, or 5) timing constraints. Do the learning experiences have to be provided between eleven o'clock and one o'clock? Or, can they be designed to fit in an evening, or over a series of evenings? The selection of learning experiences flows out of the foundational bases that have already been treated, with the curricular issues identified in the preceding chapter.

Learning experiences should be selected around a set of key expectations. These expectations include: 1) the potential of the learner to discover what is to be learned, 2) the active use of the intended learning, 3) the reinforcement of the intended learning with other learning objectives, 4) the potential for the present learning experience to stimulate the learner to go beyond the present objectives, and 5) a minimizing of distractions or negative results.

It is always preferable that the learner "discover" the intended learning rather than having it spelled out for him. Discovery makes the learning personal. Commenting on the impersonal alienating characteristics of a city, a person from Nairobi walking down the street in Pasadena observed that no person sells newspapers. Newspapers are only sold through machines. In some places one can find a row of as many as ten paper-dispensing machines. In many cities of the world newspapers are always sold by a person. The insight about "the impersonalization, and the alienation in a city," was discovered on a walk down Colorado Boulevard in Pasadena.

"One learns what one does." It's not what the teacher does that provides the learning. Rather it is what the learner does. The active use of the intended learning is critically important. This action should employ as many of the senses as possible. Sight, touch, taste, smell, hearing—all contrib-

> The Harambee Center provides learning experiences for community leaders to learn how to organize the community by doing it. Emerging leaders work alongside existing leaders in both nonformal structured ways and informally observing as apprentices.

63 Learning by Doing

ute to learning. The senses should be employed in the practice of the learning. The practice may be analogous, that is, something like what the person is to do, or it may be equivalent, doing the same thing. The learning experiences should simulate as closely as possible what the person is to do, should simulate the situation in which the person is to do it, and should provide opportunity for the learner to practice the activities and knowledge and attitudes that are the expected outcome. One will never learn to play a guitar by talking about it. One will never learn to swim without getting in the water. One will not learn to work with dysfunctional families where chemical dependency is present without being involved with such families. One will probably not learn to start new churches without doing it.

Any given learning experience may carry both positive and negative learning outcomes. The expected outcomes need to be anticipated for the learners. What might be a very desirable learning experience for an instructor may be totally inappropriate for the projected learners. Or, the outcome may prove so overwhelming negative, in spite of positive aspects, that it will have to be discarded.

Learning experiences should be expected to have multiple outcomes. Those multiple outcomes should be expected to have multiple positive outcomes, not only for the specific objective for which they were selected but for related objectives as well. As a person is learning to organize new small groups, the involvement with the groups provides opportunities for practicing the teaching and interpersonal skills that may be treated in other kinds of learning experiences.

> Instructors at the Bresee Institute expect several kinds of outcomes from a given learning experience. The assignment of an emerging leader to assist with a feeding project may provide lessons in how to distribute food equitably, relational skills in dealing with the poor, and the discovery of the need to know about nutrition to help people plan adequate diets. In addition to these positive outcomes, the emerging leader may also experience criticism, anger, bitterness, and a sense of being taken advantage of from those who receive the food on a handout basis.

64 Multiple Outcomes

Learning experiences should be selected with the expectation that the learning experiences will provide minimal distractions or minimal negative results. The playwright's phrase, "Accentuate the positive—eliminate the negative," applies to the selection and expectation of learning experiences. With these kinds of expectations, learning experiences will generate increasing motivation and readiness to learn on the part of either an adult learner or a younger person. The expectations of the learning experiences should always keep the learner in view. Will the experiences provide the learner with opportunities for discovery? Will they stimulate discovery? Will they allow for the active use of the learning? Will they reinforce the learning that is underway? Will they stimulate questions and insight into new areas of learning without providing distraction or discouragement?

Learning experiences should be selected with the expectation that the learner will have "Ah, ha!" flashes of insight that relate to many issues, that would go well beyond the present objectives. Learners should be encouraged to look for the serendipitous, to reflect on those insights that not only relate to the objectives at hand but to other related issues. Often the Lord provides new insight into one's hermeneutic for interpreting Scripture in a particular way. Often the Lord provides insight into new ways of understanding the community through a learning experience that is not focused on that issue at all.

> **Recommendation: Select learning experiences around key expectations.**

Organizing the Learning Experiences

Tyler's categories continue to instruct us about the principles for organization.[2] He suggests three organizing principles, which certainly apply in the design of a curriculum for equipping urban Christian leaders. He suggests that the learning experiences should be organized to show continuity, sequence, and integration.

Continuity

Continuity is the reinforced repetition of themes, concepts, and foundational building blocks throughout the learning experiences. Continuity provides the essential "redundancy" which prevents information overload and facilitates review and integration. Continuity in the learning experience provides that which is known

> CEFI is committed to church growth. All of its workshops focus on helping the church grow.
>
> The Harambee program has a strong focus on justice which runs through all of its programs.

65 Continuity in Learning Experiences

as the base for linking into the unknown. Continuity in learning experiences provides the core issues around which new information or new skills may cluster. As one learns how to apply basic principles of exegesis, those principles will assist, whether one prepares for teaching Sunday school, preaching, or leading small groups. In the teaching, however, the ongoing instruction in exegesis continues.

Sequence

Sequence is the ordered progression from one element to another, from one item to another, from one learning experience to another. The sequence should fit the learning style of the learner. It should fit the content of the subject being addressed. The sequence may be chronological; it

> The Church on Brady begins with post-baptismal instruction, then moves on to equipping one to establish small groups, and then work with them both to multiply them and join them into a congregation.

66 Sequence in Learning Experiences

may be geographical; or, it may address the subject in some other logical way. The sequence should be clearly understood by the learner as well as the instructor. Some subjects are much more conducive to an internal structuring which shows sequence—for example, mathematics. One begins with addition and subtraction before going to multiplication and division. The sequencing should be related to the primary purpose at hand. If one is to learn how to establish new congregations, an implicit sequence may exist for the process in a given context. Learning through that sequence may be very important. The appropriate sequencing of learning experiences seldom just happens. It must be planned.

Integration

Integration provides the linkage among the various learning experiences so that they form a whole. An integrated curriculum will link the overnight experiences with the homeless with the lectures in the well appointed lecture room. It will link the counseling experience with the Yuppy family whose young teenager is experimenting with drugs, with both biblical exegesis and the counseling experience one has recently had with the runaways who are living on the streets.

> The integration of the learning experiences into a comprehensive picture is seen in the impact of the lives of people who are emerging from these training programs. Alumni from the Harambee Center serve in churches in northwest Pasadena as church leaders and as community leaders working toward justice, reconciliation, and the strengthening of the church. Alumni from the Church on Brady are starting new Bible studies that lead to house churches, and then to larger congregations. Alumni from the ABI are starting new large churches in the cities of Peru.

6 7 Integration in Learning Experiences

Again, integration does not just happen, but rather is structured into the organization of the curriculum. Integration requires planning in the selection, the organizing, the sequencing, and the design of continuity in the learning experiences.

Recommendation: Organize the learning experiences deliberately to show continuity, sequence, and integration.

Balancing the Learning Experiences

The balance of learning experiences should be seen in at least two different ways: 1) balance among the component parts of learning experiences, and

2) balance among the basic educational approaches to the learning experiences.

Balancing the Components

The component parts that need to be balanced in any given method of equipping include: 1) the input, which would include information, skills, attitudinal instruction, 2) experience in ministry, 3) reflection about the input and experience, and 4) spiritual formation. These issues have been treated briefly in an earlier chap-

> The Bresee Institute in cooperation with APU, has designed its training program to include a balance of the components. Classroom experience, required ministry experience and regular reflection combine with worship and practice of the spiritual disciplines to form a holistic or balanced approach to leadership development.

68 Balance in Learning Experiences

ter. A given situation will require a somewhat different focus, but all four component parts must be balanced if the design for equipping is to be effective. Many training programs focus heavily on information, on skill development, or on attitudinal development. Often, attitude development is basically an input orientation that relies heavily on the teacher rather than on the learner. Even if the emphasis is shifted to the learner, where the learner is focusing on the input, the learning will not be complete without

the other three components. Experience along the way is a critical component and should be facilitated in the design of the equipping program. However, a common mistake in seminaries and training programs is that, while field experience is expected and there is a great deal of input, the two are hardly related. Reflection, therefore, is a component that can perhaps reduce the need for input and maximize the contribution of both the input and experience. What does the experience suggest that one needs to learn in terms of

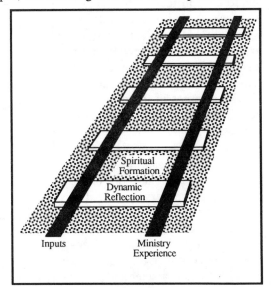

FIGURE SIX
Adapted Two Track Analogy

input? In what ways do the inputs relate to the ministry experience? All of these three contribute to the formation of character, the spiritual formation of the person, which leads then to the ongoing ministry formation of the person. Balance among these four components is a critical issue for an effective equipping program.

Frederic Holland suggests these four elements be depicted[3] as the parts of a railway. The foundational road bed on which all else is built is spiritual formation. The parallel rails of inputs and ministry experience provide the substance of the learning, and the contexts for both learning and practice. The dynamic reflection provides the integrative link between the inputs and experience. This integration provides a means of solidifying the inputs, motivation for learning, and a means to facilitate further spiritual and ministry formation. The reflection should continue at regularly spaced intervals to link these key functions.

Senyimba's African Pot Analogy depicts the same elements. However, it more clearly shows how the inputs (skills, information), ministry experience, and dynamic reflection contribute to spiritual formation. Leadership then emerges out of spiritually formed persons who have experience based competence.

Clearly, the content, the ongoing ministry experience, and regular reflection should contribute to the spiritual formation process. As one's character matures spiritually both one's capacity for influence and the expectations for one's influence by others are likely to increase. Spiritual authority emerges in the process of facilitating the whole leadership process.[4]

A key critical insight emerging from the African Pot Analogy is the sequential dimensions of the processing. Leadership potential emerges out of demonstrated competence and trustworthiness in ministry, and out of one's spirituality. This spirituality is evidenced through one's character and the quality of one's relationships.

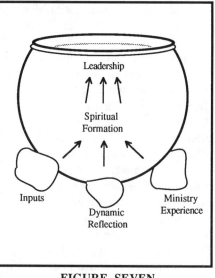

FIGURE SEVEN
African Pot Analogy

The input and reflection may be done formally, nonformally, or informally. The ministry experience may be structured as a part of a formal or nonformal program. However, to rely solely on informal (unstructured) means for any one of these critical components reduces accountability and expected effectiveness.

Typically, a well designed leadership development program will balance all three modes to fit the purpose and other key variables and will also balance the four critical components. The Bresee Institute in Los Angeles, for example, balances all three modes in a unique way in delivering the input in the ministry context as well as in a classroom. Students have opportunities to serve in the context in a variety of learning ministries. Times of reflection allow them to interact in sharing both their wounds and their victories.

> Peter B. Morehead, in *An Analysis of the Leadership Training Program at the Church on Brady,* describes the balance of four critical components: **Input** comes through sermons, CTP courses (organized under maturity, message, ministry, and mission), specific ministry training, and ministry tasks. Input is geared to match the level of experience and responsibility of the learners. **In-Ministry-Experience** . . . [is] designed to offer experience focused on individual gifts. Heavy emphasis is put on using training to serve others. **Dynamic Reflection** is present in the form of seminars, homework assignments, and informally through the reflection prompted by the example of leadership. **Spiritual Formation** comes through counseling in early stages of growth, worship times, nurture in small groups, and individualized interviews with the ministry director using growth profile sheets.

69 Balance of Critical Parts

> **Recommendation: Design the learning experiences so that the input, the ministry experience, the regular reflection, and spiritual formation all fit together in a balanced way.**

Balancing Educational Approaches

While any given program may be more formal or nonformal or may have more informal dimensions, the balancing of these to fit all of the curricular issues mentioned in a previous chapter is critically important. Each of these basic approaches to education has key weaknesses which can be addressed

> CEFI aims at balancing the educational modes to have a maximum impact on the in-service leaders who are in their seminars and workshops.

70 Balance in Educational Modes

easily by the other two approaches. Formal education tends to be theoretical. It lacks immediate practicality. It is expensive because of being resource intensive. Nonformal education is often criticized for the lack of theory, for being too focused on the present and on functions. Informal education, which occurs as enculturation in the context of relationships, is not structured. It lacks structured accountability. One never knows what really has been learned informally without giving a lot of time to it. However, when these three different basic approaches are combined in a balanced way, there is adequate theory, adequate practicality and application, and the formation of values and relationships. There is accountability and change. The balance helps one to avoid the basic weaknesses of each approach and optimize their strengths.

Recommendation: Balance the formal (theoretical), nonformal (functional), and informal (relational) dimensions of the program around the purpose.

Notes

1 The basic theory undergirding this chapter comes from Ralph Tyler's *Basic Principles of Curriculum and Instruction* (Chicago: University of Chicago Press, 1949).

2 Tyler.

3 Frederic Holland, *Theological Education in Context and Change* (D.Miss. dissertation, Fuller Theological Seminary, 1978), p. 13; and J. Robert Clinton, "Leadership Training Models Manual" (Altadena, CA: Barnabas Resources, 1984), pp. 40–49.

4 Authority may be understood as the "right to exercise power or influence." The Holy Spirit delegates authority, or that right to influence, to leaders. This delegated authority contributes directly to the emergence of a person as a leader. As one matures spiritually, spiritual authority increases. A follower's allocation of authority to a spiritual leader and his recognition of a leader's spiritual authority emerge from the recognition of God's working in and through the life of the leader to influence others for good toward God's purposes. This "delegated" and "allocated" spiritual authority is not based on one's own status or power. Rather than emerging out of such commonly expected forms of power as expertise, information, organizational connections, personal charisma, or control of rewards and punishments, it flows out of a committed servanthood (Mt. 23:1–12).

CHAPTER EIGHT

CONTENT, SKILL AND BEING ISSUES FOR EQUIPPING URBAN LEADERS

This chapter outlines and illustrates some generic recommended "content," "skill," and "being" recommendations for metro-based ministries. Three sets of perspectives are offered to present a wholistic approach. All three must be developed in a wholistic way for the urban leader to be effective.

Strategic Content for Equipping Urban Leaders

To be effective urban leaders must have a certain knowledge base from which to work. This book has identified many components of that knowledge base. This section will identify some of the levels of that cognitive base and highlight a few key components of the essential strategic content for every type of leadership.

Levels of Content Mastery

Bloom's cognitive taxonomy provides the standard means to clarify cognitive learning from the perspective of the learner.[1] Not every issue must be "known" at the highest level. However, as one asks the basic journalistic questions—why, how, when, what, where, who, and how much—of the urban ministry for which a person is being equipped, a higher level of competence will likely emerge than has been common for most training programs. Emerging leaders will not be satisfied nor competent to simply be able to recognize or interpret critical concepts for their ministries. They need to apply, analyze, synthesize, and evaluate from this new knowledge as well.

To achieve the higher levels of knowledge requires active participation in a real or closely simulated context. Jesus' methods of teaching led His disciples to the highest levels of learning. The disciples were not allowed just to listen and take in information, they were active participants who were sent out to try what they had learned. They then received feedback about what happened. By obedient discipling of others their own growth toward maturity was assured. They were expected to change their world-view to match what Jesus was teaching, not just to apply or analyze. They were expected to see life and evaluate their experience from that new perspective.

Key Content Topics

The primary content topics have been addressed in this book and could be identified under the categories of basic journalistic questions: why, how, when what, where, who, and how much. A summary of our perspectives about these primary questions will lay a base for some specific recommendations.

Who are the actors in this arena of ministry the emerging leader needs to know? 1) The sovereign Lord God is the primary person whom the emerging leader needs to know and serve. 2) The emerging leader must also know himself/herself and the relationships which exist with God, the church, the people who are the focus of ministry, and the environment. A clear understanding of one's self serves as an essential foundational element. 3) The emerging leader must know the people with whom he/she serves—their needs, their deep level spiritual commitments, and their hope. 4) The emerging leader must know the situation in which he/she is to work. The political, economic and religious structures with their accompanying principalities and powers must be understood, not only to facilitate effective communication, but to understand both what is either friend or foe in the transformational task the Lord has given to him/her.

Recommendation: The emerging leader should know who is involved with whom.

"*What* is to be done?" should be clearly understood by every emerging leader. The specific tasks for which one must give account must be understood in terms of how they contribute to the mandates to disciple all the nations and to love one's neighbor. Clarifying the task ultimately rests on God's revelation of Himself, but existing leaders discern His guidance through the written word of God and through observing what He is doing in the world today. The written word remains the normative guide for discernment of what God is doing and wants done today.

Recommendation: The emerging leader should know what the task is.

Knowing *how* the task is to be done takes the emerging leader not only into the Scriptures, but into the social sciences, history, and philosophy. The emerging leader from the West risks falling into a technological mind-set in which the technique or well-constructed method is the answer. The ancient answer remains the basis for effective urban ministry today: "'Not by strength or might, but by my Spirit' says the Lord Almighty" (Zec. 4:6). Spiritual guidance and power which shapes and energizes our plans may be effective. However, simply devising clever marketing schemes without employing God's power will sell out the church without the nations having "bought in."

Techniques should not be despised. However, a theme repeated by successful spiritual leaders from Abraham until the present is, "the battle is the Lord's." Joseph's repeated deliverance can only be attributed to the Lord. The secret of Moses' success against the Amalekites (Ex. 17:8–15) was his prior recognition of whose battle it was. What could be said of Moses could be said of Joshua and Jericho, of Gideon and Midianites, of David and Goliath, of Esther and Ahasuerus, of Nehemiah and the rebuilding of the wall, of Jesus and resurrection, of Peter and John and their encounter with the Sanhedrin, of Paul in Ephesus or of other early leaders. Omar Cabrera's "success" in evangelism in Argentina has been seen as an outstanding example of a particular strategy aimed at nominal Catholics. However, one would be greatly misled if the days of fasting and intercessory prayer for the immediate city were overlooked. The "how" is by the hand of the Lord as we work with Him to discover the myriads of possibilities He has at His disposal.

Recommendation: Emerging leaders should know how the task is to be done in terms of the Lord's battle plan.

The *where* of urban leadership development must in part include the answer, "where the people are." Leaders emerge into influence in real social and spiritual situations with real people in real time, with a real task, and with real values. Cloistered, sequestered, removed, distant, extractionist leadership development won't work. Genuine leadership can never be completed until the emerging leader enters into the reality of the situation and the followers authenticate his/her leadership.

> **Recommendation: Emerging leaders should know where they can become leaders.**

ASAP appears on many leaders' memos addressing the question of *when*. "As soon as possible" (ASAP) is the approach to take in the development of leaders in every type and place. Henrietta Mears, one of the greatest of American leader developers of a previous era, would create and assign a person to a ministry to begin the leadership empowerment process on the first hint of availability or willingness. As soon as a person accepts Christ as Lord, then service begins. As soon as faithful service in small matters has been demonstrated, the process of leadership development should continue. This principle is not a once-for-all approach, but rather an "as needed" or "as appropriate" recurring approach. The answer to "when?" is "whenever possible."

> **Recommendation: Emerging leaders should expect to develop a sense of "ASAP."**

How much content is required? The question must be linked to the questions of "why," "who," "when," and "where." The basic principle for deciding may be established as a minimal training perspective. At least enough content should be provided so that the emerging leader can begin to function in his/her status and role and so that he/she can with practice develop competence in that role. The risk for emerging leaders is often that of being overloaded with information without personal experience or reflection. Schools greatly enhance this risk.

> **Recommendation: Emerging leaders should have mastered only the basics for their initial role before they begin serving.**

The beginning and ending question is *why?* The emerging leader should be able to answer the why of his/her actions both in terms of the immediate task and of the biblical mandates. The vision, aim, purpose, goal, and object are all driven by the question, "Why?" When the why is unclear, integration of all the other issues falters and the leadership development design will likely fail.

> **Recommendation: Emerging leaders should always be able to answer "why" in terms of their immediate task and the broader biblical mandates.**

Each type (e.g., Types I–V) of urban leader must know the answers to each of these questions, from both the biblical perspective and from the perspective of the ministry context in which he/she serves. The answering of these primary questions will take the emerging leader into spiritual warfare in the city.

The cognitive basic training in a Bible institute, Bible college or seminary education should not be faulted at this point. A thorough grounding in the Bible, theology, church history, communication, pastoral theology and ethics must not be bypassed. However, because of the blindness of many who come to the city to serve with a Western worldview, the issues of spiritual warfare must be consciously added to the curriculum.

Preparing an emerging leader to enter the spiritual battle which is raging in the cities requires mastery of content which often seems strangely foreign. Entry into witnessing, caring for a poor person, or addressing political or economic structures takes a person into spiritual encounters. Objections to abortion may lead to ridicule or jail. Even placing Jesus over Santa Claus within a church school embroiled one church in Southern California in intense media criticism. Effective Christian leadership, whether focused on the evangelistic mandate or the cultural mandate, will engage the enemy in conflict.

Charles H. Kraft's description of three types of encounter in Christian witness provides a significant theoretical content base from which one may begin to address the spiritual warfare in the city. This perspective identifies content, skill, and spiritual maturity issues for the equipping Christian leaders.

People who live in cities fall prey to the same spiritual battles as do people who live in any other setting. The task for which leaders must be prepared in the city remains a spiritual task. Christian leaders must take care not to be diverted into thinking that economic, political, or educational issues present the primary constraints, tasks, or needs of people living in cities. The primary task is a spiritual one requiring spiritual awareness, a certain quality of life, and well developed skills.

To prepare leaders to lead effectively in this spiritual battle they should be equipped to engage in three different kinds of encounters or confrontations. Each of these encounters contributes to the effectiveness of the other two.

Kraft clarifies these three encounters and shows how they interrelate to empower Christian leaders in ministry. Each of these encounters employs spiritual power and aims at the *missio dei*. He describes the primary encounters as—1) power, 2) truth, and 3) allegiance or commitment.[2]

Kraft describes the nature and aims of these three kinds of encounter:

> The encounters are not of the same nature. Each differs from the other two and serves a different purpose. But each is intended to initiate a process crucial to Christian experience and aimed at a specific goal. The concern of the truth encounter is understanding, and the vehicle of that encounter is teaching. The allegiance encounter is focused on relationship and is mediated through witness. Freedom, then, is the aim of the power encounter, and spiritual warfare is its vehicle. Though the correspondence is not exact, it may be noted that truth and understanding have a lot to do with the mind. Allegiance and relationship rest primarily in the will, and freedom is largely experienced emotionally.[3]

Three leadership goals for Christians must be freedom, correct understandings, and commitment in relationship to Jesus Christ. To facilitate these goals, Christian leaders need to be equipped with the knowledge, skill, appropriate attitude, and spiritual maturity to effect these encounters. Kraft asserts, "Any total approach to Christian ministry needs all three encounters. And they need to be employed together, not separately."[4]

Evangelical Christians have in the past strongly employed the truth encounter. Charismatics and Pentecostals have realized the importance much more of the power encounter. Often within the Christian community we have neglected the allegiance encounter, and so syncretism has continued. Nominalism has flourished, and the church has stagnated.

While all three kinds of encounter are appropriate and needed in modern Western cities, cities now have an increasing number of people from the Two-Thirds World, whose worldview expects demonstrations of spiritual power. Demonstration of spiritual power by itself will not bring allegiance or commitment. Commitment or allegiance may be shallow without demonstrations of power and without truth. A proved argument may not bring commitment. All three are required.

Recommendation: Equip leaders for every type of power, truth, and commitment or allegiance encounter.

Skill Issues

Urban leaders need a wide range of skills to function effectively. All of the skills relate to the task at hand and to the ministry context. The skills should be developed around a person's giftedness. Some specific skills can be identified for people who would serve in any urban area. Other skills must be identified by genre only. The skills identified in this section include exegetical skills and contextually required skills.

Contextual Interpretive Skills

Any city is too complex to assume that any local resident will fully understand it. The emerging leaders who will be equipped for ministries in the city will nearly always come from that city. They can be expected to understand many of the characteristics of that city. Those understandings should be shared among the whole group of emerging leaders. However, because of the complexities of any city it should not be assumed that any given group will understand the city in terms of optimal ways to lead in ministry in that city.

Bakke laments what occurs in typical theological education programs:

> Pastors are not given methods of diagnosis—the capacity to survey, observe, analyze, and interpret either their complex multicultural communities or their churches. Diagnostic training equips the pastor to "custom build" a ministry around the realities of the community being served. Instead of offering a standardized food product, the effective minister will study the local food needs of the community, identify the deficiencies in the local diet, and design a new food product for those people who are being served badly or not being served at all.[5]

> The second feature of theological training fosters on the prescriptive approach by managing the standard outlets. Most theological schools teach or imply that all environments are culturally neutral. All that the colleges need to do is to pre-package formulae for ministry which will work anywhere. Much of theological education is middle class culture with a smattering of the gospel. What students are given works only in cultures similar to those in which their professors live and work.[6]

No single discipline, whether sociology, urban anthropology, theology, history, or education can be expected to provide the breadth and depth of understandings that will be needed in a given ministry context. Insights from all of these disciplines serve to provide a wholistic perspective out of which ministries may be developed. Few of the people who are being equipped for urban ministries as Type I, Type II, or Type III leaders will be specialists in any of these disciplines. However, insights from a multidisciplinary approach can be used to equip even volunteer leaders in an urban setting.

Type IV and perhaps Types III and V leaders who would design the training for Types I and II should have enough knowledge or understanding about the city in which the leaders are being equipped to allow them to discover the critical insights required in each of the following categories. The purpose for looking at the following categories is not to develop bodies of knowledge in each area, but rather to provide a wholistic picture of how to engage in ministry in that particular urban setting. The sources for the following seven different categories of information come from a wide range of people, institutions, and resources. One should expect to find published information in libraries. Current publications such as daily newspapers, publications of the chamber of commerce, government planning or zoning commissions, and other media such as television and radio also provide information related to the urban center being considered.

A valid interpretation of the city must take the leading of the Spirit and the discernment He provides. Spiritual discernment in interpreting an urban setting is an important part of preparing for spiritual warfare.

Dawson writes, "Spiritual warfare does not operate in a vacuum. It is the air force that covers the soul winner and the evangelist, and all evangelism must be conducted using all the available information."[7] The point he makes is to get the facts about the city where the ministry is to be done.

The following categories, then, while not intended to be comprehensive, do provide suggestions for an initial understanding of the city. These initial concerns include the physical geography, history, cultural composition, religious composition, networks, and their potentials for influence, needs, and as resources.

> **Recommendation: Equip leaders of every type to interpret their ministry contexts.**

Physical Environment

The Bresee Institute helps learners understand the physical environment of the city as its leaders walk with them in the neighborhoods and talk with the local people.

The local environment contributes significantly to any given urban context. The local environment probably has contributed significantly to the history of the development of that particular city, whether it be a coastal port city, a city that has depended on river transportation, or a city that has been built around some other physical geographical characteristic.

The climate and the local environment affect every dimension of the city's life. A given culture is often described as a people's response to coping within a given environment. An understanding of the local environment and its relationship to the broader environment within the country or the region is always a beginning point for understanding an urban area and region.

> **Recommendation: Equip leaders to understand the physical environment.**

History

One can never understand a city without understanding its history. Many general historical questions arise, such as how, when, and why was the city formed? Who were the people who first settled the city? Who were the people who moved into the city or who moved out of the city? What were the major events that shaped the city? Every city serves certain functions within its environment. What are those functions? How have they changed over the years? Is the city historically a city of commerce? Is it a political center? Is it a military center? Is it a religious center? Is it a center for transportation? Is it a center for communications? Is it a center for education? What combinations of functions historically has this urban area served? Dawson asks, "Is there any thing in the roots of the city that could be bringing God's judgment rather than his blessing?"[8] In order to examine this historical question about a city's spirituality in more detail Dawson lists twenty questions.[9] He suggests,

> five areas of essential knowledge in which today's Christian worker must walk: 1) Know the history of the church in your nation . . . 2) Know the history of the church in your city . . . 3) Know the history of ministry to your target subculture or ethnic group . . . 4) Know the history of the type of ministry in which you are involved . . . 5) Know the history of your movement.[10]

As one looks at the historical setting, trends begin to emerge over history. As one looks at trends, then projections into the future may be possible—trends that relate to population growth, trade, culture, and worldview change. An understanding of the past helps us understand the present. An understanding of the past gives us perspectives for action into the future.

> **Recommendation: Equip leaders to understand the local history.**

Cultural Composition

The question of who lives in the city is critical. What ethnic groups comprise its population? How are they distributed numerically? How are they distributed geographically? Do they live in groups? Do they live mixed among other ethnic groups? The question of who is important to know.

What is the relationship of each ethnic group in terms of status and role to the overall community? Does a given ethnic group have a particular ascribed or achieved status within the community? What are the roles it serves within the community? For

> The Church on Brady helps the learners learn about the cultural context in the city by living in, learning in, and ministering in the kind of urban situation which will be the focus of ministry.

71 Understanding Cultural Context

example, immigrants from Kerala in South India in the 1970s and early 1980s included many nurses, and so nurses moved into health care jobs, both in hospitals and primary health care in communities. As their families joined them, many of their husbands and extended families included professionals, educators, doctors, attorneys, and business people.

As one looks at the city, if the city has been long established, a dominant worldview perspective may pervade across subcultural lines. An understanding of the dominant worldview themes provides many clues to ways of working within that city and constraints within which to work. An understanding of the worldview also provides a base line for identifying worldview change and potential receptivity to the gospel.

Recommendation: Equip leaders to understand the local cultural context.

Religious Context

The religious context of a city requires an understanding of many complexities for effective urban ministry. What is the range of religious beliefs held and practiced within the city? How are the various religious groups distributed geographically and in terms of population? How are they distributed by age and by ethnic group?

> The Bresee Institute equips the learners to discover the religious context in which they will work by teaching how to "exegete" the city, both in the classroom and on the streets in interactions with members of the community.

72 Understanding the Religious Context

This description of religious composition requires a careful "spiritual mapping" of the ministry area to be served.

One might be tempted to look at the religious composition of a city only in terms of major religious groups, such as Christian, Muslim, Buddhist, and Hindu. However, subcategories must also be included to show major divisions and the distribution of these divisions within each of the categories, as well as the religious affiliation that is commonly practiced among those who would be nominal in any one of these groups. What is the folk religious practice in the city? What is its range? One must understand the religious formation to understand questions of resistance and receptivity to the gospel. One must understand the religious context in order to design appropriate ministry strategies and appropriate goals to meet one's purpose.

Linthicum suggests a set of four questions about the "economics, politics and religion" aimed at laying the base for an integrated wholistic ministry in the city.[11] Emerging leaders should be equipped to answer these questions about the city and ministry where they will serve.

McClung correctly asserts,

> We must know if we are battling demonic powers or dealing just with sin and its consequences in the culture. The two are not always the same. Further, if the battle is against demonic powers, what kinds of powers are we fighting? It is important to know the exact kinds of strategies Satan is using, and how they go rooted in the culture. I have found that a relationship usually exists between demonic bondage in a city or nation and the sins that have been committed there on a large scale in the past. Sometimes we have to go back centuries to find the roots of some spiritual bondages.[12]

Often church leaders are tempted to rely solely on the social sciences and the humanities to understand the religious context. While these human sciences are helpful, they offer only a dim or distorted view of the spiritual world and its impact on the daily lives of people, social structures, and communities.

Spiritual Mapping then is a skill and perspective needed to understand the religious context. An understanding of the cultural and sociological factors such as demographic distributions, economics, and worldview of the people in the urban area to be served provides a critically important base for strategic planning. However, knowing all of the sociological and cultural factors is not enough to position a person for effective ministry. The Apostle Paul wrote to the church in Ephesus that "we do not wrestle against flesh and blood, but against principalities and powers" (Eph. 6:10ff).

Dawson cautions about "spiritual mapping" based on the references to the "Prince of Persia" in Daniel and the "beasts at Ephesus":

... this should not be taken as a mandate for the development of spiritual maps in which we seek knowledge for the sake of knowledge. God will reveal what we need to know when we need to know it.

There has always been a danger of either denial of satanic activity altogether or of focusing on it too much. If we fain knowledge of the name and nature of an evil spirit and publish it broadly, the enemy will only attempt to glorify himself openly or to instill fear among the immature. Joshua warned the Israelites about this temptation. "You shall not make mention of the name of their gods" (Jos. 23:7).

Morbid fascination is a carnal appetite that can drive us to search out the hidden knowledge of the evil realm ... However, the privilege of knowing God Himself should be the center of our desire.[13]

The urban ministry for which men and women are to be equipped is primarily a spiritual struggle. The evidence of the struggle is evident in the poverty, alienation, crime, homelessness, hopelessness, oppression, drugs, apathy, and other major dysfunctions of any city.

Men and women to be fully equipped must understand the spiritual context in which they will work. At least two levels of understanding serve to form this critical base. First, one should know the general religious situation as described in local census studies and general references about the dominant religious beliefs and practices. Unfortunately, this general knowledge, while essential, is as far as many in ministry ever go. A second level is even more important. One should be equipped to prepare a spiritual map of the primary ministry area. This map should locate all of the spiritual allies one has in terms of churches, Christian agencies, and Christians. The map should also locate all of the major spiritual centers which oppose the gospel. The mapping process should include a careful description of each one. For example, all of the non-Christian places of worship such as temples, shrines, places of sacrifice, mosques, spirit houses, Masonic temples, religious reading rooms, cultic centers, Mormon and Jehovah Witness "churches, satanic centers, palm readers, and New Age Centers should be located geographically. They should then be described in terms of local influence. The political, economic and cultural impact of each of these groups should be known in terms of their extent, comprehensiveness, and depth.

When seeking to equip emerging leaders to discern the local spiritual context, McClung suggests caution be exercised. He writes,

The Scriptures say very little about the nature and names of demon powers, so we must be cautious about naming spirits over places. We can, however, recognize evil in the systems, institutions and lives of people in the city, and how that evil spirit manifests itself. Because of the association of evil and the demonic in

> Scripture, we may refer to the "spirit of greed" or "the spirit of violence" or whatever evil spiritual power seems to be manifesting itself in unusual dimension in a city or nation.[14]

> ... it is vital to recognize that principalities and demonic powers seek to use wickedness in a city as a launching pad to attack Christians. It is essential that we do not enter the "battle arena" without arming ourselves with the full armor of God. It is foolish to attempt God's work without a sufficient prayer base and an understanding of the spiritual weapons at our disposal.[15]

> ... four important characteristics [are] helpful in discerning the work of principalities and powers on a broad scale in cities and nations: spiritual blindness and hardness toward the Gospel; obsession with certain forms of evil throughout vast portions of the population; bondage to particular sins and behavior that cannot be controlled by normal means used by societies to govern themselves; and compromise and defeat in the Church (Ro. 1:18–32).[16]

Some spiritual mapping and contextual descriptions can only be discovered over an extended period of time. However, with only a minimal effort the broad outlines of the local context can be detected by simply observing and asking local residents.

The Apostle Paul suggests the nature of what is being sought in this exercise: "We do not look at the things which are seen, but at the things which are not seen. For the things which are seen are temporary, but the things which are not seen are eternal" (2 Co. 4:18). There is a difference between the temporal, or the seen, and the spiritual and the unseen.

The Greek tragedies illustrate this difference. While the mortals acted on one level of the stage, the "gods" acted on another. The audience saw a split-level stage with two simultaneous plays, total interrelated, but visually distinct. Likewise, the spiritual realm is unseen but real, intertwined with the lives of ordinary men and women.

The equipping of Christian leaders for working in an urban area should then include not only the content of the spiritual mapping of the area, but the skills for continuing to more fully understand the spiritual arena in which they will be engaged. The three kinds of Christian encounter mentioned in the section above may form a useful grid for part of the spiritual map.

Recommendation: Equip leaders for the spiritual mapping of the urban area where they will serve.

Networks and Their Potential for Influence

One characteristic of an urban area is the complexity of interlocking networks. Some of these networks include communications, political, service, trade, education, religious, and crime networks. Some networks are formally and

> The Bresee Institute and the Harambee Center both build networks among their students and members of the community at every level.

73 Understanding Networks

legally structured. Other networks are outside of the legal arena. All of these networks relate to people and the complexities of relationships.

Within an urban area other infrastructural networks which are physical and material in nature also contribute to the complexity of the city. To understand the city one must also understand these networks—roads, distribution of electric power, systems for water and waste disposal. The physical infrastructure of a city is also a critical part of what needs to be understood, because it influences every person who lives in or travels to the city.

Through these networks and other networks that could be mentioned people exercise influence. They use their power to lead for good or ill in a city.

Significant potential power for good and for enhancing the whole range of Christian ministries emerges when Christians, churches, and Christian agencies are linked or networked to act in unity. God blesses the community where Christians work together. The sum of their potential influence far outweighs their combined strength in influencing both the political, economic and religious structures, and the principalities and powers. Networking should not be seen for pragmatic means only, but as a key ingredient for spiritual warfare as well. Floyd McClung suggests that spiritual authority or the right to use God's power at a community level is related to the unity of the Christians in that community.[17] Dawson asserts, "An individual ministry or church can achieve a cone of victory within its sphere of service, but the prevailing evil spirits will dominate the secular culture unhindered until the principle of agreement based on harmony in relationships is employed."[18] Jesus said, "If a kingdom is divided against itself, that kingdom cannot stand" (Mk. 3:24).

> **Recommendation: Equip leaders to facilitate the building of and linking to local networks.**

Needs

The needs of the individual, family, community, metropolitan region, state, province, and nation should be understood to inform the person who is equipping others for ministry. "Projected needs," "felt needs," needs as "gaps to be filled," "constraints to development," "life processes," or "developmental stages" require attention so the emerging leader will be equipped and empowered to work with the individuals and community to resolve these needs appropriately.

> The Harambee program seeks to work with the needs of the community by addressing family concerns, and issues of justice and employment of the people who live nearby.
>
> **74** Understanding Needs

The spiritual needs of the community must be assessed along with the other physical and social needs at a personal level. These needs are closely interrelated to the physical and social needs. They are also related to the structural needs at a community or cultural level.

Recommendation: Equip leaders to understand local needs.

Potential Resources

Overwhelming needs may threaten the person who would serve in the city. Whether the city is Los Angeles, Bangkok, Nairobi, or Quito, the needs and the opportunities for ministry are overwhelming. However, one must also look at the resources that are available to support the ministry that is to be done in the city. As one becomes aware of networks of Christian agencies, educational institutions, nonformal ministry development programs, and government resources, it is possible to see a wide range of resources that may be used for ministry and ministry development.

The statement, "It's not what you know, but who you know that makes the difference," is true. Key resources in the city are not just financial, but relational and networking. Unity within the Christian community often releases unexpected spiritual, politi-

> The Church on Brady views the use of resources in a reproducible way. Money is not spent until it is in hand. Credit is not sought for the church. It is a pay-as-you-go policy.
>
> **75** Attitude Toward Resources

cal/social/structural, and economic resources. As the relational resources are developed, not only do financial resources become available, but facilities and equipment as well.

The equipping models cited in this book approach the question of resources in different ways. However, one commonality runs through them—they are designed so that the community being served provides the critical long term resources. As the proverb suggests, "A cord of three strands is not quickly broken" (Ecc. 4:12).

> **Recommendation: Equip leaders to assess available local resources for ministry.**

Summary

Whether the person being developed as a leader is to lead a small group, to lead several small groups, to serve as a congregational leader or as a regional leader, these kinds of information are vital in developing the person. These kinds of information form one of the critical content bases for leadership development in the city. While other content is important for the specific ministry, this information is important for fitting the person into the context.

Part of the developing of an emerging leader is the formation of an attitude to be inquisitive, to ask those journalistic questions of the context regularly, the questions of who, where, why, how, what, and how much.

> **Recommendation: Equip emerging leaders to interpret their ministry context.**

Technical Skills

Technical skills required for the context relate specifically to the task at hand in that context. These skills may include simple manual skills or highly complex skills related to the administration or operation of complex equipment. The skills may include mental tasks such as study, the preparation of teaching materials or a wide range of other kinds of technical skills. Existing leaders cannot assume that emerging leaders have these skills.

Sometimes the skills that a person has in one context may not transfer well into another context because of emotional differences, attitudinal differences, or adjustment to the new culture. It is always safer to have demonstrated the skills within that context before fully disengaging from the development program for the emerging leaders.

Recommendation: Equip emerging leaders with all of the up-to-date technical skills needed for their ministry.

Recommendation: Equip leaders to continue to upgrade their skills.

Social Survival Skills

Social survival skills are required in any situation in which a person is going to live and work. One may assume that these skills have been developed by the time a person is an adult. However, if one changes contexts and the culture is radically different, a person may be reduced to a stage of incapacity in that new culture. One may not be able to speak the language or communicate in any meaningful way. Moving from the suburbs to the inner-city may bring that drastic a change, as may moving from the thirtieth story of a high rise office building to the street may be that different. Language skills and multicultural adjustment skills are required for the person who is to work in an urban setting. It is never enough to know about the people with whom one works as an outsider. One must know the people, work with them and view life from their perspective. The adjustment skills to move into that new culture must be developed as part of the social survival skills required.

Social survival skills emerge from a basic attitude of respect for the people in the ministry context, even though they may differ significantly in their worldview and culture. This attitude of respect is foundational for two character traits which lend to social survival in a diverse community: 1) tolerance of ambiguity and 2) a high level of empathy. Equipping leaders who can tolerate ambiguity in others, that is, not always fully understanding but seeking to understand them from their perspective, positions them to develop contextually appropriate survival skills. These skills will serve not only to build and maintain interpersonal relationships, but organizational and community relationships as well. These relationships form the base for ministry.

Another set of social survival skills are "hermeneutical adjustment skills." A person needs to understand the local worldview well enough to be able to interpret empathetically both local experience, perceptions of outsiders, and the Scriptures in that context with the community . . . and, from the community's perspective. One's own worldview always conditions his/her hermeneutical approach. One's way of interpreting or hermeneutic must exhibit a range of flexibility. One must learn how to adjust that way of interpreting so it fits within the community. With differences in worldview one may with integrity interpret the same experience or the same text in different ways. In fact, one would not have integrity were he/she to interpret it consistently when there are differences of worldview.

For a person to be optimally effective in any ministry that person should follow the incarnational lead of Jesus and live in the community to be served. Floyd McClung makes a strong case for living in the community of ministry.[19] Spiritual authority is not only delegated from God Himself, it is recognized and allocated by the people who grant the right to be influenced. Giving this right is generally reserved for the people who are known and respected. It is reserved for people who have demonstrated their commitment in the community, not only by what they say, but by where they live and what they advocate for the community, its needs and its people. McClung writes, "Authority to speak about people's lives comes from our commitment to live among them as servants."[20] Participation in the local structures—educational, political, economic, and religious allows one to build the credibility and understanding that encourage others in the community, even nonbelievers, to allocate/recognize a person's spiritual authority. The role of the outside prophet is valid, but the role of the incarnational servant, shepherd, and steward of the gospel is critical.

Recommendation: Equip emerging leaders with social survival skills.

General Ministry Skills

No two theological educators will agree about a listing of basic ministry skills. For the purpose of this text we will list four general ministry skills: interpretive, communicational, team building, and spiritual warfare skills. The basic training for a soldier of the cross must include equipping in these four areas.

Interpretive Skills

Regardless of the kind of ministry involved, whether it be a social ministry or an evangelistic ministry, the leader should have well developed interpretive skills. The leader should be able to understand the Scriptures and how to apply them to his/her ministry context, both as an outsider and as a member of the community. That dual role and dual perspective can bring creative tension and help within the community.

> **Recommendation: Equip emerging leaders with interpretive skills.**

Communicational Skills

A second set of skills required for anyone in ministry is communicational skills. They must fit one's status, role, and type of leadership. One should have the appropriate communicational skills for the interpersonal, the organizational, and the extra-organizational relationships that are required in a particular kind of ministry or type of leadership. These general ministry skills again are highly affected by the context and by the people with whom the emerging leader is working.

It is unlikely that appropriate skills for ministry can be developed effectively outside of the ministry context. "Generically" developed skills in other contexts will only fit "generically."

> **Recommendation: Equip emerging leaders with communicational skills.**

Team Building Skills

Urban ministries nearly always involve a team comprised of people with different gifts, different levels of experience, different levels of spiritual maturity, and differences in perspective as to how the ministries are to be done. The more people who are involved, the greater the need for the development of team building. The negative effects of spiritual warfare can nearly always be seen in the weaknesses of a team. When the diversity of the team is not brought together to function in harmony toward a common purpose, the team will move toward dysfunctionality and dissolution. Emerging leaders need to be taught the basic skills of team building.

> **Recommendation: Equip leaders to build ministry teams.**

Spiritual Warfare Skills

Describing the full range of skills needed for spiritual warfare goes beyond the scope of this book, as do the full descriptions of the interpretive, team building, and communicational skills. However, the previous skills are foundational to spiritual warfare skills. Some skills to be developed include "how to's" in each of the following arenas: intercessory prayer, deliverance from demonization, "strategic" level prayer, discernment of evidence of spiritual warfare, spiritual mapping of local urban structures and geographical areas of ministry, personal spiritual and ministry formation, worship, meditation, fasting, "putting on the armor" (cf. Eph. 6:10–20), and demonstrating obedience without complaint (cf. Jude 11). Dawson suggests worship is the point of beginning in spiritual warfare, but that "opposite behavior—murmuring and complaining—is a sin that God will not tolerate. Such conduct poisons the atmosphere, robs others of their faith and produces death and defeat."[21]

McClung provides a description of the foundations of equipping for spiritual warfare:

> Spiritual warfare can never be divorced from the basics of trusting in the Lord Jesus Christ for salvation, living a holy life, applying God's Word and God's character to our business dealings and relationship, fellowshiping with other believers, reading the Scriptures daily and being filled with the Holy Spirit. The spiritual armor for the believer that is described in Ephesians 6 speaks to the importance of a right relationship with the Lord and others. Unless our minds are protected with the helmet of salvation, our hearts covered with the breastplate of righteousness, our innermost beings girded with truth, our feet prepared to bring the Gospel of peace to others, and unless we hold up the shield of faith with which we quench the accusations and attacks of the enemy, we are vulnerable.[22]

Recommendation: Equip emerging leaders with the essential skills for spiritual warfare.

Strategic Skills for Equipping Urban Leaders

Donald A. McGavran has suggested several strategic principles for effective urban evangelism.[23] These keys to church growth not only apply to strategic planning, but to the development of leaders as well. The development of each of these skills will position the emerging leaders for significant urban ministries.

Carl George, director of the Charles E. Fuller Institute of Evangelism and Church Growth, has carried McGavran's theories even further.[24] His "metachurch theory" provides the theoretical framework for linked house churches, the equipping of a balanced leadership, and virtually unlimited growth potential. The foundational organizational structure is the cell group or "house" church. The primary leadership is found in the small group leader, that is, the lay leader, rather than the highly trained professional. The leadership development approach is on site, in service, at a convenient time, and with hands-on practical learning. The development of these skills will not only serve the evangelistic mandate, but will establish the church so that the cultural mandate can be effectively addressed as well.

"Linked House" Churches

Christians everywhere need to assemble. The reasons for assembly are clearly spelled out in the book of Acts—fellowship, breaking of bread, the apostles' doctrine, and prayer (Ac. 2:42). The writer of Hebrews (10:25) encourages, "Do not forsake the assembling of yourselves together." However, assembling presents a problem. In many cases regular assembly requires a building, and buildings cost money. How does one plant churches without buildings? Or, how does one finance the high cost of urban property and construction in an economy where inflation may run to three digits?

Many congregations have left the city centers. Many affluent people moved out to the suburbs, and so church buildings were emptied. As these church buildings were emptied, in some cases the properties were sold. In some parts of the Two-Thirds World churches have never existed in the urban centers. The loss of property, people, and support seems to make the use of private homes, store fronts, yards, public buildings, theaters, hotels, or parks a virtual necessity.

> The Church on Brady equips church planters by teaching them to establish a small group from which other small groups emerge. These small groups are linked by the emerging leader to a growing partnership. As they emerge they learn to pool their finances in a common bank account and begin to share increasingly in ministry.

Experience seems to indicate that when believers meet in nonreligious surroundings where not-yet-Christians can attend without provoking hostility or feeling threatened, and where Christians are able to conduct the services, conversions multiply, and new neighborhoods are penetrated with the gospel. Once again the house church movement is being seen as having great potential, not only in the West but in the rest of the world as well.

However, small independent congregations find it difficult to survive the pressures of the city. When they are linked integrally with others, their potential for multiplication rises geometrically. For example, in the Vision of the Future Church in Argentina, the focus is on cell groups. In Korea the Yoido Full Gospel Church links more than 50,000 small cell groups to form one large congregation. The training focus is on the equipping of leaders for small linked house churches.

> **Recommendation: Equip emerging leaders to link other house church leaders.**

Develop Unpaid Lay Leaders

Monte Sahlin suggests that the leaders of growing urban churches lead by example as they equip other leaders. Sahlin emphasizes that the pastor gathers the small

> The CCCMTI provides the majority of its training programs for unpaid or volunteer leaders.

proportion of the church membership that is ready to make a commitment and encourage them to a high level of participation. The emphasis here is on the development of local leaders."[25]

No Nazarene work existed in New Delhi five years ago. A layperson began a small group ministry in that city. Today, over thirty small groups exist all over the city. All of them are led by lay people.

The Church on Brady has built a church of six hundred on lay leadership. They consciously shepherd these men and women through several levels of leadership development. Using primarily the small group concept, the church, in addition to its own growth, has planted more than thirty churches in the Los Angeles area and also trained and sent missionaries to at least five world areas.

Korean church growth is based in the cities and has spread into the rural areas using lay leadership and small group concepts. The same is true of Latin American churches.

Luz de Cristo, a charismatic renewal ministry to recent Hispanic immigrant groups, relies entirely on their own leadership. They have the only two-year Bible Training Institute in California, which is exclusively for students who have an average education level of third to fourth grade. The Institute trains both in biblical knowledge and practical ministry skills. With a senior pastor who has an M.Div. and two assistants, this ministry is equally divided between evangelism and social responsibility ministries.

Using the leadership typology described above, the greatest priority for leadership development is for Type I leaders. Type I leaders lead small groups. Type I leaders lead house churches. They can be equipped effectively using a combination of inexpensive informal, and nonformal means.

The second priority for developing unpaid lay leaders is for Type II leaders. Type II leaders are the leadership links among the "linked house churches" or small groups. Type II leaders typically do not need formal education, but can be multiplied through nonformal means.

> **Recommendation: Equip and orient emerging leaders to develop Types I and II leaders.**

Train for Discernment

As Types III, IV, and V leaders are equipped to work in the city, they need to understand the city. The city is a mosaic of cultural groups. Some pieces of the mosaic are more receptive than others. Campus Crusade found that its ministry in West Berlin was not bearing fruit. They commissioned a few students, who were social scientists, to do a study on which students were more responsive to the gospel. Their findings were that natural science students tended to be more open than their social science counterparts. As a result, they began to focus their efforts in the universities specializing in the natural sciences. The ministry flourished.

Types III, IV, and V leaders should be trained to discern the difference between resistant pieces of the mosaic and responsive parts of the mosaic. As they understand who is responsive, then the Types

> LMI in Lima has developed its whole strategy utilizing the principle of reaching the responsive first and then moving out from them to other segments of the population.

I and II leaders can be encouraged to focus their resources among the responsive peoples. As they identify those parts of the population who are resistant, different strategies for communicating the gospel can be designed to attract them to the good news of Jesus Christ.

Kingdom work exacts a heavy price when ministry in the city concentrates its energy on unresponsive people. Workers become discouraged; God's financial resources are wasted; and even worse, people whom God has prepared to receive the gospel go unevangelized. One key question for identifying probable responsiveness is, "Where is social change occurring most intensely?"

A tremendous influx of Armenian immigrants from both Lebanon and Soviet Armenia has come to Southern California. Experience has shown that the Soviets are more responsive than their more secularized-westernized Lebanese counterparts. The Armenian Bible College took on the project of evangelizing the Soviet Armenian immigrants in Southern California, and within a few months had as many as 200 people in their services.

Discernment of the level of receptivity is one key training issue for emerging leaders. However, learning how to discern the ways the emerging leaders' followers will fit into their contexts is another important training issue. Every type of leader needs to be equipped to be discerning. However, the issues to be discerned for each type of leader requires different kinds of attention and training.

Table Four shows some of the discernment related contrasts for training. (See p. 235).

Training for discernment aims at providing the critical understandings needed of the ministry context, of the people who are to be led, and of God's will in that situation. This training then seeks to equip emerging leaders for the prophetic function of interpreting God's will in a specific situation from a kingdom perspective. It should fit in the present and provide clear, valid, and reliable guidance into the future. "Trust in the Lord with all your heart, and lean not on you understanding; in all your ways acknowledge Him, and He shall direct your paths" (Pro. 3:5–6).

Recommendation: Train emerging leaders to be discerning and to equip others to be discerning.

Equip For Communications Specificity

People worship best and receive the gospel by faith most readily in the language and culture which are closest to their heart. The present tremendous influx of peoples into urban centers of the world is presenting one of the greatest challenges the Church has ever faced. Such immigration brings unbelievable change. In the US alone every year more than 600,000 people now arrive legally, and more than 400,000 enter illegally. These people have to live somewhere. They move into our neighborhoods, or they move into someone else's neighborhood, and those displaced people move into our neighborhood. The pluralistic society affects every person. The impact is almost entirely urban.

> The Church on Brady equips people within the context in the language in which they will be serving.
>
> The Bresee Institute serves as the training arm for the First Church of the Nazarene in Los Angeles, which has four different ethnic congregations who "equally" comprise that church.

76 Communicationally Specific

To communicate effectively, specific communication strategies must be designed. These strategies must address cultural differences, language

TABLE FOUR
TRAINING FOR DISCERNMENT

Type I	Type II	Type III	Type IV	Type V
How to discern interpersonal relationships and communications within a given small group in a specific subculture. Leader should be an insider in that subculture.	How to discern interpersonal relations and inter-group relations. How to discern community functions so that small groups may be linked together. How to discern whether a small group is in a responsive situation or a resistant situation. How to discern the difference between inappropriate methods with little response and resistance. This leader should be a subcultural insider with some experience outside of that subculture.	How to discern so as to facilitate multiple small group cohesiveness both biblically appropriate and culturally acceptable without "suboptimizing," i.e., giving preferential treatment to any particular small group. How to discern which parts of a given community or subculture are most receptive. How to discern the training needs of Type I leaders. This kind of leader should be a subcultural insider with wide experience within the broader culture.	How to discern the implications of situational traits for local strategic planning. How to discern the training needs of Type II leaders. How to discern the overall leadership balance in a large congregation or region and the steps needed to optimize that balance. This person should be familiar with the diversity of cultures within the region.	How to discern the training needs of Types III and IV leaders. How to discern the events and trends for receptivity in new unreached regions. How to discern what would be appropriate strategies for ministries in new regions or cultures. This person should be able to strategize or evaluate strategies designed for new cultural groups on the basis of potential effectiveness. This person may or may not be an insider.

differences, and worldview differences. While not prescribing homogeneous unit churches as the perpetual ideal, churches that are contextually
appropriate will win the hearts and minds of people. These churches and
Christians can then be led out of a narrow ethnicity to accept each other as
brothers and sisters in the Lord.

Specific equipping for specific ethnic groups requires working in an
"incarnational" way. Learning about people is not the same as learning to
work from within with those people.

> **Recommendation: Train leaders to communi-
> cate to specific groups with a receptor
> orientation.**

Equip to Surmount the Property Barrier

Several viable reproducible models exist for providing meeting places in
urban areas. Whether the strategy is the formation of many small house
churches or multiple large congregations, the leaders need to be equipped
for that specific strategy. Specific skills and attitudes will differ among the
various strategies.

Existing facilities may be
used by multiple congregations, as
is seen with the First Church of
the Nazarene in Los Angeles or the
Anglican Church in Juba, Sudan
where five congregations who
speak different languages comprise one "local church" and share
the same building. Congregations
may join together to provide property and build buildings for new

> LMI trains leaders to go beyond self sup-
> port to the support of the purchase of
> property and the provision of buildings for
> other churches.
>
> The Church on Brady teaches leaders how
> to start house churches without outside
> support.

77 Addressing Urban Property
Needs

congregations, as is seen in the LMI strategies in Lima, Peru. Cell groups
may be linked into a large congregation which meets in rented facilities,
such as a sports arena or theater, as demonstrated by the Boston Church of
Christ or the Vision of the Future Church in Argentina or Christ's Church
of the Valley in Phoenix, Arizona. Congregations may also combine the use
of a central campus with the use of nearby homes and rented theaters as
Christ's Church of the Valley in West Covina, California does. Other
churches convert their campus office space to educational or meeting space
and rent off-campus office space. An Assembly of God Church in downtown Nairobi rented hotel banquet rooms on Sunday morning for space.

Some smaller urban churches have taken the initiative to rent space from older declining churches.

This need for a place to meet regularly makes the use of private homes, storefronts, yards, or parks a virtual necessity in the city. In the Southern California climate, Scott Chamberlain, pastor of a church on the border of skid row has been able to take the church to the park. They minister to the homeless and the skid row people where they live. The important thing is to have a regular place for worship where all can attend conveniently.

Conversions multiply and new neighborhoods are penetrated with the gospel when several basic conditions are met for the location: 1) Where groups of believers meet in natural-neutral urban surroundings, 2) when they meet in places where people who are not yet Christians can attend without provoking hostility, 3) when they meet without feeling threatened, 4) where lay Christians are able to conduct the services, and, 5) where the people being served can have easy access.

House churches probably will be the most common organizational form in which Christianity grows in Two-Thirds World cities for the remainder of this century. Whether temporary or long range, house churches are a vital part of nearly every successful urban strategy around the world, including cities in Latin America, Africa, and Asia.

> **Recommendation: Equip leaders to surmount the property barrier.**

Equip to Communicate Commitment

Each of the ministry equipping models presented in this book present Jesus Christ as the central person and the message of salvation. Churches of fervent faith (conviction, commitment, confidence) make cities tremble and nations know that Christ is Lord. The city-conquering churches of the first centuries were churches that believed that Jesus was Lord and were willing to seal their belief with their lives. Their intense conviction, confidence, and commitment appealed to the peoples of the cities in that time. The same is true today.

Commitment, conviction, confidence, faith—these are the cornerstone of effective leadership. Leaders communicate this faith by demonstration, more than by exhortation. Modeled commitment motivates faith.

> **Recommendation: Equip leaders to communicate commitment.**

Provide a Theological Base for a Just Society

The Harambee Center addresses the issues of justice in all of its programs, whether in job training for single mothers or seminars for local community leaders.

McGavran asserts that Christianity provides the perfect base for the emerging masses.[26] Indeed, the only place where common people dare hope for justice has been the Christian faith.

In the city, as nowhere else, the church must articulate biblical answers to the burning social questions raised by members of different segments of the society. If we fail in the urban arena, we shall have failed indeed.

> **Recommendation: Provide a solid biblical theological base for wholistic ministry for the leaders.**

Intercession

Equipping emerging leaders to intercede not only for their ministries but for the people they will equip as leaders remains a high priority. Dawson, emphasizing the importance of intercession for the people one would lead, shows that intercession was the first of six responsibilities Jethro taught Moses.[27]

Spiritual leaders today continue to have a "priestly" responsibility. Even biblical leaders who were not priests demonstrated this critically important mediation role with God; consider Abraham, Moses, Daniel, Nehemiah, Jesus, and Paul. Intercession releases God's power to influence individuals as wells as the principalities and powers.

McClung writes, "The most powerful influence the Church can have on society is through prayer. But without a biblical perspective on the city, our prayers will be filled with unbelief."[28]

> **Recommendation: Train emerging leaders to intercede for everyone their ministries may influence.**

Being Issues

Two different sets of perspectives combine to form the basis for this section: learning in the affective domain and spiritual formation. The formation of one's attitude actually moves into worldview change. Krawthwol's taxonomy[29] clearly delineates the process and extent of conversion required in the affective domain for one to function well in a metro setting. Another way of looking at "being" issues centers around the issue of spiritual formation and ministry maturity. Clinton's *The Making of a Leader*[30] and *Leadership Emergence Theory*[31] provide a clear research base from which to evaluate one's spiritual and ministry maturity. His generalized "timeline" provides a means by which to assess a person's stage of maturation. With each period in a person's life certain kinds of "process items" or learning experiences can generally be expected. For the person who is concerned about the development of leaders, some of these kinds of learning experiences may be either designed or facilitated. Kraft's perspective on Christian encounters[32] also contributes to the formation of character and commitment. Samaan's biblical analogies and metaphors provide a rich picture of the means, content, and results of spiritual formation.[33]

The quality of a person's relationship with God and an obedient learning posture before Him provide the bases for empowerment to engage the enemy. A mature relationship with God positions a person to confront not only individuals with the good news of the gospel, but to confront the economic, political, and religious systems of the city as well.

> To confront the systems at any level which promises change means that, unavoidably, one is confronting the principalities and powers of that city. That means spiritual warfare!

> Essential to that spiritual warfare needs to be our recognition that the principalities and powers, sensing their exposure by and consequent vulnerability before the church, will attack us with all the forces at their disposal. The principalities will always choose to attach us at our most vulnerable point. That most vulnerable point for most urban Christians is our capacity to sustain ourselves in ministry. To remain optimistic, hopeful, and full of humor is the most difficult task in urban ministry. Thus the principalities will seek to make us feel overwhelmed, exhausted, and pessimistic about what the church actually can accomplish against the systems and structures. Once our hope has been destroyed, we have been destroyed![34]

God will continually renew our hope if we remain close to Him in our inmost being. Our hope will also be renewed as we work with other Christians in unity.

> The battle of our city is a battle between God and Satan for the soul of our city. Precisely because it is a spiritual warfare, because we Christians are the only ones who understand that warfare for what it is, and because we Christians are caught in the center of that warfare when we choose to minister responsibly in the city, the principalities and powers chose to attack us at our most vulnerable point. We urban Christians are most vulnerable in sustaining ourselves in ministry.[35]

Affective Development

Krawthwol lists five affective stages that can be applied to the formation of an urban leader in a new context. Because of prior experience a person may be found at any point and needing to progress through the succeeding stages. But assuming that one is an outsider to a situation, he/she can expect to go through all five developmental stages. One may be subverted, diverted, or interrupted at any stage. However, anything less than reaching the fifth stage will be less than satisfactory to the people who live within the ministry context.

Krawthwol's five affective stages are listed as follows:

1) Receiving

The person must be willing to listen, read, observe, and/or otherwise receive information about the people and ministry situation. Without being open to listen and learn, no progress, no adjustment, and no relationships will emerge.

> The Bresee Institute will take learners for an "urban plunge" to allow them to receive new impressions of the city.

78 Attitude of Receiving

2) Responding

The second stage is an active response to what is being perceived. In some cases this response may be contextually inappropriate, but no correction is possible until an active response is evident.

> After an "urban plunge" time is structured to reflect and elicit responses among the Bresee students.

79 Eliciting Response

3) Valuing

If the response is favorable, the person who continues to receive and respond may come to value that which is new. One may come to say that the perspective of the city dweller is valid and good.

> In the Bresee Institute as people continue to reflect, they are encouraged to look for the good and the valuable aspects of the context.

80 Forming "Valuation"

4) Organizing

At this point the person consciously acts on the basis of the new values. A *conscious* reordering of actions and attitudes occurs.

> After the students have been in the program at the Bresee Institute for a while, they are expected to begin to act appropriately and to reorder their behavior to fit the situation.

81 Organizing around Value

5) Changing Worldview

At this point one is working out of an insider's perspective where the values have been assumed and internalized. To a certain extent, this is a worldview change. This new worldview forms the unexpressed base of action.

> The intention for Bresee graduates is that they will habitually see the city with new eyes—eyes that interpret the situation in terms of ministry opportunities and a commitment to that ministry.
>
> **82** Behaving out of New Worldview

The focus on the person (being) not only focuses on worldview change, but also on the specific shape of that conversion. One is expected to be "transformed by the renewing of his/her mind" (Ro. 12:1–3). The formation of one's character (cf. Ro. 5) to be "Christlike" is an active goal of leadership developers for spiritual formation.

> **Recommendation: Equip leaders with a view to transforming their worldview.**

Spiritual and Ministry Formation

Some specific information will be needed in the process of spiritual formation. In addition to the mastery of information which contributes to an understanding of the truth, other encounters are also expected. Allegiance or commitment encounters which lead toward a heightened personal relationship are also required for the emerging leader. Clinton refers to these kinds of encounters which occur frequently in the life of an emerging leaders as "integrity process items." These encounters test the heart's intent and lead toward commitment. Power encounters which free the individual from spiritual enslavement may also be needed.

Samaan writes,

> There is no set discipline or means which automatically accomplishes spiritual formation. A means is useful only if it helps a believer reach his/her potential in Christ. Methods should be appropriate to one's character, culture, calling, and circumstance.[36]

Linthicum adds, "The task of spiritual disciplines is to turn, to enrich and make fecund the soil of our lives so that, as Christ does His work in us, we will be receptive people in whom God's presence can spring up into an abundant harvest."[37]

The methods for addressing spiritual formation may be suggested from the metaphors which are used in the Scriptures. Samaan writes,

Different metaphors are appropriate for each of the arenas [of spiritual formation]. For example the metaphors: disciple, soldier, journey, and athlete hold special insights for small groups. The metaphors: growth, journey, and suffering servant are appropriate to the individual. The metaphors: learner, disciple, friend, medicine, and holy person apply to a one-on-one relationship. The metaphors: servant, holy person, and growth are appropriate to the corporate Body of Christ. And finally, the metaphors: ambassador, servant, holy person, and soldier apply to the relationship of the Christian to his/her world.[38]

Recommendation: Intentionally focus on the spiritual formation of emerging leaders.

Recommendation: Equip emerging leaders to address spiritual formation among the people with whom they serve.

Equip Lasting Leaders

The goal of equipping leaders for urban ministries must be leaders who will serve faithfully and effectively for a lifetime. One of the serious problems facing urban ministries today is the high dropout rate. The whole leadership development program training should be designed to put people on a track which will see them finish well after a lifetime of service. Many Bible college and seminary graduates drop out of effective leadership, not because God has called them elsewhere, but because of serious problems in their ministries which could have been addressed developmentally early in their ministry formation.

The characteristics of leaders who finish well has been the subject of extended study.[39] These issues can and should be addressed developmentally in our curricula and modeled by those who would presume to participate in the equipping of others.

J. Robert Clinton describes leaders who last:

a. They maintain a personal vibrant relationship with God right up to the end.
b. They maintain a learning posture and can learn from various kinds of sources—life especially.
c. They evidence Christlikeness in character.
d. Truth is lived out in their lives so that convictions and promises of God are seen to be real.
e. They leave behind one or more ultimate contributions [as saint, stylistic practitioner, mentor, public rhetorician, pioneer, crusader, artist, founder, stabilizer, researcher, writer or promoter].

      f. They walk with a growing awareness of a sense of destiny and
see some or all of it fulfilled.[40]

While these may not be all the characteristics of leaders who finish
their ministries well, this list provides a means of reflection for people who
would design leadership development programs. During the early formative time of a person's ministry development, it is important to develop a
mental picture of what a Christian leader is like. During this formative period an emerging leader can be challenged to set his/her life goal on being
faithful to the end. During the time of high idealism in younger emerging
leaders, older leaders can help them develop these habits which will not
only shape their ministries for effective service, but will position them for
a lifetime of service. No one sets out to fail. However, some, without planning ahead, begin destructive habits early in their ministries. The wise
older leader will help emerging leaders develop habits and perspectives that
will serve for a lifetime.

> **Recommendation: Develop leaders who are
> committed to remain faithful to the end of
> their lives.**

Equip Visionary Transformational Leaders

What is needed now in urban ministries are visionary transformational leaders who will take advantage of the era in which they live. The Church des-
perately needs visionary leaders who can and will lead through the maze of
obstacles facing the church today in the cities of the world. The Church needs
transformational leaders who will change the whole context of ministry.

The writer of Hebrews helps us understand the kind of person who is
needed. This vision is described as faith: "Now faith is being sure of what
we hope for and certain of what we do not see" (He. 11:1). After presenting a long list of visionary men and women who demonstrated their faith,
the writer of Hebrews writes, "Remember your leaders, who spoke the
word of God to you. Consider the outcome of their way of life and **imi-
tate their faith.**" (He. 13:7).

Visionary leaders anchor their hope in the coming kingdom while act-
ing responsibly as citizens and ambassadors of the kingdom now. The kingdom will be consummated in the future, but we can act now out of the
knowledge of what that future will be. Urban leaders are to act in the present as citizens, ambassadors, and agents of that kingdom. Visionary leaders
act in the present out of a future perspective.

Vision is the perspective that Moses had when he stretched out his hand over the Red Sea. Vision is the perspective that Joshua had when he began leading the march around the city of Jericho. Vision views God as able to save to the uttermost those who believe; to deliver from the most difficult situation—as the three were delivered from the fire; to provide all of the resources needed even in the midst of hardship; to present us fault-less before his glory with great joy.

Vision anchors hope in the future. Again, the writer of Hebrews helps us understand: "We have this hope as an anchor for the soul, firm and se-cure. It enters the inner sanctuary behind the curtain, where Jesus, who went before us, has entered on our behalf. He has become a high priest for-ever, in the order of Melchizedek" (He. 6:19–20). The picture of an anchor here is used for steerage through a channel where the currents or the wind threaten the ship's survival. Christ as an "anchor for the soul" provides that point in the "inner sanctuary" toward which we are guided into the future. Vision is linked to a living person who speaks and acts for us—Jesus. Vi-sion is hope.[41]

> Vision is the internal force that guides an individual through unforeseen difficul-ties or stimulates a person to act when he is too tired or too ambivalent to take the next step toward reaching the goal. Vision is the characteristic that is the re-sponsibility of a leader and sets the leader apart from his followers.[42]

> Vision is not so much *what* you think as *how* you think. Vision is less a matter of content than of process. It is thinking in a very special way, tuning your mind. Vision is moving away from micro-management, from 'flyspeck man-agement,' to macro-leadership. Vision is not necessarily having a plan, but hav-ing a mind that always plans.[43]

> . . . the vision articulates a view of a realistic, credible, attractive future for the organization, a condition that is better in some important ways than what now exists."[44]

A leader's vision functions to provide the means of organizing infor-mation into a meaningful perspective, thus integrating the mission with existing opportunities. It serves as a base for formulating a plan of action, and as a filter for evaluating feedback.[45] Vision serves to enhance the lead-ership potential of a leader by producing a strong future orientation, en-hancing optimism, nurturing creativity, building on assets, attracting and motivating new participants, and meeting unmet needs.[46] Vision will help the leader by giving a sense of direction, providing a base to evaluate pro-gress, avoiding needless conflict and duplication of effort, and helping him/ her change the focus of the group off of activities and onto outcomes.[47]

Leaders without vision are reactive frequently doubting themselves, quick to blame others. They follow fads without passion. They seldom take personal risk. Often leaders without vision take care of their own perks, status, and titles as they protect their own turf. They focus on their status more than their role, preferring to be served above serving. They delegate without participation. They act out of a "Scarcity Paradigm;" that is, they do not believe that others can be empowered on a win-win basis or that success can come without someone else having to fail. They think "win-lose." They fear failure. They focus on problems and the past. They emphasize remediation while trying to cut costs. They often produce frustration stimulated goals. When criticized they respond with self-justification. They seek to be understood rather than to understand others. Unfortunately, they work with no clear end in mind. They often fear change and avoid improvement.[48]

Visionary leaders, on the other hand, make their vision simple and understandable for followers. They show the vision's compatibility with the followers. They make it observable as they show the vision's advantage for the followers. They always communicate the vision "in a hundred ways a thousand times." They encourage questions. Visionary leaders use clear, direct, strong, simple, suitable, specific, unexpected language with a focus on the future. They focus on possibilities and opportunities. They take risks as they build other people. They think "win-win" as they test for understanding and acceptance. They give attention to understanding before seeking to be understood. They are noted for their passion as they think beyond the present situation and followers to broader contexts and to the future. They give attention to the formation of character knowing that both trustworthiness and competence are expected by people who would follow them into new ways. They are sure of what they hope for and certain of what they do not yet see.

Visionary leaders transform their situations. They bring change, not only in their immediate followers, but in the broader situation as well. They are often willing to use unconventional strategies.

Visionary transformational leaders accurately assess the situation both of the followers and the broader context where they function. They give time to discernment and understanding the situation where they serve. They communicate self-confidence with conviction. Paul wrote, "I am convinced that . . ." (Ro. 8:38–39). Peter said, "There is no other name . . ." (Ac. 4:12).

Transformational leaders use power appropriately. They will be viewed as transformational if they use of all three kinds of power (personal, positional, spiritual) for the followers and the good of the broad situation to accomplish God's purposes, rather than for personal benefit.

Transformational leaders motivate toward revealed values such as unity in the faith, mature Christlikeness. They consistently exhibit integrity, and behave in loving ways. They motivate toward commitment, regardless of whether the effects immediately benefit the followers.

Transformational leaders move beyond mere exchange or transactional leadership to changing the favorability of the situation. They do not just lead for the benefits they receive (e.g., power, money, pride, position, organizational results) (cf. 1 Pe. 5:1–5). They seek to influence, not for personal benefit, but as servants of the Lord whose purpose is higher.

Visionary or transformational leaders move beyond the immediate context to address the larger frames of reference. Transformational leaders realize that the broader cultural issues which affect their followers must be addressed over the long term for lasting effectiveness.

Transformational or visionary leaders look from a multigenerational time perspective. They act from a future perspective with the vision ever before them. Rather than reacting to the aftermath of a problem they act in the "beforemath;"[49] that is, they act now as if the future were already realized. They address this multigenerational perspective by shaping their organizational culture and influencing the broader culture.

They address long term and multigenerational transformational change in their situation in several ways. They give attention to their priorities with the group. People know these priorities by what the leaders praise, plan, inquire about, measure, criticize, monitor, evaluate, and otherwise attend to.

The transformational leader's reaction to crisis provides a clear picture of the undergirding values and priorities. Crises will occur and transformational leaders will face them head on.

They provide the key role models of what the followers are not only to do, but what they are to become. Transformational leaders communicate values and expectations by their own actions and attitudes. The Apostle Paul writes six times "Look at me. Follow my example." They model integrated integrity.

Transformational leaders will participate in the allocation of rewards in the groups they lead. These rewards are not just monetary, but include praise, encouragement, and recognition. The withholding of rewards demonstrates what is not acceptable, and serves to discourage certain actions, and bringing negative reinforcement.

They help set the criteria for selection and dismissal. Long term change is affected by the selection of leaders and the dismissal of people who are dysfunctional. Transformational leaders will engage in the structuring of the criteria for these changes.

They will attend to designing organizational structures so they empower others. The organizational structures along with their policies and procedures will be changed over time to reflect the values of the leader. They will participate in the formation of formal statements such as creeds, charters, brochures, and bylaws. Even the physical facilities will not escape the attention of a true transformational leader. As they remain with the group they will help shape its hope for the future by telling and retelling stories, legends, and myths of the group.[50]

A major part of the task for urban ministries must be seen as equipping *visionary* leaders. Existing leaders begin equipping by *personally modeling* visionary leadership. The description of visionary leadership applies to educators as well as to the people who would equipped to lead in urban ministries. They can be equipped as visionary leaders by helping them develop a vision. A theological perspective of hope in which God is both able and willing to act in the present is critical for today's cities. They can be helped by developing a kingdom perspective which has both present and future implications. It is in a very real sense a "Back to the Future" perspective.

Existing leaders and educators can help emerging leaders to become visionary by expecting, entrusting, empowering them to address that vision. We begin by providing the conditions of empowerment for the learners within the institution as the institution becomes a model of empowerment.

Remember that empowerment requires the establishing of three critical relationships—with God, with others, and with the social organizations in which people serve. Begin with a focus on spiritual formation and helping people develop personal growth relationships with God through Christ.

Existing leaders will help them establish win-win agreements and structures both with individuals and the social systems in which they will lead. Again, existing leaders will take responsibility to help establish helpful structures and systems with the person being served in mind rather than the institution. Equippers continue by helping them to establish and practice "self-supervision" in a spirit of high accountability.

Existing leaders will continue to empower by giving opportunities for the emerging leaders to do important work on crucial tasks; providing the resources they need; allowing them discretion over the use of those resources. Empowerment is enhanced by helping to build key relationships for them with mentors. Recognition of their growing accomplishments provides encouragement and further empowerment. Finally, existing leaders can assist in the equipping of visionary leaders by consciously changing their relational status from superior instructors to peer participants in the cause.

Visionary and transformational leaders cannot be "trained," but they can be developed as others are willing to build expectations, hope and faith. They can be developed as existing leaders assist in the development of those key empowering relationships. They can be developed as they have an increasingly clear view of the future.

Recommendation: Equip visionary transformational leaders.

Summary

Effective ministry or leadership over the long term flows out of who the person is, not just what he/she knows or can do. Integrity emerges out of consistency of character, not out of the rehearsal of information or skills. One cannot expect to be effective in spiritual warfare if one's own spiritual maturity is not being continually transformed by the Spirit of God.

One may fail to master any particular fact or skill, but a failure in one's character will destroy potential for influence in the Christian community and even more so in the non-Christian community. Spiritual authority and ministry maturity relate closely to the emergence of character.

The Lord uses a wide range of learning experiences over time to shape the person. These experiences may be expected to have continuity (recurring themes), sequence (every pressing one toward the more demanding and difficult) and integration. Over time the experiences fit together in wholistic patterns related to ministry formation and around one's gifts and calling. One can expect the Lord to work in every circumstance for good (Ro. 8:28) if one is faithful

Personal spiritual disciplines focusing on trust and obedience facilitate this spiritual growth. Prayer, meditation, Bible study, worship, praise, witnessing, and the serving of others all contribute to growth. Faithfulness in the midst of opposition, disappointment, joy, temptation, or any other circumstance will contribute over time to spiritual maturation. Spiritual maturity may be expected, but it does not come automatically nor without significant personal cost.

Leadership is always based on relationships, including the relationship one has with God, with other people, and with the community that is to be influenced. The development of a skill base, a knowledge base, and a Christian character forms the primary prerequisites for leadership. However, leadership potential is a combination of trustworthiness and competence as perceived by the people who are to be influenced. For a person to emerge as a leader in a community, he/she must be seen by that community to be trustworthy and competent. The task of the person who is facilitating the development of another person as a leader will focus the skill, knowledge, and character development in ways which will relationally empower him/her in that setting.

Notes

1 Benjamin S. Bloom, ed., *Taxonomy of Educational Objectives: The Classification of Educational Goals Handbook I: Cognitive Domain* (New York: Longman, Inc., 1956), pp. 201–207.

1.00 Knowledge
1.10 Knowledge of specifics
1.11 Knowledge of terminology
1.12 Knowledge of specific facts
1.20 Knowledge of ways and means of dealing with specifics
1.21 Knowledge of conventions
1.22 Knowledge of trends and sequences
1.23 Knowledge of classifications and categories
1.24 Knowledge of criteria
1.25 Knowledge of methodology
1.30 Knowledge of universals and abstractions of a field
1.31 Knowledge of principles and generalizations
1.32 Knowledge of theories and structures

2.00 Comprehension
2.10 Translation
2.20 Interpretation
2.30 Extrapolation

3.00 Application

4.00 Analysis
4.10 Analysis of elements
4.20 Analyses of relationships
4.30 Analysis of organizational principles

5.00 Synthesis
5.10 Production of a unique communication
5.20 Production of a plan, or proposed set of operations
5.30 Derivation of a set of abstract relations

6.00 Evaluation
6.10 Judgments in terms of internal evidence
6.20 Judgments in terms of external criteria

2 Jesus Christ confronts Satan

Concerning power resulting in power encounters to release people from Satanic captivity and bring them into freedom in Christ.

Concerning allegiance resulting in allegiance encounters to rescue people from wrong allegiances and bring them into relationship with Jesus Christ.

Concerning truth resulting in truth encounters to counter error and bring people to correct understandings (Charles H. Kraft, "Encounters for Christian Witness," *Evangelical Missions Quarterly* 27 (1991): 258–265.

3 Ibid.

4 Ibid.

5 Raymond J. Bakke, *The Urban Christian: Effective Ministry in Today's Urban World* (Downers Grove, IL: InterVarsity Press, 1987), pp. 52–53.

6 Ibid.

7 John Dawson, *Taking Our Cities for God: How to Break Spiritual Strongholds* (Lake Mary, FL: Creation House, 1989), p. 116.

8 Ibid, p. 86.

9 1) What place does your city have in this nation's history?
   2) Was there ever the imposition of a new culture or language through conquest?
   3) What were the religious practices of ancient peoples on the site?
   4) Was there a time when a new religion emerged?
   5) Under what circumstances did the gospel first enter the city?
   6) Has the national or city government ever disintegrated?
   7) What has been the leadership style of past governments?
   8) Have there ever been wars that affected this city? *wars of conquest * wars of resistance to invasion or * civil war
   9) Was the city itself the site of a battle?
   10) What names have been used to label the city, and what are their meanings?
   11) Why was the city originally settled?
   12) Did the city have a founder? What was his dream?
   13) As political, military, and religious leaders have emerged, what did they dream for themselves and for the city?
   14) What political, economic, and religious institutions have dominated the life of the city?
   15) What has been the experience of immigrants to the city?
   16) Have there been any traumatic experiences such as economic collapse, race riots, or an earthquake?

17) Did the city ever experience the birth of a socially transforming technology?
18) has there ever been the sudden opportunity to create wealth such as the discovery of oil or a new irrigation technology?
19) Has there ever been religious conflict among competing religions or among Christians?
20) What is the history of relationships among the races (Dawson, p. 85)?

[10]   Dawson, p. 85.

[11]   1.   What are the forms of emperor worship to which you believe your city is tempted to succumb?
2.   How does your city marry its economics, politics, and religion in order to worship its emperor? What are the results of this unholy marriage? Who in your city end up benefiting the most from this marriage? Who end up becoming its victims? Who end up being martyred?
3.   What role(s) do you see the church as institution playing in this marriage? What role(s) do you see the people of God playing?
4.   The vision for the new Jerusalem sets forth a definite quality of life for the city.
a.   If such a quality of life became the focus of your church's ministry to individuals, how would that affect your ministry?
b.   If such a quality of life because the focus of your church's ministry, how would that affect the ways your church would relate to your city's systems and structures?
c.   If such a quality of life became the focus of your church's ministry, how would that affect your perceptions of and the ways you would deal with your city's principalities and powers? Linthicum, p. 290.

[12]   Floyd McClung, *Seeing the City with the Eyes of God* (Terrytown, NY: Chosen Books, Fleming H. Revell Company, 1991), p. 30.

[13]   Dawson, pp. 156–157.

[14]   McClung, pp. 30–31.

[15]   Ibid., p. 31.

[16]   Ibid., p. 33.

[17]   Ibid., pp. 52–57.

[18]   Dawson, p. 100.

[19]   McClung, pp. 103–110.

[20]   Ibid., p. 106.

[21]   Dawson, p. 164.

[22]   McClung, p. 39.

[23]   Donald A. McGavran, *Understanding Church Growth* (Grand Rapids: William B. Eerdmans Publishing Company, 1990).

[24]   Carl George, interviewed by Edgar J. Elliston, February 22 1991.

[25]   Monte C. Sahlin, "A Study of Factors Relating to Urban Church Growth in the North American Division of Seventh Day Adventists" (n.p., 1986), p. 15.

[26]   McGavran, pp. 195–209.

[27]   Dawson, p. 205.

[28]   McClung, p. 16.

[29]   David R. Krawthwol, ed., *Taxonomy of Educational Objectives: The Classification of Educational Goals Handbook II: Affective Domain* (New York: David McKay Company, Inc., 1964).

[30]   J. Robert Clinton, *The Making of a Leader* (Colorado Springs: NavPress, 1988).

[31]   J. Robert Clinton and Katherine Haubert, *The Joshua Project: A Study in Leadership Development, Leadership Transition and Destiny Fulfillment* (Altadena, CA: Barnabas Resources, 1990).

[32]   Charles H. Kraft, "Encounters for Christian Witness."

[33]   Lynn Elizabeth Samaan, *Images of Missionary Spirituality: A Study of Spiritual Formation* (M.A. thesis, Fuller Theological Seminary, 1990).

[34]   Robert C. Linthicum, *City of God, City of Satan: A Biblical Theology of the Urban Church* (Grand Rapids: Zondervan Publishing House, 1991), p. 278.

[35]   Ibid., p. 235.

[36]   Samaan, p. 172.

[37]   Linthicum, p. 243.

[38]   Samaan, pp. 174–175.

[39]   J. Robert Clinton, *A Personal Ministry Philosophy: One Key to Effective Leadership* (Altadena, CA: Barnabas Resources, 1992).

[40]   See J. Robert Clinton's research which is in part reported in *Leadership Emergence Theory: A Self-Study Manual for Analyzing the De-*

velopment of a Christian Leader (Altadena, CA: Barnabas Resources). The research to which he refers includes directed autobiographies of about 400 international leaders, surveys of about 300 published biographies and character studies of all of the leaders of the Bible.

41 See Robert Tremaine's "Visionary Leadership" (n.p., 1991) for a review of the literature related to visionary leadership.

42 George Barna, *The Frog in the Kettle: What Christians Need to Know about Life in the Year 2000* (Ventura, CA: Regal Books, 1990), pp. 80–81.

43 Peter Koestenbaum, *Leadership: The Inner Side of Greatness: A Philosophy for Leaders* (San Francisco: Jossey-Bass Publishers, 1991), p. 84.

44 Warren Bennis and Burt Nanus, *Leaders: The Strategies for Taking Charge* (New York: Harper and Row Publishers, 1985), p. 89.

45 George Barna, *The Barna Report: What Americans Believe* (Ventura, CA: Regal Books, 1991), pp. 169–170.

46 Lyle Schaller, *The Change Agent* (Nashville: Abingdon Press, 1979), pp. 101–103.

47 Edward R. Dayton and Theodore W. Engstrom, *Strategy for Leadership* (Old Tappan, NJ: Fleming H. Revell, Co., 1979), pp. 56–58.

48 See Tremaine for a review of the literature related to visionary leadership.

49 This term, "beforemath," comes from Stanley Davis' book entitled, *Future Perfect* (Reading, MA: Addison-Wesley Publishing Company, 1987), pp. 220–228.

50 See Gary Yukl, *Leadership in Organizations*, 2nd ed. (Englewood Cliffs, NJ: Prentice Hall, 1988), pp. 210–231 for his treatment of transactional and transformational leadership. See Stephen R. Covey, *Principle-Centered Leadership* (New York: Summit Books, 1991), pp. 278–287 for another helpful treatment of transformational leadership which shows its visionary character based on a commitment to basic principles.

BIBLIOGRAPHY

Adams, Arthur Merrihew. *Effective Leadership for Today's Church.* Philadelphia: Westminster Press, 1978.

Alexander, John F. "Making People Aware," *The Urban Mission: Essays on the Building of a Comprehensive Model for Evangelical Urban Ministry.* Edited by Craig W. Ellison. Washington, D.C.: University Press of America, Inc., 1983, pp. 83–91.

Allen, Frank W. "Toward a Biblical Urban Mission," *Urban Mission* 3 (January, 1986): 6–13.

Arinze, Francis, Cardinal. "Globalization of Theological Education," *Theological Education.* 23: 1 (Autumn, 1986): 7–42.

Augsburger, Myron S. "Theological Twists," *The Urban Mission: Essays on the Building of a Comprehensive Model for Evangelical Urban Ministry.* Edited by Craig W. Ellison. Washington, D.C.: University Press of America, Inc., 1983, pp. 69–78.

Azusa Pacific University Graduate School of Theology *Catalog.* Azusa, CA: Azusa Pacific University, 1984.

Badaracco, Joseph L., Jr. and Elsworth, Richard R. *The Quest for Integrity in Leadership.* Boston: Harvard Business School Press, 1989.

Baker, Robert L. and Schutz, Richard E., eds. *Instructional Product Development.* New York: Van Nostrand Reinhold Company, 1971.

Bakke, Raymond J. "A Biblical Theology for Urban Ministry" *Metroministry.* Edited by David Frenchak. Elgin, IL: David C. Cook, 1979, pp. 12–25.

_____. "The Challenge of World Urbanization to Mission Strategy: Perspectives on Demographic Realities," *Urban Mission* 4 (September, 1986): 6–17.

_____. "The City and the Scriptures," *Christianity Today* 28: 9 (June 15, 1984): 14–17.

_____. "Faithful to the Cities of the World," *Faithful Witness: The Urbana '84 Compendium.* Edited by James McLeish. Downers Grove, IL: InterVarsity Press, 1985, pp. 88–98.

_____. "Strategy for Urban Ministry," *TSF Bulletin* 8: 4 (March–April, 1985): 20–21.

_____. "A Theology as Big as the City," *Urban Mission* 6 (May, 1989): 8–19.

_____. "Toward a Theology of the City," *Institute on the Church in Urban-Industrial Society: Occasional Papers* 7 (1977): 1–12.

_____. *The Urban Christian: Effective Ministry in Today's Urban World*. Downers Grove, IL: InterVarsity Press, 1987.

Barclay, William. *Educational Ideals in the Ancient World*. Grand Rapids: Baker Book House, 1974.

Barna, George. *The Barna Report: What Americans Believe*. Ventura, CA: Regal Books, 1991, pp. 169–170.

_____. *The Frog in the Kettle: What Christians Need to Know about Life in the Year 2000*. Ventura, CA: Regal Books, 1990, pp. 80–81.

Barrett, David. *World-Class Cities and World Evangelization*. Birmingham, AL: New Hope, 1985.

Bass, Bernard, ed. *Stogdill's Handbook of Leadership*. New York: The Free Press, 1981.

Bauer, Walter. *A Greek-English Lexicon of the New Testament and Other Early Christian Literature*. Translated and adapted by William F. Arndt and F. Wilbur Gingrich. Chicago: The University of Chicago Press, 1957.

Bellack, Arno A. and Kliebard, Herbert M., eds. *Curriculum and Evaluation*. Berkeley: McCutchen Publishing Corporation, 1977.

Benefiel, Ronald. "Multi-Congregational Structure for First Church of the Nazarene, Los Angeles, California." n.p., 1989.

_____. Transcript of interview by Timothy J. Kauffman, July 28, 1986, p. 12.

Bennett, David W. "Images of Emergent Leaders: An Analysis of Terms Used by Jesus to Describe the Twelve." n.p., March, 1990.

Bennett, Janet Marie. "Modes of Cross-Cultural Training: Conceptualizing Cross-Cultural Training as Education," *Theories and Methods in Cross-Cultural Orientation*. Edited by Judith N. Martin. Special issue of the *International Journal of Intercultural Relations*. New York: Pergamon Press, 1986, pp. 117–134.

Bennett, Milton J. "A Developmental Approach to Training for Intercultural Sensitivity," *Theories and Methods in Cross-Cultural Orientat-*

ion. Edited by Judith N. Martin. Special issue of the *International Journal of Intercultural Relations.* New York: Pergamon Press, 1986, pp. 179–196.

Bennis, Warren. *On Becoming a Leader.* Reading, MA: Addison-Wesley Publishing Company, 1989.

_____. *Why Leaders Can't Lead.* San Francisco: Jossey-Bass Publishers, 1990.

Bennis, Warren and Nanus, Burt. *Leaders: The Strategies for Taking Charge.* New York: Harper and Row Publishers, 1985.

Beukema, George G. *The Servant's Community: A Study of the Development of a Servant Style Ministry in the Inner-City.* D.Min. dissertation, Western Theological Seminary, 1982.

Bloom, Benjamin S., ed. *Taxonomy of Educational Objectives: The Classification of Educational Goals Handbook I: Cognitive Domain.* New York: Longman, Inc., 1956.

Boan, Rudee, et al. "Annotated Bibliography on the Urban Church," *Review and Expositor: A Baptist Theological Journal* 80 (Fall, 1983): 583–594.

Bonthius, Robert H. "Impact of the Urban Crisis on Pastoral Theology," *New Shape of Pastoral Theology: S. Hiltner.* Edited by W. B. Oglesby. Nashville: Abingdon Press, 1969, pp. 101–120.

Bosch, David J. *Transforming Mission: Paradigm Shifts in Theology of Mission.* Maryknoll, NY: Orbis, 1991.

Bresee Institute. "Promotional Literature." Los Angeles: Bresee Institute, n.d.

Bruce, Alexander B. *The Training of the Twelve.* Grand Rapids: Kregel Publications, 1971.

Burns, J. M. *Leadership.* New York: Harper and Row, 1978.

Callahan, Kenneth L. *Effective Church Leadership: Building on the Twelve Keys.* New York: Harper and Row, 1990.

Carroll, Jackson W. "The Professional Model of Ministry: Is It Worth Saving?" *Theological Education* 21 (Spring, 1985): 7–48.

Church on Brady. *Day of the Congregation.* Los Angeles: The Church on Brady, 1990.

Claerbaut, David. "A Theology for Ministry to the Urban Poor," *Covenant Quarterly* 38 (May, 1980): 29–37.

Developing Leaders for Urban Ministries

Clinton, J. Robert. *Leadership Emergence Patterns.* Altadena, CA: Barnabas Resources, 1986.

_____. *Leadership Emergence Theory: A Self-Study Manual for Analyzing the Development of a Christian Leader.* Altadena, CA: Barnabas Resources, 1989.

_____. *Leadership Training Models Manual.* Altadena, CA: Barnabas Resources, 1984.

_____. *The Making of a Leader.* Colorado Springs: NavPress, 1988.

_____. *A Personal Ministry Philosophy: One Key to Effective Leadership.* Altadena, CA: Barnabas Resources, 1992.

Clinton, J. Robert and Hauber, Katherine. *The Joshua Portrait: A Study in Leadership Development, Leadership Transition and Destiny Fulfillment.* Altadena, CA: Barnabas Resources, 1990.

Coe, Shoki. "Learning in Context: The Search for Innovative Patterns in Theological Education," *Theological Education Fund* 6 (1973): 195.

Conn, Harvie M. "'Any Faith Dies in the City': The Secularization Myth," *Urban Mission* 3 (May, 1986): 6–19.

_____. "Christ and the City: Biblical Themes for Building Urban Theology Models," *Discipling the City: Theological Reflections on Urban Missions.* Edited by Roger S. Greenway. Grand Rapids: Baker Book House, 1979, pp. 222–286.

_____. *A Clarified Vision for Urban Mission: Dispelling the Urban Stereotypes.* Grand Rapids: Zondervan Publishing House, 1987.

_____. "The Kingdom of God and the City of Man: A History of the City/Church Dialogue," *Discipling the City: Theological Reflections on Urban Missions.* Edited by Roger S. Greenway. Grand Rapids: Baker Book House, 1979, pp. 9–59.

_____. "Lucan Perspectives and the City," *Missiology: An International Review* 13 (October, 1985): 409–428.

_____. "The Rural-Urban Myth and World Mission," *Reformed Review* 37 (Spring, 1984): 125–136.

Conn, Harvie M. and Rowen, Samuel F., eds. *Missions and Theological Education in World Perspective.* Farmington, MI: Associates of Urbanus, 1984.

Copeland, E. Luther. "Can the City Be Saved: Toward a Biblical Urbanology," *Perspectives in Religious Studies* 4 (Spring, 1977): 14–22.

Covey, Stephen R. *Principle-Centered Leadership*. New York: Summit Books, 1991.

_____. *The Seven Habits of Highly Effective People: Restoring the Character Ethic*. New York: Simon and Schuster, 1989.

Craig, Robert L., ed. *Training and Development Handbook A Guide to Human Resource Development*, 3rd ed. New York: McGraw-Hill Book Company, 1987.

Crichton, Iain. "Empowering for Effective Urban Ministry: The Center for Urban Theological Studies—Philadelphia," *Urban Mission* 5 (November, 1987): 33–42.

Cronbach, Lee J. "Course Improvement through Evaluation," *Curriculum and Evaluation*. Edited by Arno A. Bellack and Herbert M. Kliebard. Berkeley: McCutchen Publishing Corporation, 1977, pp. 319–332.

Davis, Robert H., Alexander, Lawrence T., and Yelon, Stephen L. *Learning System Design: An Approach to the Improvement of Instruction*. New York: McGraw-Hill Book Company, 1976.

Davis, Stanley. *Future Perfect*. Reading, MA: Addison-Wesley Publishing Company, 1987.

Dawson, John. *Taking Our Cities for God: How to Break Spiritual Strongholds*. Lake Mary, FL: Creation House, 1989.

Dayton, Donald W. and Nelson, F. Burton. "The Theological Seminary and the City," *The Urban Mission: Essays on the Building of a Comprehensive Model for Evangelical Urban Ministry*. Edited by Craig W. Ellison. Washington, D.C.: University Press of America, Inc., 1983, pp. 114–121.

Dayton, Edward R. and Engstrom, Theodore W. *Strategy for Leadership*. Old Tappan, NJ: Fleming H. Revell Co., 1979, pp. 56–58.

Dearnley, Pat and Broadbent, Pete. "Jesus Christ, the Life of the City?" *Churchman: Journal of Anglican Theology* 97: 1 (1983): 41–54.

Deaton, Charles and MacCaskey, Michael. *All about Pruning*. San Francisco: Ortho Books, 1978.

Delooz, Pierre. "Pastoral Care for Supercities," *Pro Mundi Vita Bulletin* 99 (1984): 29–52.

De Pree, Max. *Leadership is an Art*. New York: Doubleday, 1989.

DeSilva, Ranjit. "CCC Schools," *Crenshaw Christian Center: Annual Report 1990*. Los Angeles: Crenshaw Christian Center, 1990.

Dressel, Paul L. and Dora, Marcus. *On Teaching and Learning in College.* San Francisco: Jossey-Bass Publishers, 1982.

Drucker, Peter. *The New Realities: In Government and Politics/In Economics and Business/In Society and World View.* New York: Harper and Row, 1989.

Dulles, Avery, reviewer. *From New Creation to Urban Crisis: A History of Action Training Ministries, 1962–1975* by George D. Younger. *Theology Today* 43: 3 (1986): 427–430.

Eames, Edwin. *Anthropology of the City.* Englewood Cliffs, NJ: Prentice Hall, 1977.

Eck, Diana L. "True Liberty Cherishes Difference," *Los Angeles Times.* July 5, 1992, p. M5.

Ellens, J. Harold. "Church and Metropolis," *Missiology: An International Review* 3 (April, 1975): 169–175.

Ellison, Craig W., ed. *The Urban Mission: Essays on the Building of a Comprehensive Model for Evangelical Urban Ministry.* Edited by Craig W. Ellison. Washington, D.C.: University Press of America, Inc., 1983.

Elliston, Edgar J. "Biblical Criteria for Christian Leadership," *Curriculum Foundations for Leadership Education in the Samburu Christian Community.* Ph.D. dissertation, Michigan State University, 1981.

_____. "Designing Leadership Education," *Missiology: An International Review* 16: 2 (April, 1988): 203–215.

_____. "Developing Christian Leaders." Address presented to the Pan-African Conference of Christian Church/Church of Christ Missionaries, Nairobi, Kenya. July, 1985, pp. 1–2.

_____. *Home Grown Leaders.* Pasadena, CA: William Carey Library, 1992.

_____. *Missions Education in Christian Church Bible Colleges.* n.p., 1988.

Elliston, Edgar J. and Smith, W. Michael. *An Outline for Program Planning and Evaluation.* n.p., 1976.

Elliston, Edgar J., ed., *Christian Relief and Development: Training Leaders for Effective Ministry.* Dallas: Word Books, 1989.

Ellul, Jacques. *The Meaning of the City.* Translated by Dennis Pardee. Grand Rapids: William B. Eerdmans Publishing Company, 1970.

Erickson, Eric. *Childhood and Society*. New York: N. W. Norton and Company, Inc., 1950.

Everist, Norma. "New Frameworks for Seminary Education," *Trinity Seminary Review* 6 (1984): 80–93.

Ferris, Robert W. *Renewal in Theological Education: Strategies for Change*. Wheaton: The Billy Graham Center, Wheaton College, 1990.

Fiedler, Fred E. *A Theory of Leadership Effectiveness*. New York: McGraw-Hill, 1967.

_____. "The Trouble with Leadership Training is that it Doesn't Train Leaders," *Leadership and Social Change*. Edited by William R. Lassey and Richard R. Fernandez. La Jolla, CA: University Associates, 1980, pp. 236–248.

Figge, Robert J., Jr. *Responsive Urban Bible Education: Formulating Objectives for Manna Bible Institute*. D.Min. dissertation. Eastern Baptist Theological Seminary, 1988.

Fischer, Claude. *The Urban Experience*. New York: Harcourt, Brace and Jovanovich, 1976.

Ford, LeRoy. *A Curriculum Design Manual for Theological Education*. Nashville: Broadman Press, 1991.

_____. "A Manual for Designing Theological Education." n.p., 1989.

Foster, Richard J. *Money, Sex and Power: The Challenge of the Disciplined Life*. Cambridge, MA: Harper and Row, 1985.

Fritz, Paul J. "Summer Urban Church-Planting Internships for Seminary Students: Nigeria," *Urban Mission* 5 (May, 1988): 38–42.

Gabler, Neal. "Moral Relativism? You Don't Get It." *Los Angeles Times*. June 14, 1992: M1.

Gangel, Kenneth O. *Leadership for Church Education*. Chicago: Moody Press, 1970.

Gemelch, George and Zenner, Walter P., eds. *Urban Life: Readings in Urban Anthropology*. Prospect Heights, IL: Waveland Press, 1988.

George, Carl. Interviewed by Edgar J. Elliston, February 22, 1991.

Gerber, Virgil. *Discipling through Theological Education by Extension*. Chicago: Moody Press, 1980.

Gilliland, Dean S., ed. "Contextual Theology as Incarnational Ministry," *The Word among Us: Contextualizing Theology for Mission Today.* Dallas: Word Books, Inc., 1989, pp. 9–31.

Glasser, Arthur. "Confession, Church Growth, and Authentic Unity in Mission Strategy," *Protestant Cross-Currents in Mission.* Edited by Norman Horner Nashville: Abingdon Press, 1968, pp. 178–222.

_____. Syllabus: "Theology of Mission." Pasadena: Fuller Theological Seminary, 1989.

Goldingay, John. "The Bible in the City," *Theology* 92 (1989): 5–15.

Goodenough, Ward Hunt. *Cooperation in Change: An Anthropological Approach to Community Development.* New York: John Wiley and Sons, Inc., 1966.

Greenslade, Philip. *Leadership, Greatness and Servanthood.* Minneapolis: Bethany House Publishers, 1984.

Greenway, Roger S. "Cities, Seminaries, and Christian Colleges," *Urban Mission* 3: 1 (September, 1985): 3–5.

_____. "Content and Context: the Whole Christ for the Whole City," *Discipling the City: Theological Reflections on Urban Missions.* Grand Rapids: Baker Book House, 1979, pp. 85–106.

_____. "Don't Be an Urban Missionary Unless," *Evangelical Missions Quarterly.* 19: 2 (April, 1983): 86–94.

_____. "Goals of Ethnic Evangelism," *Cities, Missions' New Frontier.* Edited by Roger S. Greenway and Timothy Monsma. Grand Rapids: Baker Books, 1989, pp. 80–90.

Greenway, Roger S. and Monsma, Timothy M. *Cities: Missions' New Frontier.* Grand Rapids: Baker Book House, 1989.

Grigg, Viv. *Companion to the Poor.* Sutherland, Australia: Albatross Books, 1984.

Hall, Douglas John. "De-evangelism: Exploring the Mystery of the Deserted Urban Church," *Urban Mission* 6 (September, 1988): 6–12.

Hall, John Wesley, Jr. "Holistic Ministry Variables in Four Latin American Cities: A Factor Analysis." n.p., 1991.

Hannerz, Ulf. *Exploring the City: Inquiries toward Urban Anthropology.* New York: Columbia University Press, 1980.

Hazlett, James Thomas. *The Training of Laypersons for Positions of Leadership within the Local Presbyterian Church.* D.Min. dissertation, Fuller Theological Seminary, 1976.

Hendricks, Howard G. *Teaching to Change Lives*. Portland: Multnomah Press, 1987.

Henrichsen, Walter A. *Disciples Are Made Not Born*. Wheaton: Victor Books, 1988.

Hersey, Paul and Blanchard, Kenneth H. *Management of Organizational Behavior Utilizing Human Resources*, 4th ed. Englewood Cliffs, NJ: Prentice Hall, 1981.

_____. *Management of Organizational Behavior Utilizing Human Resources*, 5th ed. Englewood Cliffs, NJ: Prentice Hall, 1988.

Hian, Cha Wee. *The Making of a Leader*. Downers Grove, IL: InterVarsity Press, 1987.

Hiebert, Paul G. "Critical Contextualization," *International Bulletin of Missionary Research*. 11: 3 (July, 1987): 103–112.

_____. Syllabus: "Urban Anthropology." Pasadena: Fuller Theological Seminary, 1987.

Hofstede, Geert. "Motivation, Leadership, and Organization: Do American Theories Apply Abroad?" *Organizational Dynamics*. Summer, 1980, pp. 42–62.

Holland, Frederic. *Theological Education in Context and Change*. D.Miss. dissertation, Fuller Theological Seminary, 1978.

Hollander, Edwin. *Leadership Dynamics*. New York: The Free Press, 1978.

Houghton, Graham and Sargunam, Ezra. "The Role of Theological Education in Church Planting among the Urban Poor: A Case Study from Madras," *Evangelical Review of Theology* 6: 1 (April, 1982): 141–144, (Reprinted from *TRACI Journal*. April, 1981).

International Congress on World Evangelization. *The Lausanne Covenant*, Article 5. Lausanne, Switzerland: Lausanne Committee for World Evangelization, July 1974.

James, Samuel M. "Training for Urban Evangelization," *An Urban World: Churches Face the Future*. Edited by Larry Rose and C. Kirk Hadaway. Nashville: Broadman Press, 1984, pp. 189–206.

Johnson, Douglas W. *The Care and Feeding of Volunteers*. Nashville: Abingdon, 1978.

Johnson, Mauritz, Jr. "A Schema for Curriculum," *Curriculum and Evaluation*. Edited by Arno A. Bellack and Herbert M. Kliebard. Berkeley: McCutchen Publishing Corporation, 1977, pp. 3–19.

Jones, R. Review of Roger S. Greenway, ed. *Discipling the City: Theological Reflections on Urban Missions.* Grand Rapids: Baker Book House, 1979. *International Bulletin of Missionary Research* 5 (October, 1981): 184.

Jurgensen, Barbara. "Bible and Mission in an Inner-City Congregation," *Bible and Mission.* Edited by W. Stumme. Minneapolis: Augsburg Publishing House, 1986, pp. 111–119.

Keller, Suzanne. *The Urban Neighborhood.* New York: Random House, 1968.

Kelley, John. "Image of the City in Christian Tradition," *AFER: African Ecclesial Review* 20 (1978): 235–241.

Kenel, Sally A. "Urban Psychology and Spirituality," *Journal of Psychology and Theology* 15 (Winter, 1987): 300–307.

Kinsler, F. Ross, ed. *Ministry by the People.* Maryknoll, NY: Orbis Books, 1983.

Kirkpatrick, John. *A Theology of Servant Leadership.* D.Miss. dissertation, Fuller Theological Seminary, 1988.

Kittel, Gerhard. *Theological Dictionary of the New Testament.* Translated by Geoffrey W. Bromiley. Grand Rapids: William B. Eerdmans Publishing Company, 1967.

Kliebard, Herbert M. "The Tyler Rationale," *Curriculum and Evaluation.* Edited by Arno A. Bellack and Herbert M. Kliebard. Berkeley: McCutchen Publishing Corporation, 1977, pp. 56–68.

Knox, John. "The Ministry in the Early Church," *The Ministry in Historical Perspective.* Edited by H. Richard Niebuhr and Daniel D. Williams. New York: Harper and Row, 1956, p. 21.

Koestenbaum, Peter. *Leadership: The Inner Side of Greatness: A Philosophy for Leaders.* San Francisco: Jossey-Bass Publishers, 1991.

Kouzes, James M. and Posner, Barry Z. *The Leadership Challenge: How to Get Extraordinary Things Done in Organizations.* San Francisco: Jossey-Bass Publishers, 1987.

Kraft, Charles H. *Christianity and Culture.* Maryknoll, NY: Orbis, 1979.

_____. *Christianity with Power.* Ann Arbor: Servant Books, 1989.

_____. "Encounters for Christian Witness," *Evangelical Missions Quarterly* 27 (1991): 258–265.

Krawthwol, David R., ed. *Taxonomy of Educational Objectives: The Classification of Educational Goals Handbook II: Affective Domain.* New York: David McKay Company, Inc., 1964.

Kromminga, Carl G. "The Role of the Laity in Urban Evangelization," *Discipling the City: Theological Reflections on Urban Missions.* Edited by Roger S. Greenway. Grand Rapids: Baker Book House, 1979, pp. 128–150.

Lassey, William R. and Fernandez, Richard R. *Leadership and Social Change.* La Jolla, CA: University Associates, 1976.

LeTourneau, Roy. Interviewed by Edgar J. Elliston, February 10, 1991.

Linthicum, Robert C. *City of God, City of Satan: A Biblical Theology of the Urban Church.* Grand Rapids: Zondervan Publishing House, 1991.

Lofland, Lyn. *A World of Strangers.* New York: Basic Books, 1973.

Luecke, Richard H. "The City as Context for Biblical Faith," *The Christian Ministry* 20 (March–April, 1989): 10–12.

Mager, Robert F. and Kenneth M. Beach, Jr. *Developing Vocational Instruction.* Belmont, CA: Fearon-Pitman Publishers, Inc., 1967.

Mager, Robert F. and Pipe, Peter. *Analyzing Performance Problems or 'You Really Oughta Wanna'.* Belmont: Fearon Publishers, Inc., 1970.

Marchant, Colin. "The Theology of Urban Mission," *Baptist Quarterly* 33 London (January, 1989): 2–6.

Martin, Judith N. "Training Issues in Cross-Cultural Orientation," *Theories and Methods in Cross-Cultural Orientation.* Special issue of the *International Journal of Intercultural Relations.* New York: Pergamon Press, 1986, pp. 103–116.

Martin, Judith N., ed. *Theories and Methods in Cross-Cultural Orientation.* Special issue of the *International Journal of Intercultural Relations.* New York: Pergamon Press, 1986.

Maslow, Abraham. *Motivation and Personality,* 2nd ed. New York: Harper and Row Publishers, 1970.

Mayo, G. Douglas and DuBois, Philip H. *The Complete Book of Training: Theory, Principles, and Techniques.* San Diego: University Associates, Inc., 1987.

Mbea, Francois. "Training for Mission in Urban and Rural Africa," *International Review of Mission* 65 (July, 1976): 313–316.

McCaffery, James A. "Independent Effectiveness: A Reconsideration of Cross-Cultural Orientation and Training," Edited by Judith N. Martin. *Theories and Methods in Cross-Cultural Orientation.* Special issue of the *International Journal of Intercultural Relations.* New York: Pergamon Press, 1986, pp. 159–178.

McClung, Floyd. *Seeing the City with the Eyes of God.* Terrytown, NY: Chosen Books, Fleming H. Revell Company, 1991.

McConnell, C. Douglas. *The Bresee Institute for Urban Training: A Study in the Analysis of Urban Training.* M.A. thesis, Fuller Theological Seminary, 1985.

_____. *Networks and Associations in Urban Mission: A Port Moresby Case Study.* Ph.D. dissertation, Fuller Theological Seminary, 1990.

McGavran, Donald A. Lectures on Church Growth at Columbia Bible College, Columbia, SC, 1969.

_____. *Understanding Church Growth.* Grand Rapids: William B. Eerdmans Publishing Company, 1980.

_____. *Understanding Church Growth.* 2nd ed. edited by C. Peter Wagner. Grand Rapids: William B. Eerdmans Publishing Company, 1990.

McGavran, Donald A. and Arn, Win. *How to Grow A Church.* Glendale, CA: Regal Books, 1974.

McGregor, Douglas. *The Human Side of Enterprise.* New York: McGraw Hill, 1960.

McKerihan, Elizabeth. Interviewed by Edgar J. Elliston, February 19, 1991.

McKinney, Lois. "Training Leaders," *Discipling through Theological Education by Extension.* Edited by Virgil Gerber. Chicago: Moody Press, 1980, pp. 179–191.

McSwain, Larry L. "Understanding Life in the City: Context for Christian Ministry," *Southwestern Journal of Theology* 24: 2 (Spring, 1982): 6–19.

_____. Review of Roger S. Greenway, ed. *Discipling the City: Theological Reflections on Urban Missions.* Grand Rapids: Baker Book House, 1979. *Review and Expositor: A Baptist Theological Journal* 77 (Spring, 1980): 298–299.

Monsma, Timothy M. "Family, Clan and Tribe in the City," *Discipling the City: Theological Reflections on Urban Missions.* Edited by Roger S. Greenway. Grand Rapids: Baker Book House, 1979, pp. 151–174.

Morehead, Peter B. "An Analysis of the Leadership Training Program at the Church on Brady." n.p., 1986.

Neill, Stephen. *A History of Christian Missions.* New York: Penguin Books, 1964.

Nelson, Ross. "A Theology of Compassion for the City," *The Urban Mission: Essays on the Building of a Comprehensive Model for Evangelical Urban Ministry.* Edited by Craig W. Ellison. Washington, D.C.: University Press of America, Inc., 1983, pp. 39–48.

Niebuhr, H. Richard and Williams, Daniel D., eds. *The Ministry in Historical Perspective.* New York: Harper and Row, 1956.

Nouwen, Henri J. M. *In the Name of Jesus: Reflections on Christian Leadership.* New York: Crossroad Publishing Company, 1989.

Paige, R. Michael, "Trainer Competencies: The Missing Conceptual Link in Orientation," *Theories and Methods in Cross-Cultural Orientation.* Edited by Judith N. Martin. Special issue of the *International Journal of Intercultural Relations.* New York: Pergamon Press, 1986, pp. 135–158.

Palen, John J. *The Urban World.* New York: McGraw-Hill, 1987.

Pannell, William E. "Developing Evangelical Minority Leadership," *The Urban Mission: Essays on the Building of a Comprehensive Model for Evangelical Urban Ministry.* Edited by Craig W. Ellison. Washington, D.C.: University Press of America, Inc., 1983, pp. 122–129.

Pasquariello, Ronald D., Shriver, Donald W. and Geyer, Alan. *Redeeming the City: Theology, Politics and Urban Policy.* Reviewed by George D. Younger, *International Review of Mission* 74 (January, 1985): 124–126.

Perkins, John. "The Harambee Christian Family Center." n.p., n.d.

_____. *Harambee News.* 6: 2 (Summer 1991).

Peters, Thomas J. *Thriving on Chaos: Handbook for a Management Revolution.* New York: Alfred A. Knopf, 1988.

Peters, Thomas J. and Waterman, Robert H., Jr. *In Search of Excellence.* New York: Warner Books, 1982.

Pobee, John S., ed. "Ministerial Formation for Mission Today," *Ministerial Formation* 45 (April, 1989): 1–28.

Poethig, Richard P., ed. "The Shape of Urban Ministry in the 80's," *Institute on the Church in Urban-Industrial Society, SERIES: (ICUIS Occasional Paper 8).* 1979.

Rambo, David. Church Growth Lectures: "Patterns of Bible Institute Training Overseas"; "Theological Education by Extension: What is it Accomplishing?"; "Crisis at the Top: Training High Level Leaders"; "Leadership for the Cities: Facing the Urban Mandate." Fuller Theological Seminary, 1981.

Reich, Robert. *The Work of Nations.* New York: Alfred A. Knopf, 1991.

Rengstorf, K. H. *"Mathetes," Theological Dictionary of the New Testament,* IV. Edited by Gerhard Kittel, translated by Geoffrey W. Bromiley. Grand Rapids: William B. Eerdmans Publishing Company, 1967, p. 416.

Review of LeTourneau Ministries International. Los Angeles: LeTourneau Ministries International, 1991.

Richards, Lawrence O. *A Theology of Christian Education.* Grand Rapids: Zondervan Publishing House, 1975.

Riga, Peter. "Theology for the Earthly City," *Metropolis: Christian Presence and Responsibility.* Edited by P. Morris. Notre Dame: Fides Publishing, 1970, pp. 56–91.

Roberts, Vella-Kottarthil. *The Urban Mission of the Church from an Urban Anthropological Perspective.* D.Miss. dissertation, Fuller Theological Seminary, 1981.

Rooy, Sidney H. "Theological Education for Urban Mission," *Discipling the City: Theological Reflections on Urban Missions.* Edited by Roger S. Greenway. Grand Rapids: Baker Book House, 1979, pp. 175–207.

Rose, Larry and Hadaway, C. Kirk, eds. *An Urban World: Churches Face the Future.* Nashville: Broadman Press, 1984.

Sahlin, Monte C. "A Study of Factors Relating to Urban Church Growth in the North American Division of Seventh Day Adventists." n.p., 1986.

Samaan, Lynn Elizabeth. *Images of Missionary Spirituality: A Study of Spiritual Formation.* M.A. thesis, Fuller Theological Seminary, 1990.

Schaefer, Herbert G. "Theological Education and the Mission of the Church," *Theology and Life* 10 (December, 1987): 17–31.

Schaller, Lyle. *The Change Agent.* Nashville: Abingdon Press, 1979.

_____. *Forty-four Questions for Church Planters.* Nashville: Abingdon Press, 1991.

Schmidt, Stephen. "On Christian Nurture: Urban America, Chicago, USA," *Parish Religious Education: The People, the Place, the Profession.* Edited by M. Harris. Mawah, NJ: Paulist Press, 1978, pp. 135–147.

Schuller, David S., ed. "Mission, Spirituality, and Scholarship," *Theological Education* 17 (Autumn, 1980): 1–84.

Scriven, Michael. "The Methodology of Evaluation," *Curriculum and Evaluation.* Edited by Arno A. Bellack and Herbert M. Kliebard. Berkeley: McCutchen Publishing Corporation, 1977, pp. 334–371.

Senyimba, Michael S. Ndawula. *An Appropriate Curriculum for Developing Types I and II Spiritual Leaders in Namirembe Diocese, Uganda.* Th.M. thesis, Fuller Theological Seminary, 1987.

Shenk, David W. "The City Is a Gift," *Urban Mission.* 4 (September, 1986): 39–40.

Siebert, Rudolf J. "Urbanization as a World Trend: A Challenge to the Churches," *Missiology: An International Review* 13 (October, 1985): 429–443.

Simkins, Tim. *Nonformal Education and Development.* Manchester, England: University of Manchester Department of Adult and Higher Education, 1977.

Sinnott, Thomas G. "Theological Reflections on Housing," *Currents in Theology and Mission* 11 (June, 1984): 176–179.

Smith, Fred. *Learning to Lead: Bringing out the Best in People.* Waco: Word Books, 1986.

Smith, Linda. *An Awakening of Conscience: The Challenging Response of American Evangelicals toward World Poverty.* Ph.D. dissertation, American University, 1987.

Smith, Timothy L. *Called unto Holiness.* Kansas City: Nazarene Publishing House, 1962.

Stake, Robert E. "The Countenance of Educational Evaluation," *Curriculum and Evaluation.* Edited by Arno A. Bellack and Herbert M. Kliebard. Berkeley: McCutchen Publishing Corporation, 1977, pp. 372–390.

Stanley, Paul and Clinton, J. Robert. *Connections.* Colorado Springs: NavPress, 1991.

Steele, Robert E. "Toward the Development of Adequate Training Programs for Urban Ministry," *Journal of Psychology and Theology* 6 (Fall, 1978): 291–297.

Steinbruck, John F. "Bible and Mission in a Center-City Congregation," *Bible and Mission*. Edited by W. Stumme. Minneapolis: Augsburg Publishing House, 1986, pp. 173–184.

Stogdill, Ralph M. "Personal Factors Associated with Leadership: A Survey of the Literature," *Journal of Psychology* 25 (1948): 35–71.

Stufflebeam, Daniel L. "Educational Evaluation and Decision Making," *Educational Evaluation: Theory and Practice*. Edited by Blaine R. Worthen and James R. Sanders. Worthington, OH: Charles A. Jones Publishing Company, 1973, pp. 128–150.

Teague, Dennis J. *An Annotated Bibliography on Christian Leadership Development for Urban Ministries Using Andragogical Methods*. M.A. thesis, Fuller Theological Seminary, 1984.

Tink, Fletcher. *The Bresee Institute for Urban Training Brochure*. Los Angeles: Bresee Institute for Urban Training, 1983.

_____. "Internship Arrangements at the Bresee Institute." n.p., 1984.

Tremaine, Robert. "Visionary Leadership." n.p., 1991.

Tyler, Ralph. *Basic Principles of Curriculum and Instruction*. Chicago: University of Chicago Press, 1949.

Van Engen, Charles. *God's Missionary People: Rethinking the Purpose of the Local Church*. Grand Rapids: Baker Book House, 1991.

Vangerud, Richard D. "The Ministry Today: A Survey of Perspectives," *Word and World: Theology for Christian Ministry* 1 (Fall, 1981): 391–397.

Verkuyl, Johannes H. "The Role of the Diaconate in Urban Mission," *Discipling the City: Theological Reflections on Urban Missions*. Edited by Roger S. Greenway. Grand Rapids: Baker Book House, 1979, pp. 208–221.

Vidyasagara, Vijaya. "Urban Rural Mission of the Church," *Theology and Ideology in Asian People's Struggle*. Edited by George Ninan. Singapore: Christian Conference of Asia—Urban Rural Mission, 1985, pp. 18–47.

Vincent, John J. "Innovation in Great Britain: The Sheffield Urban Theology Unit," *Learning in Context: The Search for Innovative Patterns in Theological Education*. Edited by S. Coe, et al. Kent, England: Theological Education Fund, 1973, pp. 116–131.

_____. "Theological Education for Urban Mission," *Ministerial Formation* 27 (July, 1984): 20–22.

Wagner, C. Peter. *Leading Your Church to Growth*. Ventura, CA: Regal Books, 1984.

_____. "A Missiological View of Relief and Development," *Christian Relief and Development: Training Workers for Effective Ministry*. Edited by Edgar J. Elliston. Dallas: Word Books, 1989, pp. 115–128.

Wagner, C. Peter, ed. *Territorial Spirits*. Chichester, England: Sovereign World, Ltd., 1991.

Wallace, Darryl K. "Jesus Ain't Got No Feet: A Black Perspective on Christology," *Urban Mission* 6 (January, 1989): 13–23.

Ward, Ted. "The Church and Development." Lecture series at Daystar University, Nairobi, Kenya, 1979.

_____. "Facing Educational Issues," *Church Leadership Development*. Glen Ellyn, IL: Scripture Press Ministries, 1977, pp. 31–46.

_____. "Servants, Leaders and Tyrants," *Missions and Theological Education in World Perspective*. Edited by Harvie M. Conn and Samuel F. Rowen. Farmington, MI: Associates of Urbanus, 1984, pp. 19–40.

_____, ed. *Faculty Dialogue* 10 (Winter–Spring, 1988): 1–110.

Ward, Ted and Dettoni, John. "Increasing Learning Effectiveness through Evaluation," *Effective Learning in Non-Formal Education*. Edited by Ted W. Ward and William A. Herzog, Jr. East Lansing: Michigan State University, 1977, pp. 198–288.

Ward, Ted and Herzog, William. *New Paths to Learning*. East Lansing: Michigan State University, 1977.

Wilkes, Paul. "The Hands that Would Shape Our Souls," *The Atlantic Monthly* (December, 1990): 59–88.

Wink, Walter. *Naming the Powers: The Language of Power in the New Testament*. Philadelphia: Fortress Press, 1984.

Winter, Gibson. "Seminary in a Metropolitan Society," *The Princeton Seminary Bulletin* 1: 4 (1978): 201–212.

World Impact. "Ministry Information." Los Angeles: World Impact, Inc., n.d.

World Impact. *World Impact Bulletin*. Los Angeles: World Impact, Inc., August, 1988.

Worthen, Blaine R. and Sanders, James R. *Educational Evaluation: Theory and Practice.* Worthington, OH: Charles A. Jones Publishing Company, 1973.

Wrong, Dennis H. *Power: Its Forms, Bases and Uses.* New York: Harper and Row, 1980.

Yamamori, Tetsunao. *God's New Envoys.* Portland: Multnomah Press, 1987.

Youssef, Michael. *The Leadership Style of Jesus.* Wheaton: Victor Books, 1986.

Yuen, Bessie Kawaguchi. "Urban Poor-ology: A Theology of Ministry to the World's Urban Poor," *Urban Mission* 5 (September, 1987): 13–19.

Yukl, Gary A. *Leadership in Organizations.* 2nd ed. Englewood Cliffs, NJ: Prentice Hall, 1989.

Indexes

General Index

Author Index

Scripture Index